Magical Origami Gnomes

Books by John Montroll
www.johnmontroll.com
Instagram: @montrollorigami

Origami Symphonies

Origami Symphony No. 1: The Elephant's Trumpet Call
Origami Symphony No. 2: Trio of Sharks & Playful Prehistoric Mammals
Origami Symphony No. 3: Duet of Majestic Dragons & Dinosaurs
Origami Symphony No. 4: Capturing Vibrant Coral Reef Fish
Origami Symphony No. 5: Woodwinds, Horns, and a Moose
Origami Symphony No. 6: Striped Snakes Changing Scales
Origami Symphony No. 7: Musical Monkeys
Origami Symphony No. 8: An Octet of Cats
Origami Symphony No. 9: Ode to Australia
Origami Symphony No. 10: Lucky & Dangerous Sides of Origami
Origami Symphony No. 11: Folding on Land, Air and Sea

Animal Origami

Jungle Origami
Arctic Animals in Origami
Origami Aquarium
Dogs in Origami
Perfect Pets Origami
Dragons and Other Fantastic Creatures in Origami
Bugs in Origami
Horses in Origami: Second Edition
Origami Birds: Second Edition
Origami Gone Wild
Dinosaur Origami
Origami Dinosaurs for Beginners
Prehistoric Origami: Dinosaurs and other Creatures: Third Edition
Mythological Creatures and the Chinese Zodiac Origami
Origami Sea Life: Third Edition
Bringing Origami to Life: Second Edition
Origami Sculptures: Fourth Edition
African Animals in Origami: Third Edition
North American Animals in Origami: Third Edition
Origami for the Enthusiast: Second Edition
Animal Origami for the Enthusiast: Second Edition

Geometric Origami

The Magic of Origami Polyhedra
Origami Stars: Second Edition
Galaxy of Origami Stars: Second Edition
Origami and Math: Simple to Complex: Second Edition
Origami & Geometry
3D Origami Platonic Solids & More: Second Edition
3D Origami Diamonds
3D Origami Antidiamonds
3D Origami Pyramids
A Plethora of Polyhedra in Origami: Third Edition
Classic Polyhedra Origami
A Constellation of Origami Polyhedra
Origami Polyhedra Design

General Origami

Magical Origami Gnomes: 38 Gnomes. Infinite Fun.
Origami Fold-by-Fold
DC Super Heroes Origami
Origami Worldwide
Teach Yourself Origami: Third Edition
Christmas Origami: Second Edition
Storytime Origami
Origami Inside-Out: Third Edition

Dollar Bill Origami

Dollar Origami Treasures: Second Edition
Dollar Bill Animals in Origami: Second Revised Edition
Dollar Bill Origami
Easy Dollar Bill Origami

Simple Origami

Fun and Simple Origami: 101 Easy-to-Fold Projects: Second Edition
Origami Twelve Days of Christmas: And Santa, Too!
Super Simple Origami
Easy Dollar Bill Origami
Easy Origami
Easy Origami 2
Easy Origami 3
Easy Origami Coloring Book
Easy Origami Animals
Easy Origami Polar Animals
Easy Origami Ocean Animals
Easy Origami Woodland Animals
Easy Origami Jungle Animals
Meditative Origami

Magical Origami Gnomes

38 Gnomes. Infinite Fun.

Antroll Publishing Company

John Montroll

To Charley

Magical Origami Gnomes: *38 Gnomes. Infinite Fun.*

Copyright © 2025 by John Montroll. All rights reserved.
No part of this publication may be copied or reproduced by any means without the express written permission of the author.

ISBN-10: 1-877656-72-0
ISBN-13: 978-1-877656-72-9

Antroll Publishing Company

Introduction

Welcome, Origami-Wizard. Your adventure begins now.

Within these pages live 38 delightful origami gnomes, each one folded from a square sheet of paper, and each with a personality far too big for their tiny hats. Whether you are a curious beginner or a seasoned folder, you'll find gnomes that range from simple to intermediate, all brought to life with clear instructions and a good dose of whimsy.

All models are designed by origami master John Montroll, and each gnome comes with a short, humorous story that offers a peek into the lives of these charming, mischievous, and clever creatures. As gnomes are magical and origami is magical, the combination takes everything to another level.

Your journey will wind through five whimsical chapters:

Welcome Gnomes—Cheerful greeters with questionable hospitality skills.
Mountain Gnomes—Rugged, wise, and always a little dusty from gem hunting,
Tinker Gnomes—Inventive, eccentric, and prone to building things that usually don't explode.
Forest Gnomes—Peaceful and earthy, taking special care of mushrooms and squirrels,
Mischievous Gnomes—Tricksters who believe rules are more like polite suggestions.

You are not just folding paper, you are creating a cast of magical characters. Each springs into life, ready to be made into scenes, hidden in corners of rooms, placed on shelves, or stacked in a drawer (they're not picky).

Photos were taken of all the models folded from 9 3/4 inch square sheets of origami paper (kami). Kami is the perfect choice for gnomes because all models use paper that is white on one side and a solid color on the other. Paper with sizes of 6 or 7 inches would work as well.

The diagrams are drawn in the internationally approved Randlett-Yoshizawa style. Origami supplies can be found in arts and craft shops, or at Dover Publications online: www.doverpublications.com. You can also visit OrigamiUSA at www.origamiusa.org for origami supplies and other related information including an extensive list of local, national, and international origami groups.

Please follow me on Instagram @montrollorigami to see posts of my origami.

I want to thank to the folders who proof-read the diagrams.

Be prepared for infinite fun. Once you start, there's no turning back.

John Montroll
www.johnmontroll.com

Contents

Symbols 9
Basic Folds 10
Appreciating Gnomes 14

Welcome to the Land of Gnomes

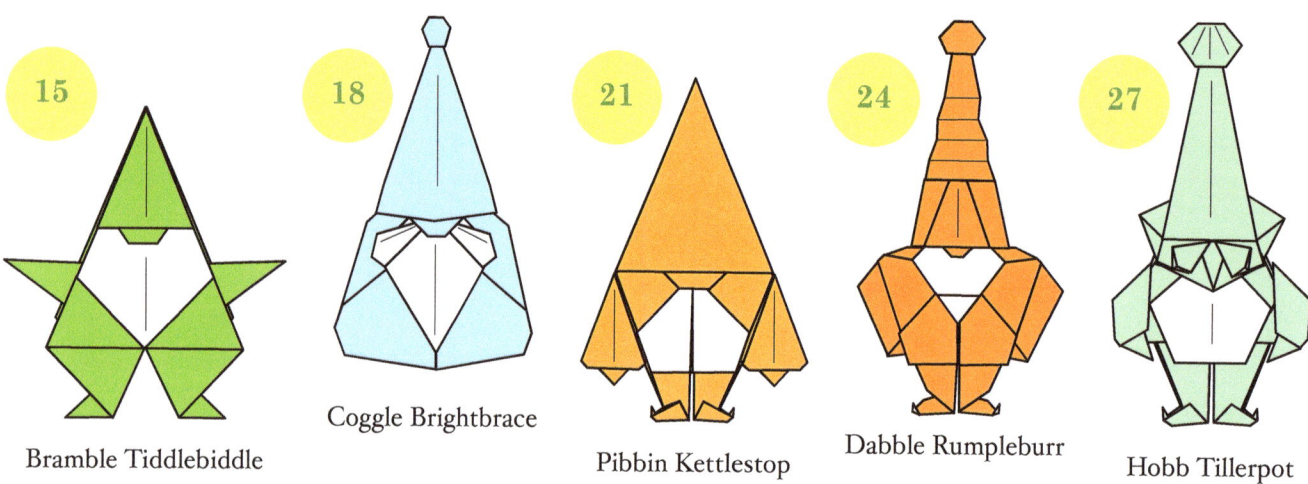

15 Bramble Tiddlebiddle
18 Coggle Brightbrace
21 Pibbin Kettlestop
24 Dabble Rumpleburr
27 Hobb Tillerpot

Mountain Gnomes of the East

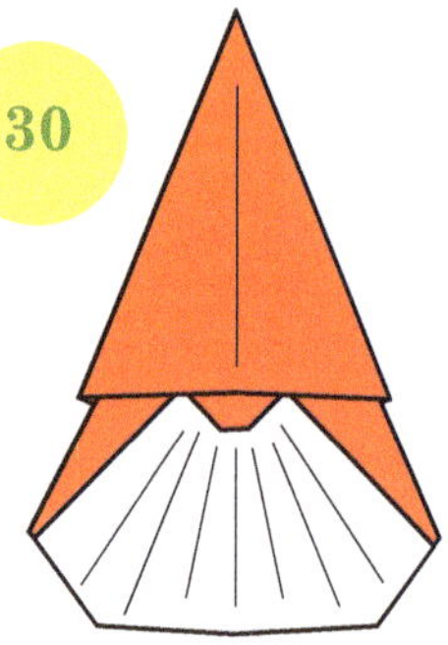

30 Varnic Thunderforge
32 Brindle Copperknot 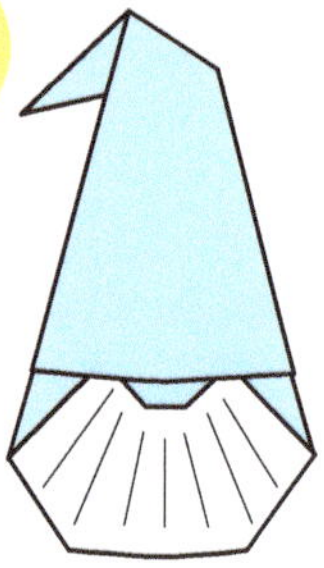
35 MountainCliffer 
38 Crystalline Ironsprocket 
41 Crystalline Flintcoil 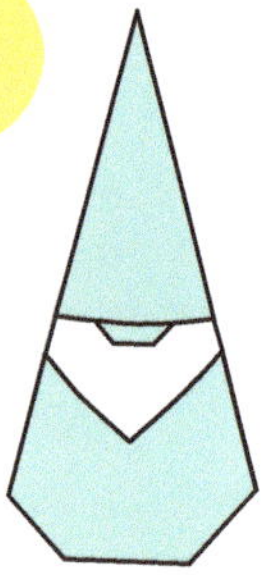

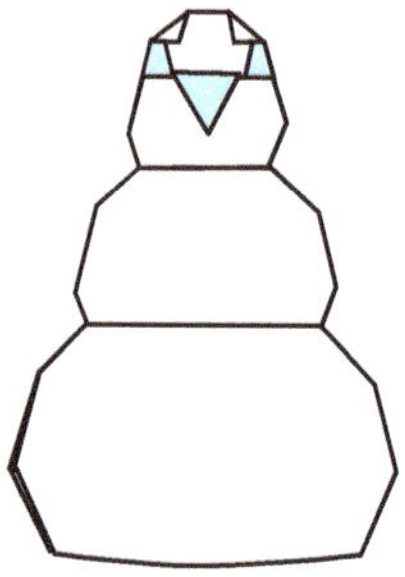

44 Snowgnome / Snowman
47 Brindle Deepdelver 
49 MetalCrafter

Tinker Gnomes of the South

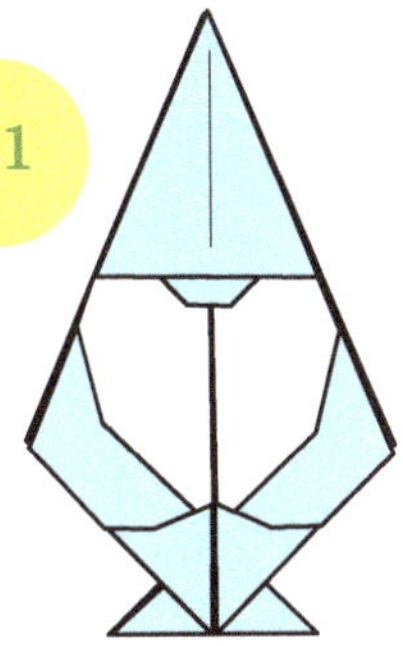

51 Mr. LaberDaber TinkerBlinker

53 Mrs. GearWhirl TinkerBlinker

56 Fribbin TinkerBlinker

59 Glimmer TinkerBlinker

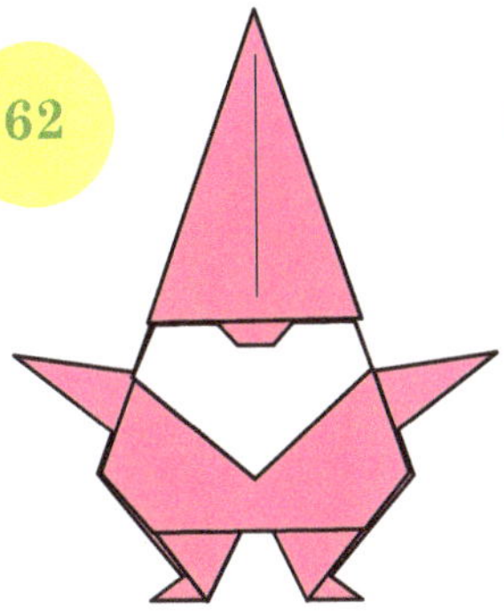

62 CoggleJam TinkerBlinker

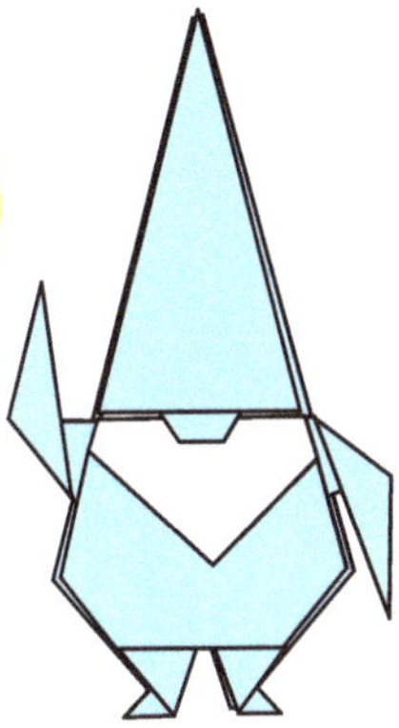

65 PlanetGranite TinkerBlinker

68 Wizzle TinkerBlinker

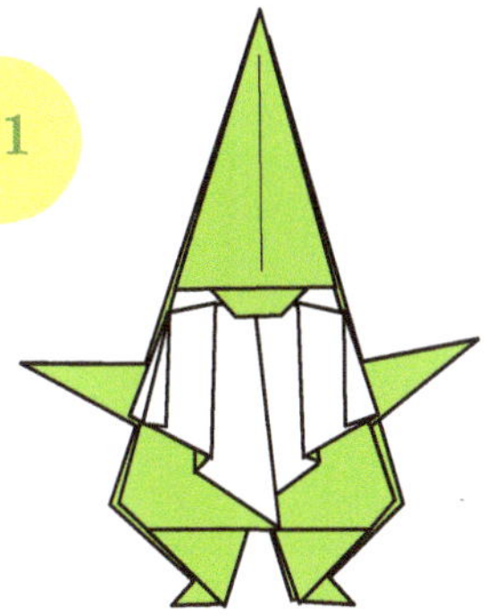

71 Bizzle TinkerBlinker

Forest Gnomes of the West

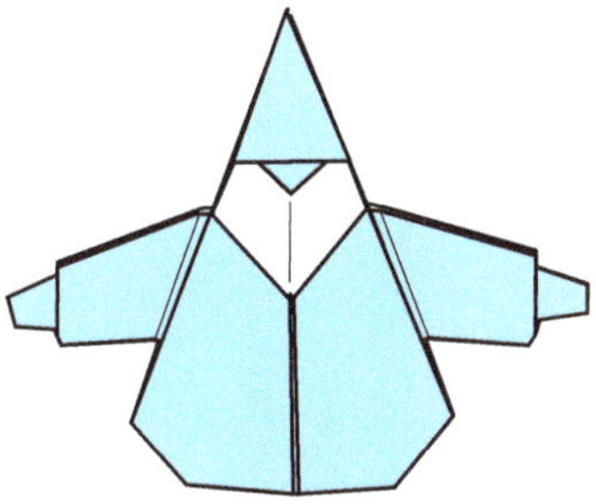

74 Wizard

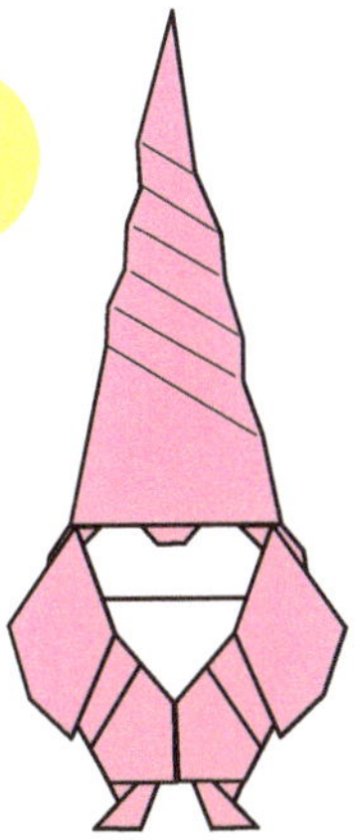

77 Tinket Greenwhistle

79 Bibble Thistlebrush

82 Jimble Underbark

More ➡

Contents 7

85	88	91	94
Grindle Mossroot	Crimble Bumbleknack	Wibbin Nutterclap	Nockle Fernpocket

Mischievous Gnomes of the North

98	101	104
Flipwig Barrelroll	Tottik Grumbleflick	Driggol Driftnettle

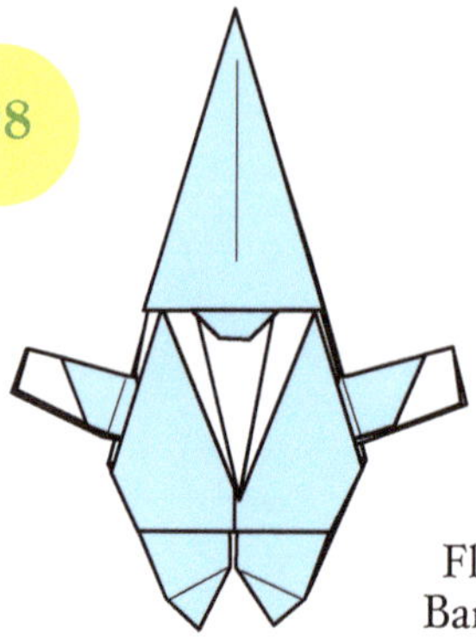

108	111	114
Margold Eggwobble	Fizzle Nimblecheek	Vibble Noodlebop

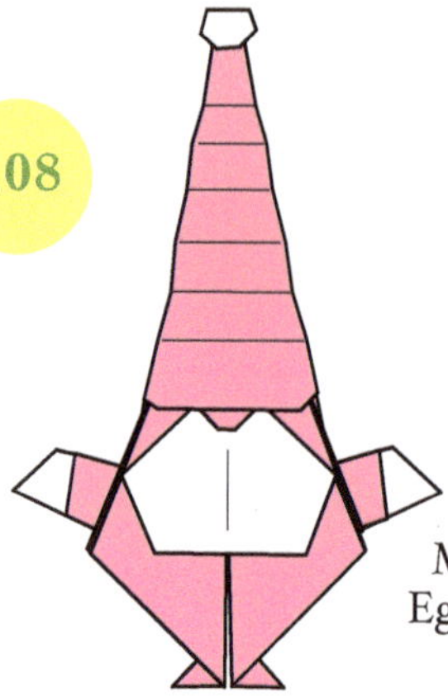

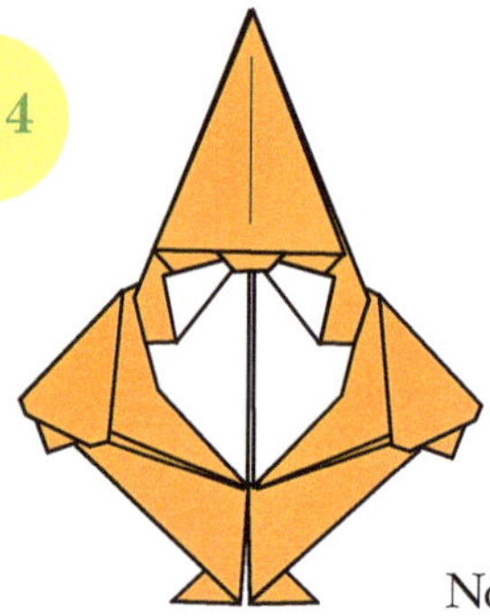

117	121	124
Zindle Snickerdash	Sprolla Mucklestomp	Jibber Kelpwhistle

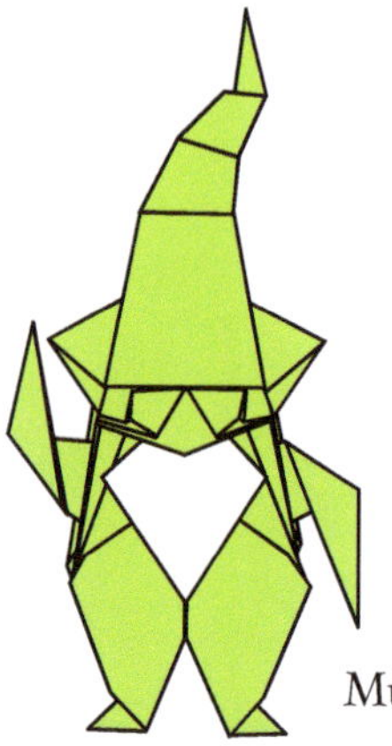

Symbols

Lines

\- \- \- \- \- \- \- \- \- Valley fold, fold in front.

—··—··—··—··— Mountain fold, fold behind.

——————— Crease line.

·· X-ray or guide line.

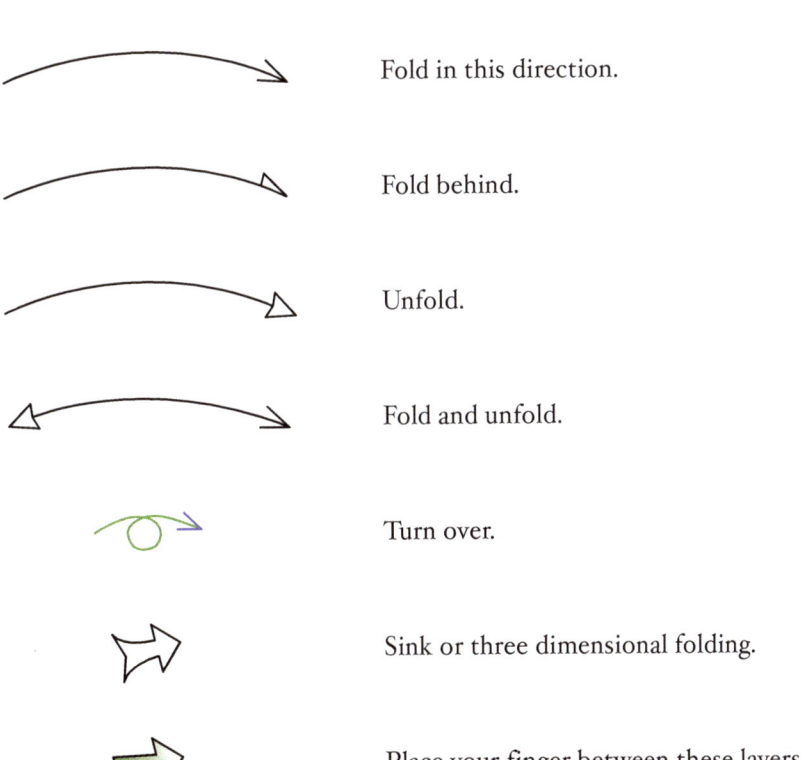

Arrows

Fold in this direction.

Fold behind.

Unfold.

Fold and unfold.

Turn over.

Sink or three dimensional folding.

Place your finger between these layers.

Basic Folds

Pleat Fold.

Fold back and forth. Each pleat is composed of one valley and mountain fold. Here are two examples.

1 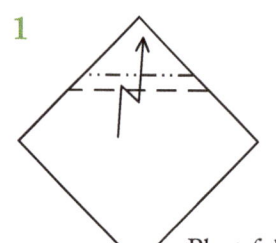 2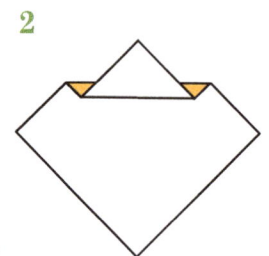

Pleat-fold.

1 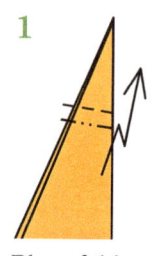 2

Pleat-fold.

Squash Fold.

In a squash fold, some paper is opened and then made flat. The shaded arrow shows where to place your finger.

1 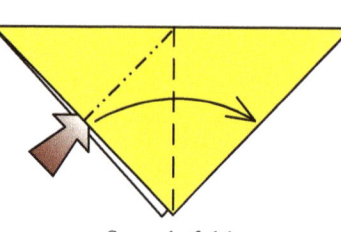 2 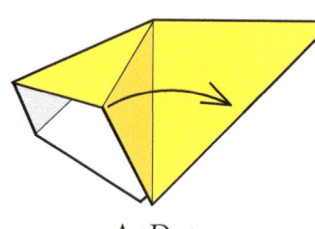 3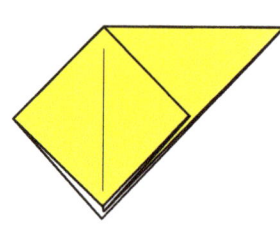

Squash-fold.   A 3D step.

Petal Fold.

In a petal fold, one point is folded up while two opposite sides meet each other.

1 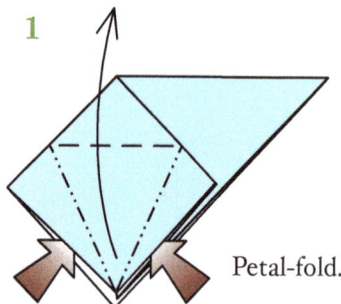 2 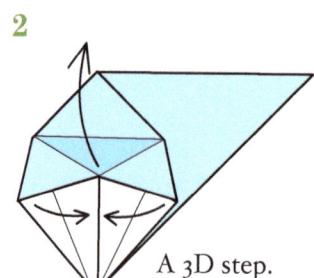 3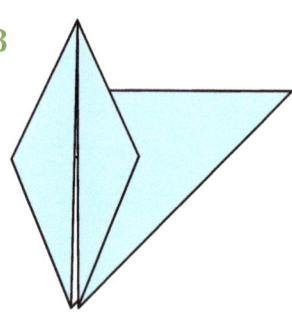

Petal-fold.   A 3D step.

Rabbit Ear.

To fold a rabbit ear, one corner is folded in half and laid down to a side.

1 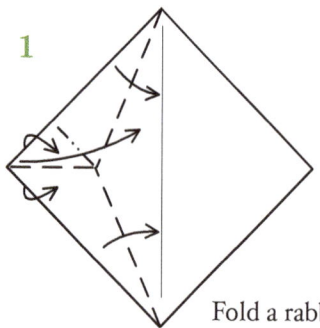 2 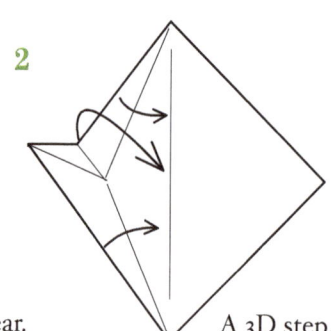 3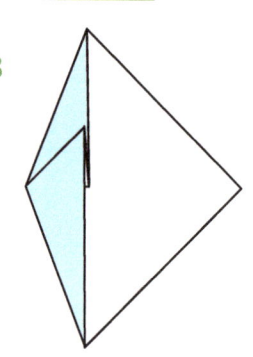

Fold a rabbit ear.   A 3D step.

Double Rabbit Ear.

If you were to bend a straw you would be folding the double rabbit ear.

1 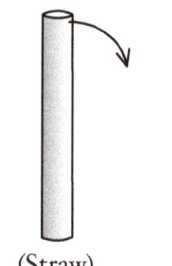 2 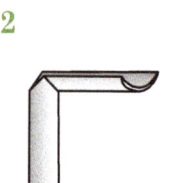   1 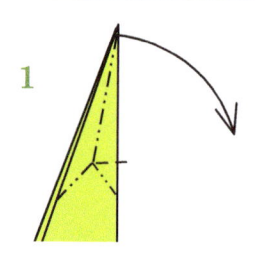 2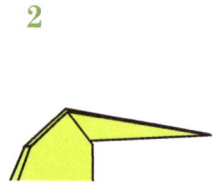

(Straw)   Double-rabbit-ear.

Magical Origami Gnomes

Inside Reverse Fold.

In an inside reverse fold, some paper is folded between layers. Here are two examples.

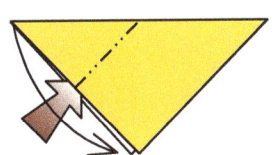
Reverse-fold.

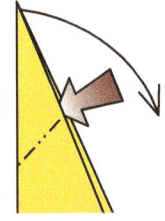
Reverse-fold.

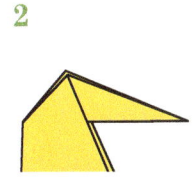

Outside Reverse Fold.

Much of the paper must be unfolded to make an outside reverse fold.

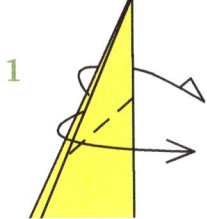
Outside-reverse-fold.

Crimp Fold.

A crimp fold is a combination of two reverse folds. Open the model slightly to form the crimp evenly on each side. Here are two examples.

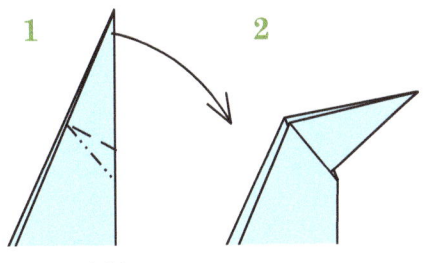
Crimp-fold.

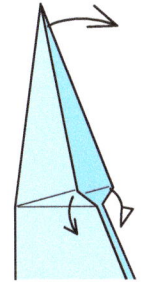
Crimp-fold.

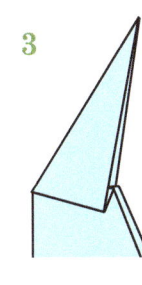
A 3D step.

Sink.

For a sink, some of the paper without edges is folded inside. To do this fold, much of the model must be unfolded.

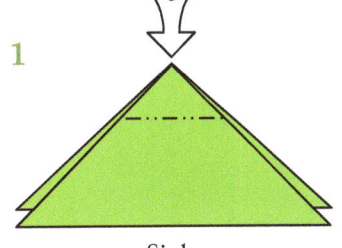
Sink.

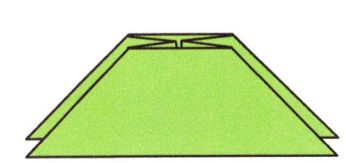

Spread Squash Fold.

A cross between a squash fold and sink fold, some paper in the center is spread apart and then made flat.

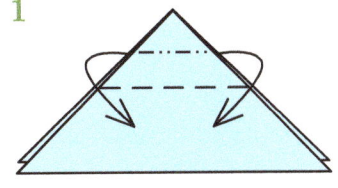
Spread-squash-fold.

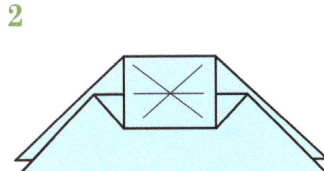

Basic Folds

Sink Nose Fold.

The sink nose fold is used in many gnomes, as a way to create the hat and nose. The diagrams will be shown as in step 8. To do this fold, the steps below show more detail.

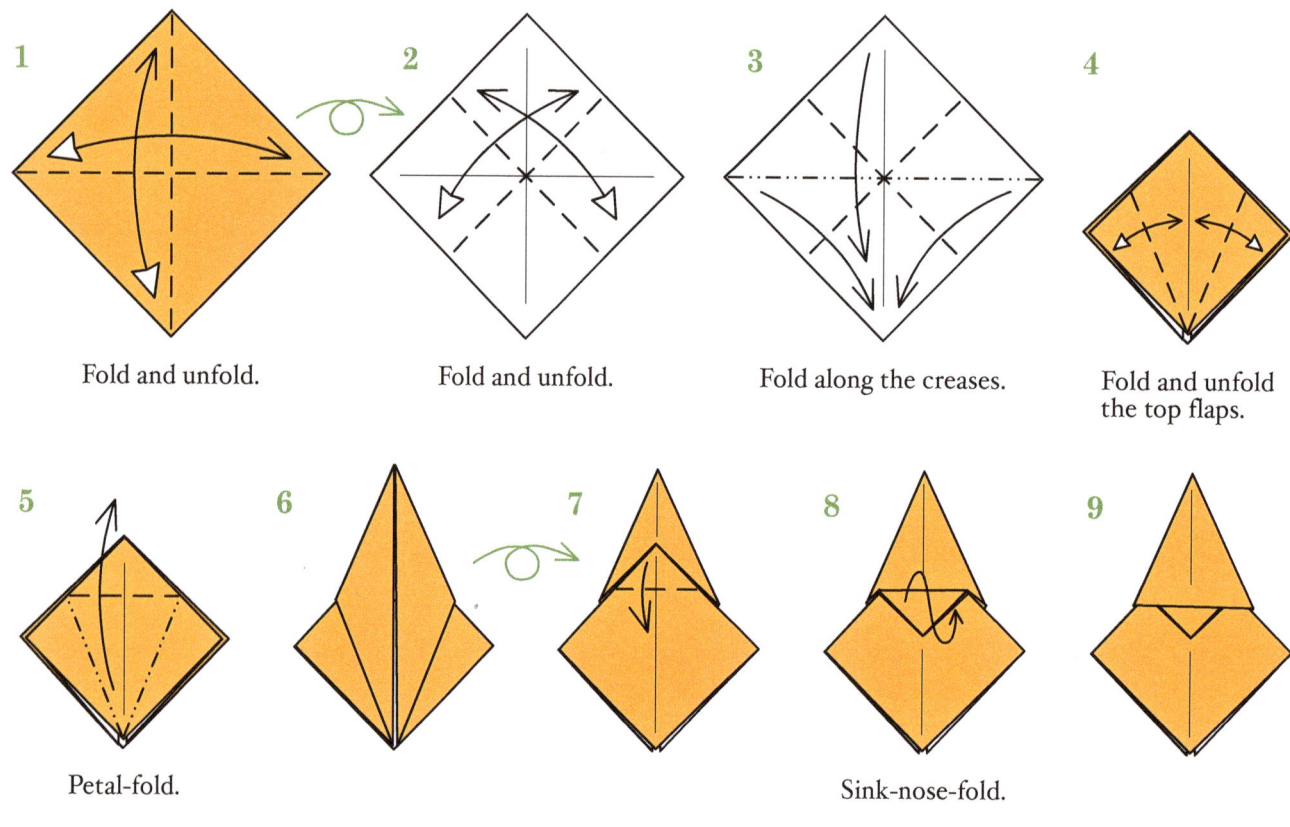

Here are the details for the sink nose fold. Begin with step 8.

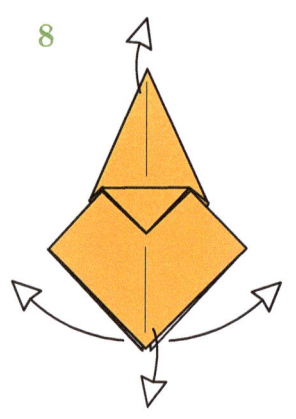

Unfold everything.

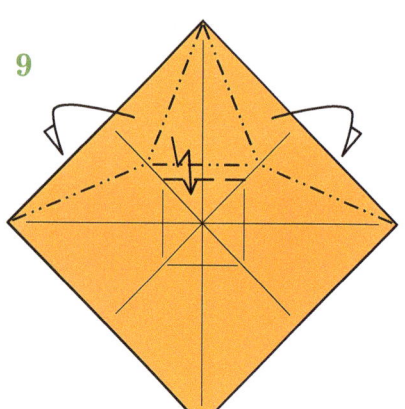

Begin at the top, folding along the creases.

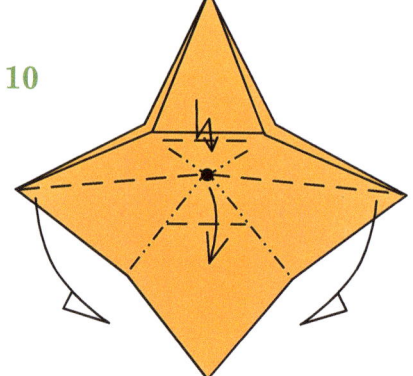

This is 3D. Puff out at the dot and fold along the creases to flatten.

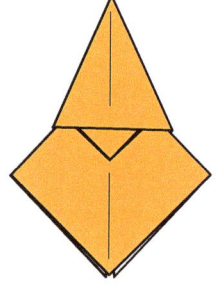

12 *Magical Origami Gnomes*

Blintz Frog Base.

This uses the double unwrap fold which is shown in detail below.

1 Fold and unfold.

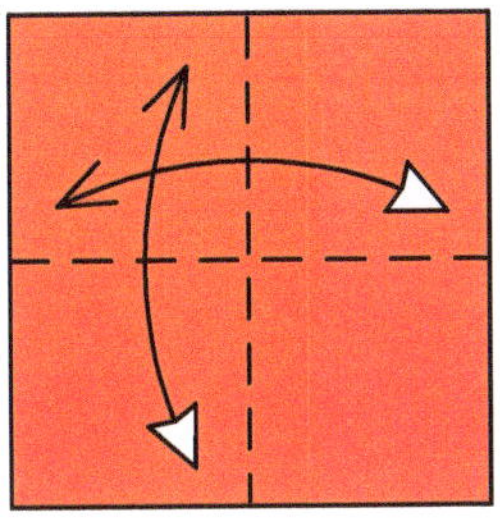

2 Blintz fold: Fold the four corners to the center.

3

4 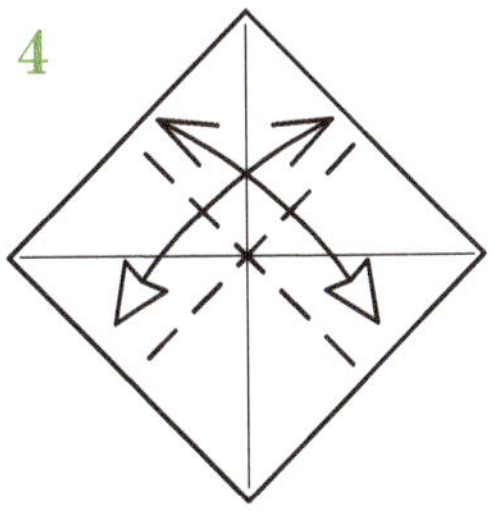 Fold and unfold.

5 This is similar to the Preliminary Fold.

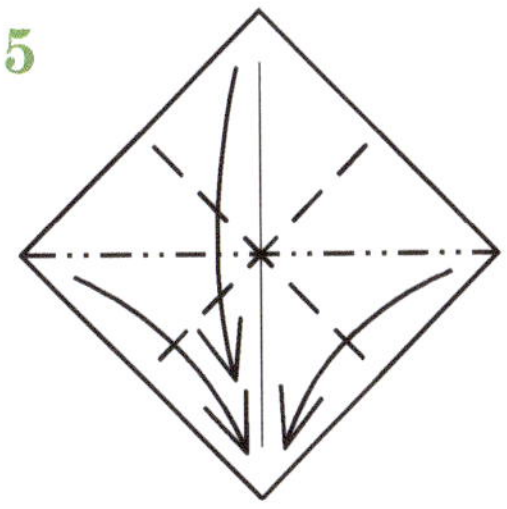

6 (Diagram enlarged.) Squash-fold.

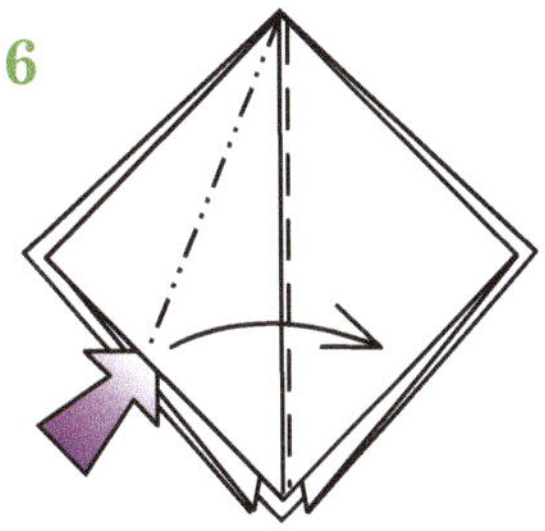

7 Petal-fold.

8 Double-unwrap-fold.

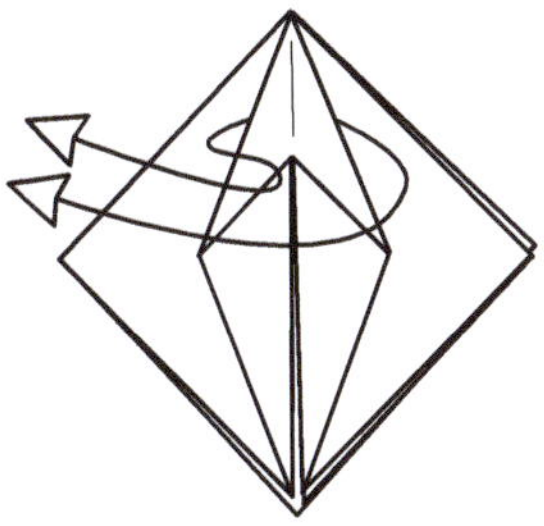

9 Repeat steps 6–8 three more times, on the back and sides.

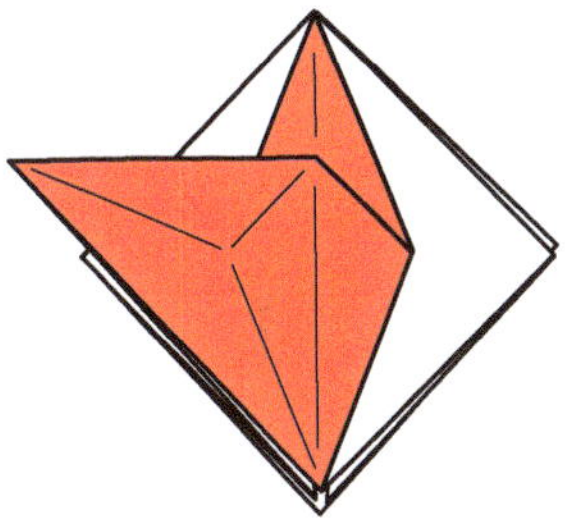

10 Blintz Frog Base

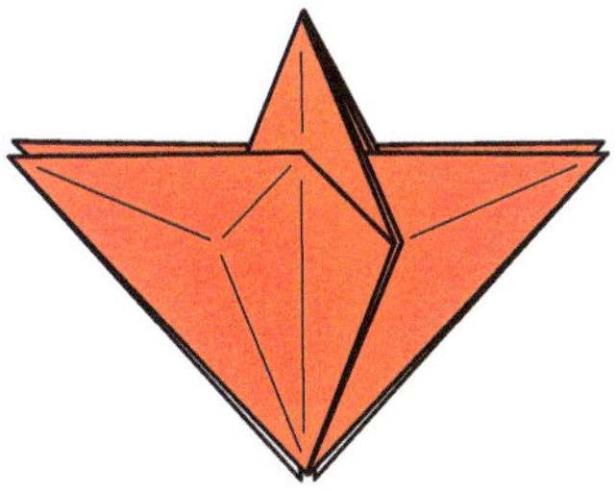

Double Unwrap Fold.

In the double unwrap fold, locked layers are unwrapped and refolded. Much of the folding is 3D. The diagrams are depicted as shown in steps 8 and 9 of the Blintz Frog Base.

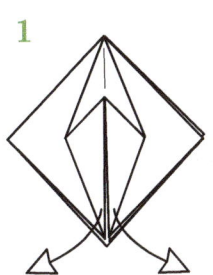

1 Begin with step 8 of the Blintz Frog Base. Spread at the bottom.

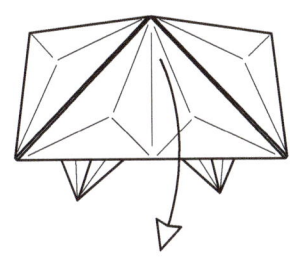

2 Unfold the top layer.

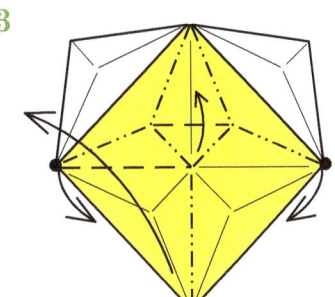

3 Refold along the creases. The dots will meet at the bottom.

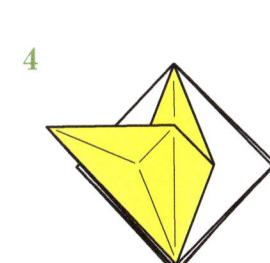

4

Basic Folds 13

Appreciating Gnomes

Gnomes have wandered through human imagination for centuries, popping up in garden corners and fantasy stories. These small, usually bearded creatures with tall hats, became caretakers of the earth, secret keepers of hidden treasures, and tricksters who remind us not to take life too seriously. Magical and mysterious, they blend nature, craft, and playfulness. Here are a few types of gnomes.

Mountain gnomes are the keepers of high peaks and craggy ridges, living in hidden caves. They are master stoneworkers, crafting intricate dwellings and crystal-lit halls. Known for their quiet wisdom, mountain gnomes guard rare minerals.

Tinker gnomes are the spirited engineers of the gnome world, forever surrounded by gears, springs, and improbable gadgets. They are happy to work on a dozen projects without finishing any. Their attempts always come with surprises.

Forest gnomes dwell beneath roots, inside hollow logs, or in snug burrows covered in moss. They are gentle herbalists, animal friends, and masters of camouflage. They protect the woodlands, ensuring balance and harmony between all creatures. These gnomes can speak to animals and will ride on the backs of wild animals.

Mischievous gnomes thrive on harmless pranks such as hiding your keys, moving your tools, or switching the sugar with salt. Their goal isn't to harm but to spark laughter and surprise. They remind us life need not be so predictable.

Small, secretive, and hidden as gnomes are, they have great power. They protect earth and nature, show the value of hard work, add mischief to magic, and bring whimsy into our daily lives. They symbolize quiet intelligence, imagination and playfulness, harmony with plants and animals, and guardians of gardens and treasures. They always bring unsuspecting joy.

Welcome to the Land of Gnomes

Welcome to the land of the gnomes. Friendly gnomes will stroll with you, teach magic basics, offer food and a place to rest. They will guide you to the enchanted mushrooms, hidden caves, and tiny cottages so you can meet more gnomes. With their magic notebooks, you can record your adventures. The ride is wild, hold on to your hats and keep safe inside your snuggly shoes.

Bramble Tiddlebiddle

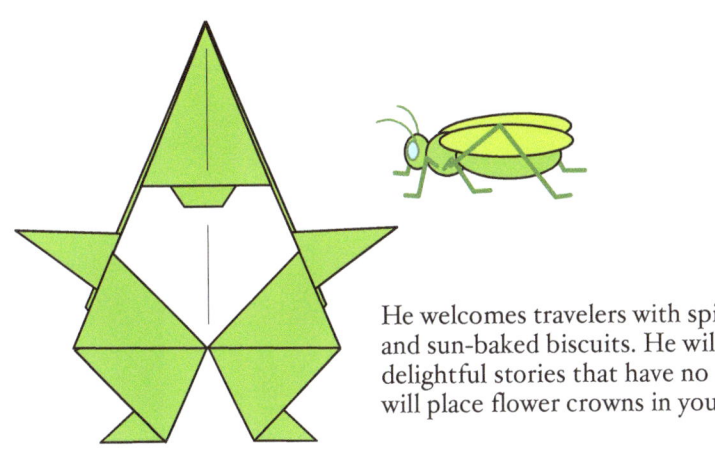

He welcomes travelers with spiced cider and sun-baked biscuits. He will tell you delightful stories that have no end and will place flower crowns in your hat.

1

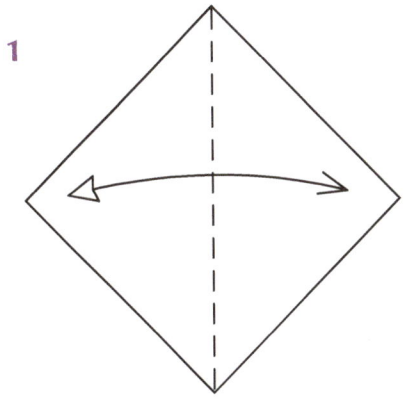

Fold and unfold.

2

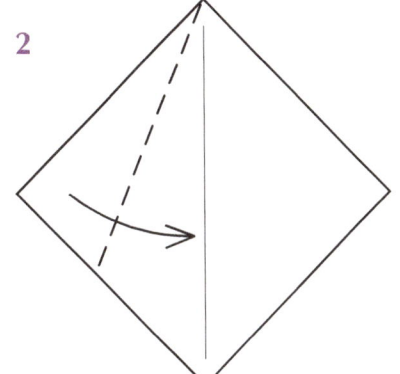

Fold to the center.

3

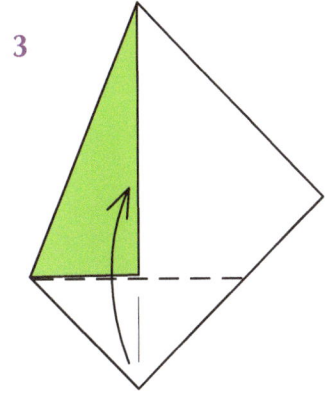

Fold up.

4

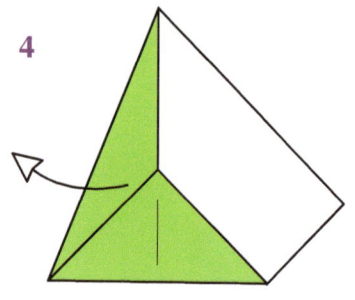

Unfold.

5

Fold and unfold.

6

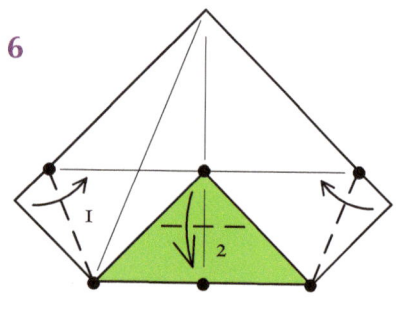

1. Fold on the left and right.
2. Fold down.

7

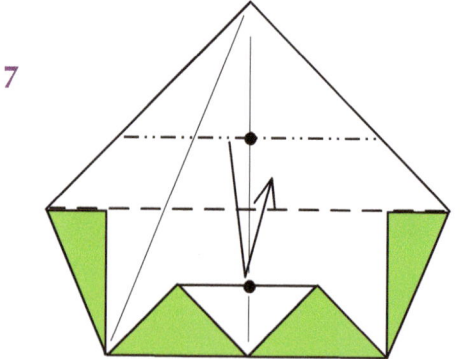

Pleat-fold so the dots meet.
Valley-fold along the crease.

8

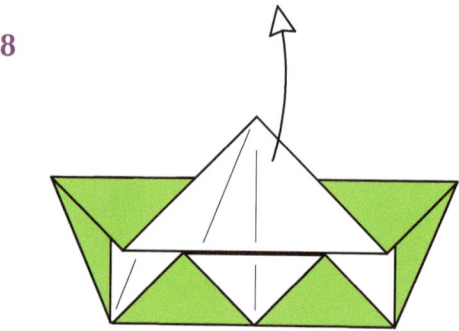

Unfold.

9

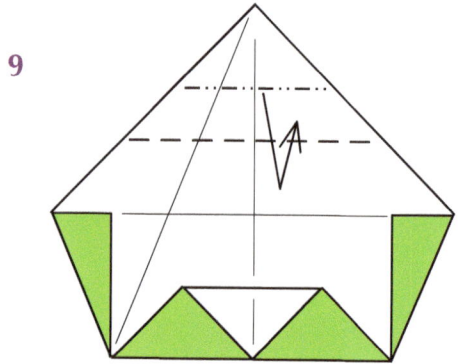

Valley-fold along the crease for this pleat fold.

10

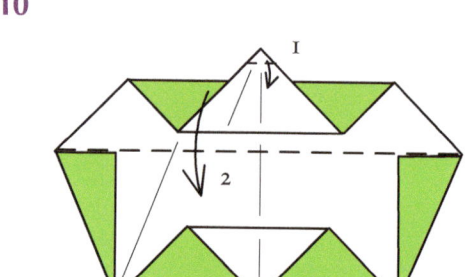

1. Fold down.
2. Fold along the crease.

11

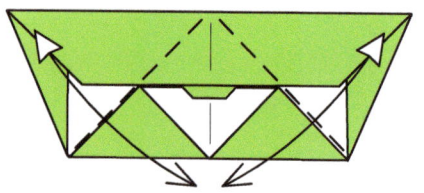

Fold and unfold.

12

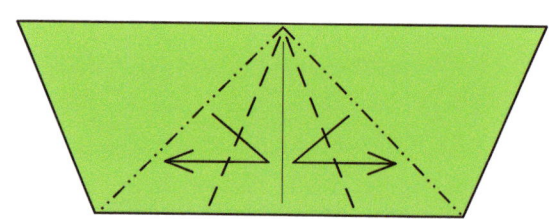

Pleat-fold to the center.

16 *Magical Origami Gnomes*

13

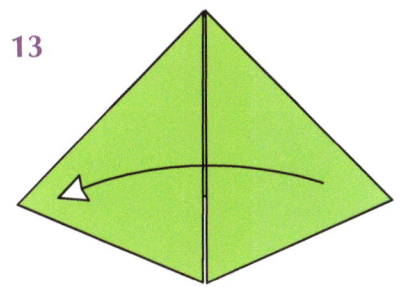

Unfold.

14

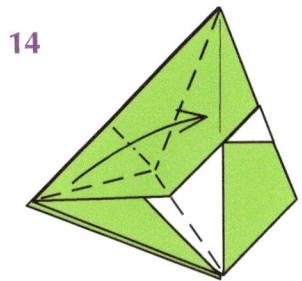

Rabbit-ear.

15

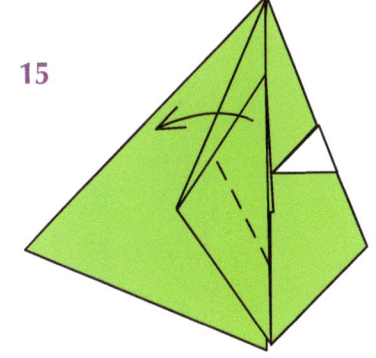

Spread-squash-fold.

16

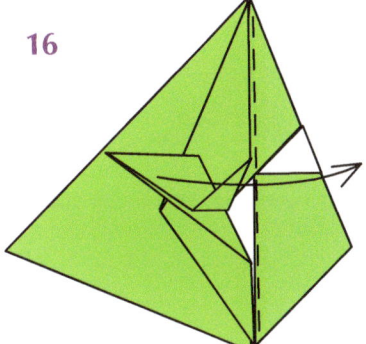

17

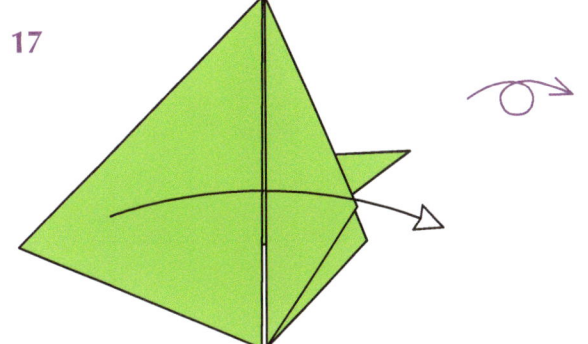

Repeat steps 13–16 in the opposite direction.

18

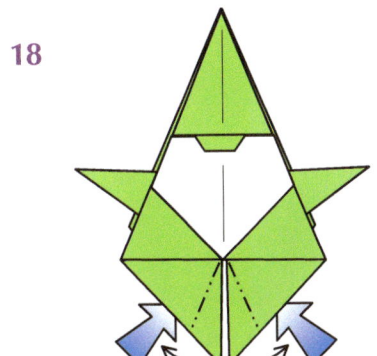

Make reverse folds.

19

Bramble Tiddlebiddle

Bramble Tiddlebiddle 17

Coggle Brightbrace

Coggle Brightbrace builds tiny wind chimes that sing sweet melodies and offers magical lanterns for safe travels. If your cart, kettle, or broomstick breaks, he will fix it with feathers and marble rocks, all while serving you gnome-made lemonade.

1

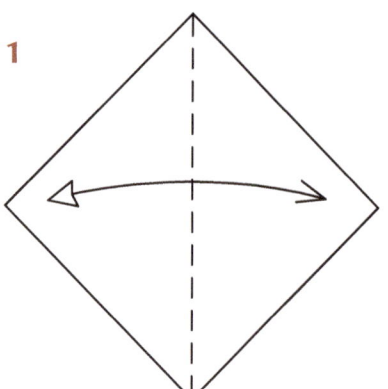

Fold and unfold.

2

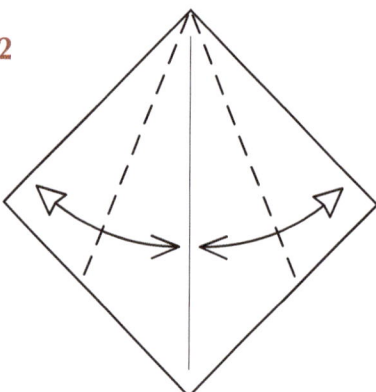

Fold to the center and unfold.

3

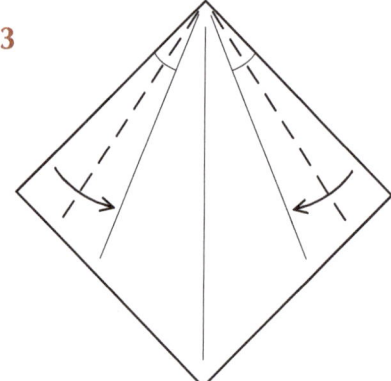

4

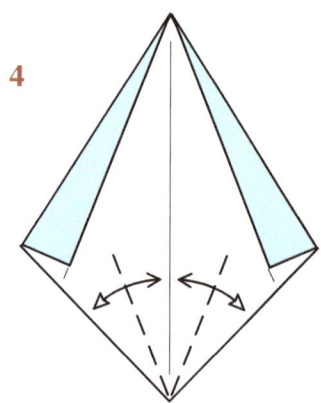

Fold to the center and unfold.

5

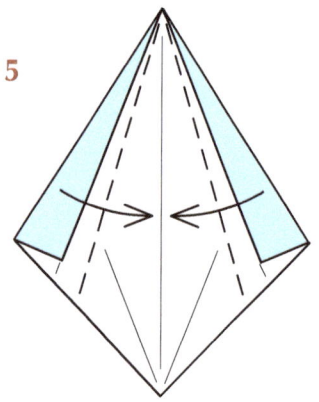

Fold to the center.

6

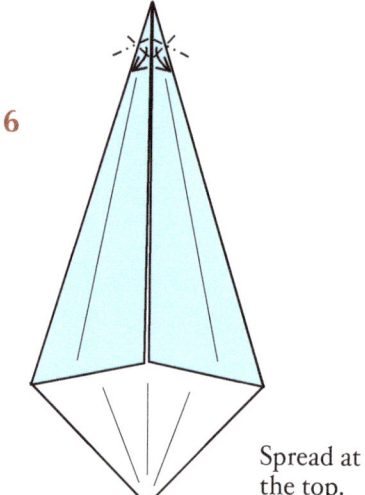

Spread at the top.

18 *Magical Origami Gnomes*

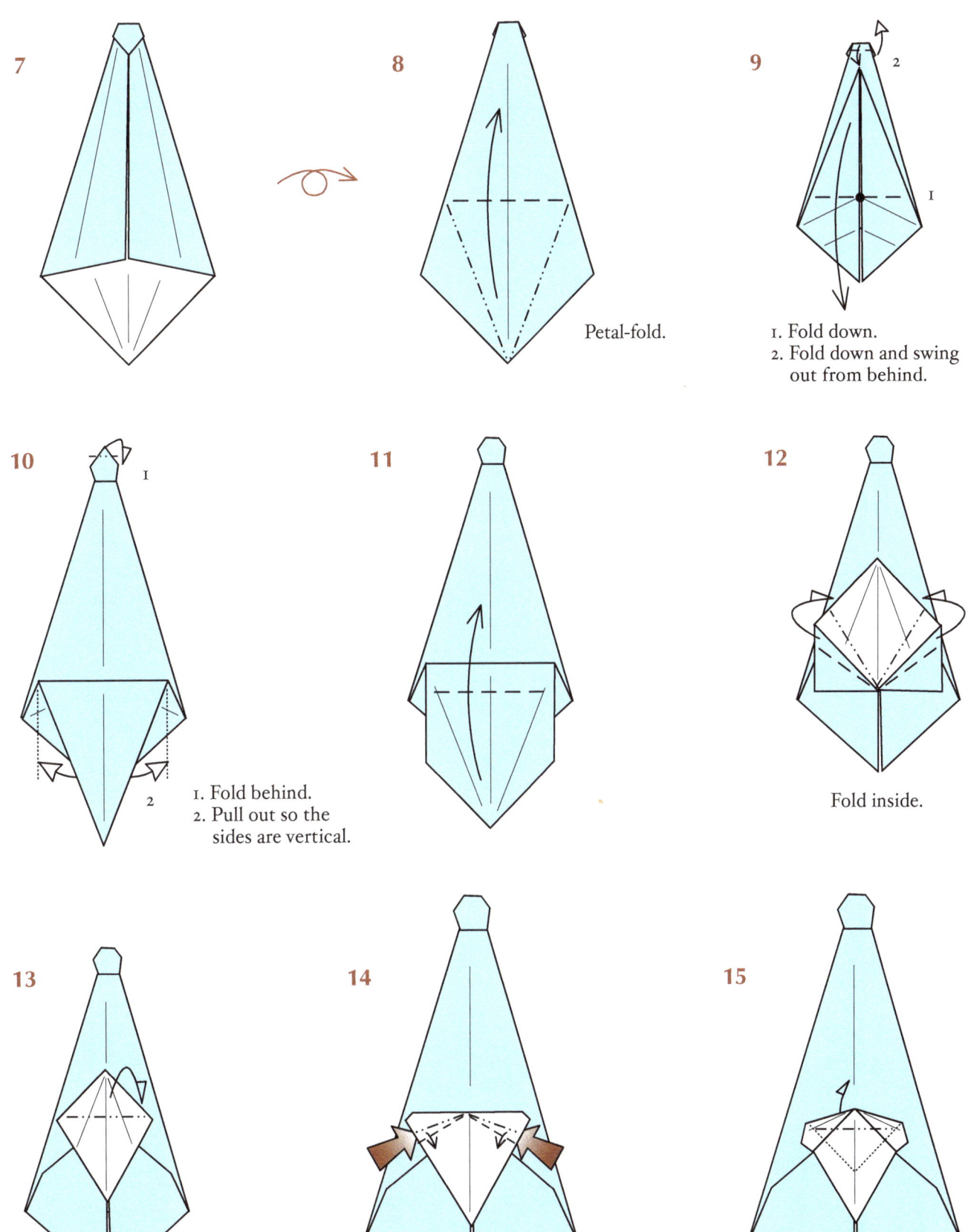

Coggle Brightbrace

16

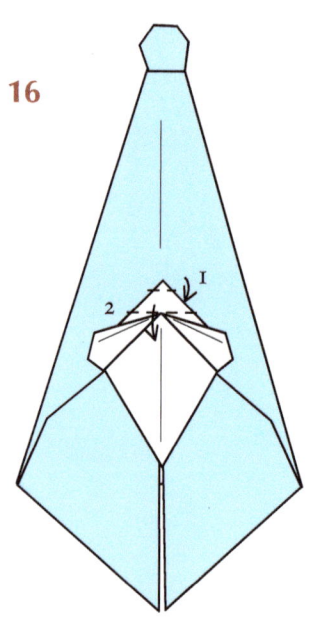

1. Fold down.
2. Fold down.

17

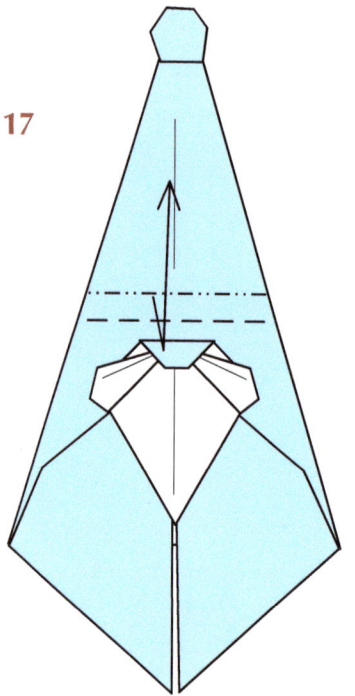

Pleat-fold to cover the top of the nose.

18

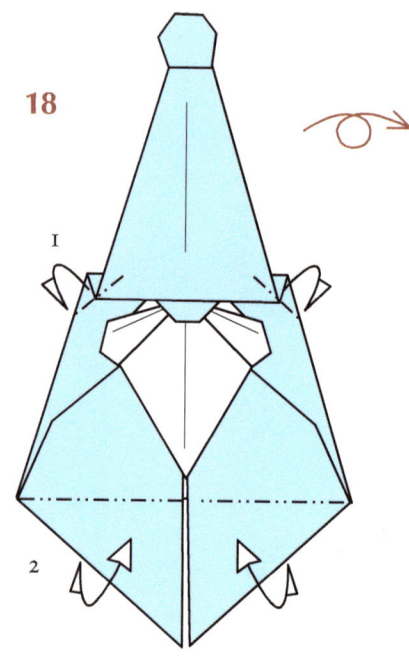

1. Fold behind.
2. Fold and unfold.

19

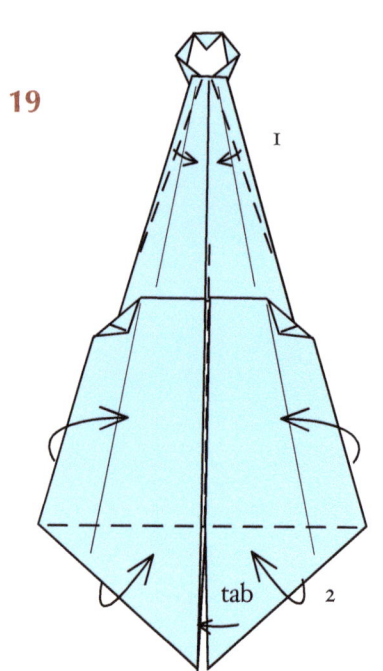

1. Fold thin strips.
2. Begin to fold the model in half to make it 3D. Lift up at the bottom and tuck the tab into the pocket.

20

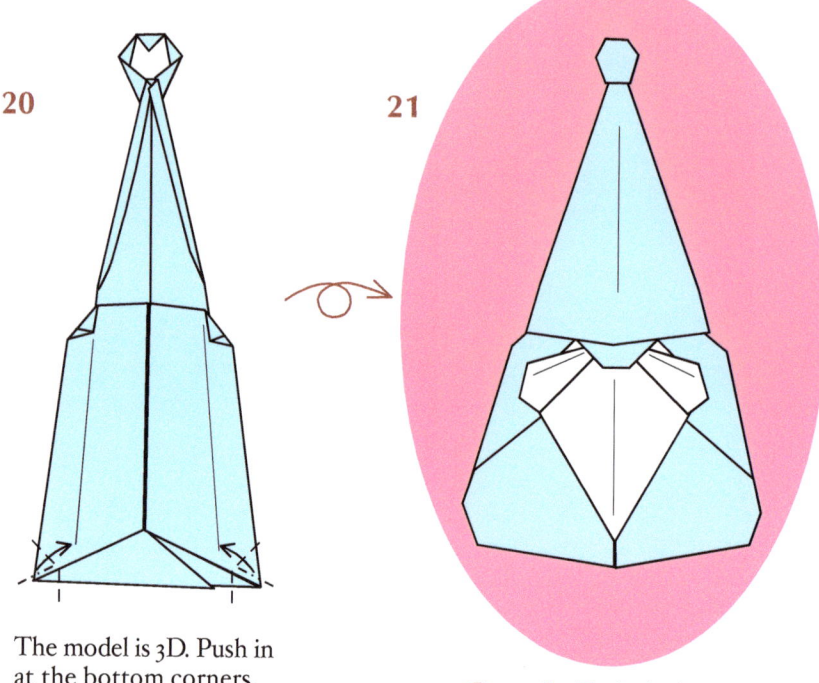

The model is 3D. Push in at the bottom corners. The model can stand.

21

Coggle Brightbrace

Pibbin Kettlestop

To keep your travels safe, Pibbin Kettlestop will offer you his glowing shoes, and show you the secrets of the sprigs and moss that will lead the way. His bubbling stew and little mushroom pies will keep you full and content.

1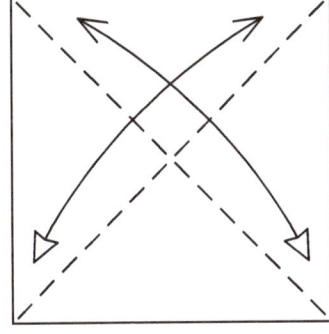

Fold and unfold.

2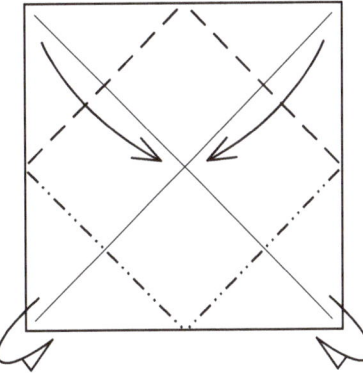

Fold to the center with two flaps in front and two behind.

3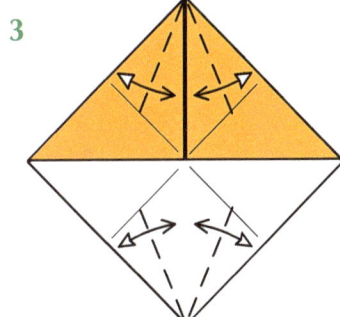

Fold to the center and unfold.

4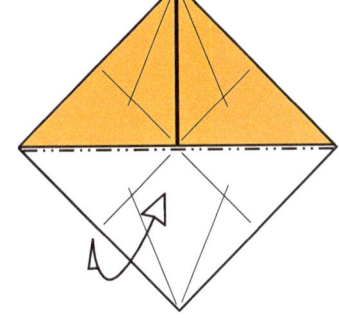

Fold and unfold.

5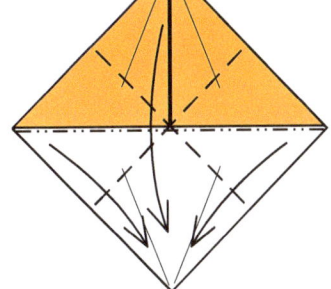

Fold along the creases.

6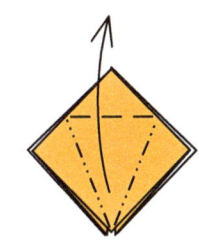

Petal-fold.

Pibbin Kettlestop 21

7

8

Petal-fold.

9

Pull out the hidden corners.

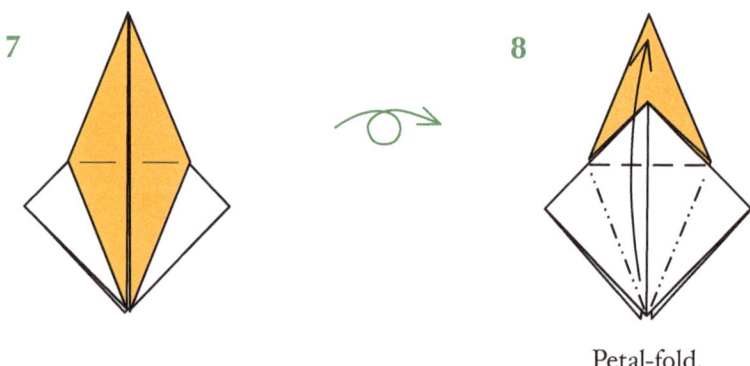
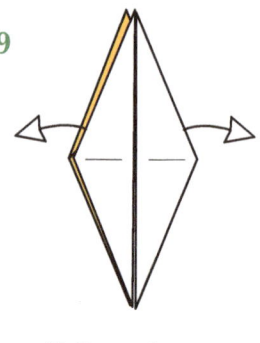

10

Fold behind and unfold.

11

12

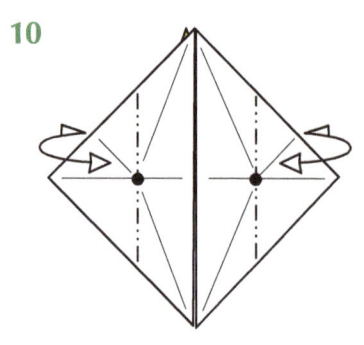
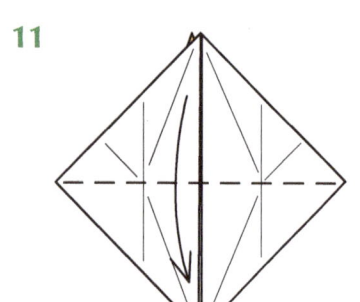
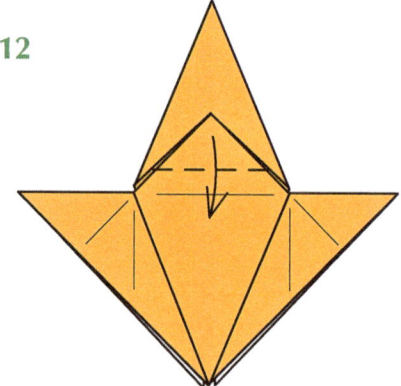

13

Sink-nose-fold.
(See page 12.)

14

Tuck inside so the dots meet.

15

Fold along the creases for these crimp folds.

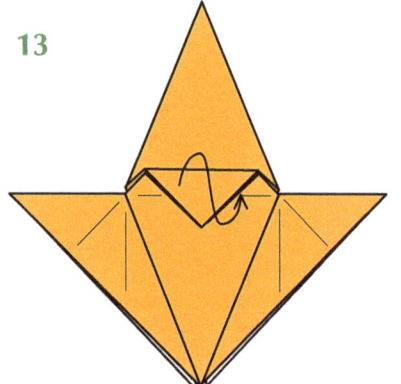
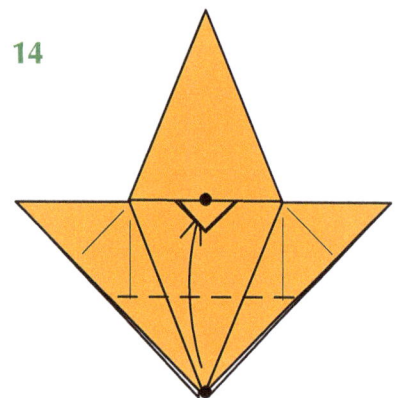
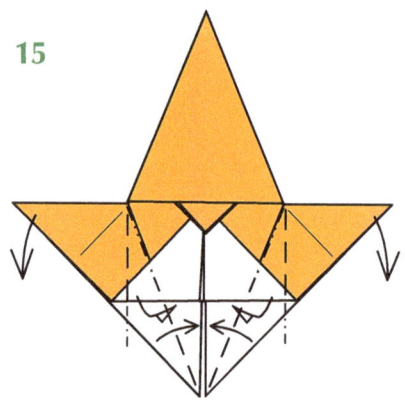

22 *Magical Origami Gnomes*

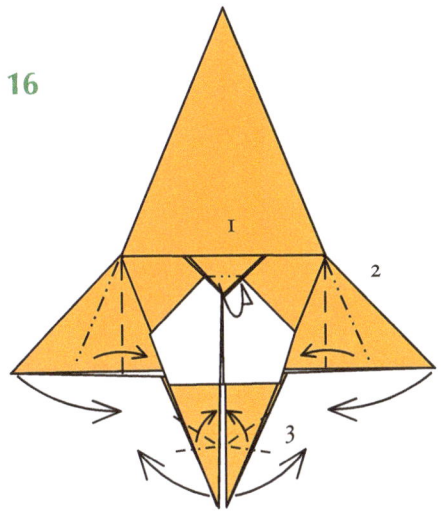

1. Fold inside.
2. Make squash folds.
3. Make crimp folds.

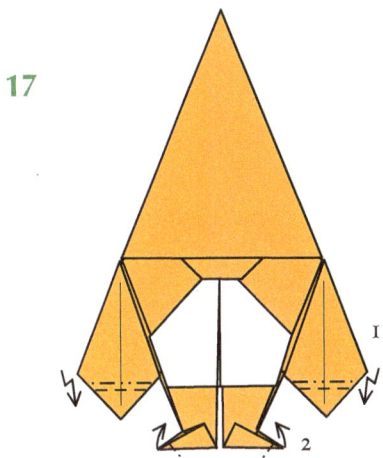

1. Make pleat folds.
2. Make reverse folds.

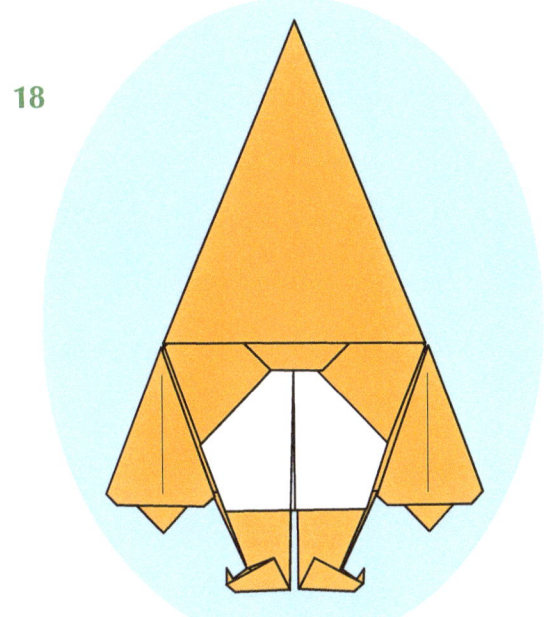

Pibbin Kettlestop

Pibbin Kettlestop 23

Dabble Rumpleburr

When tired, Dabble Rumpleburr's inn is open, ready to prepare meals of buttered blossoms and warm spicy twigs. He will slip helpful notes and little treats into your hat, along with enchanted maps that glow in the dark. With a crystal orb and floating feathers, he will tell you the best spots to visit that take the path of leaf resistance.

1

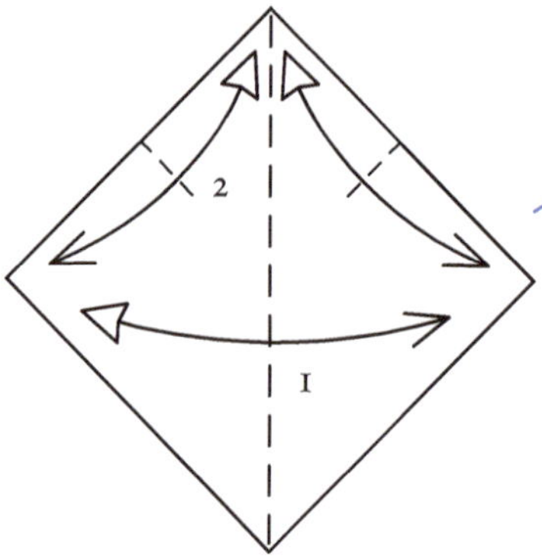

1. Fold and unfold.
2. Fold and unfold on the edges.

2

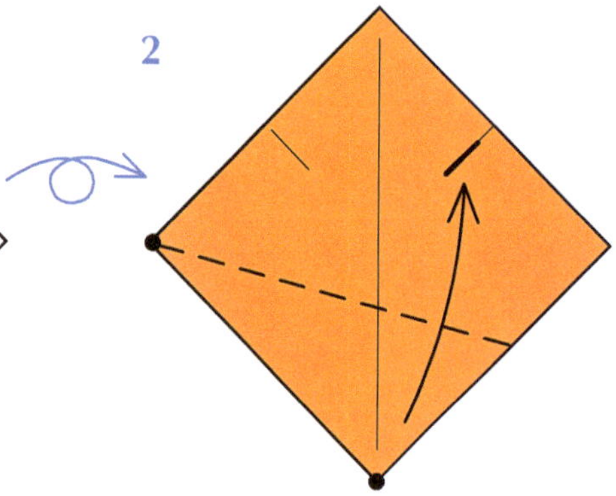

Bring the lower dot to the bold line.

3

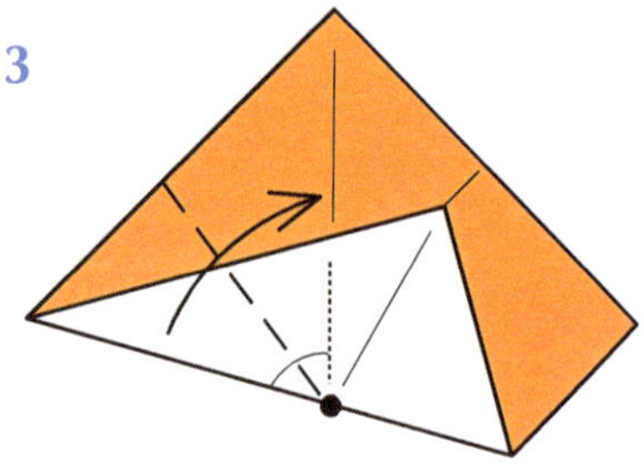

4

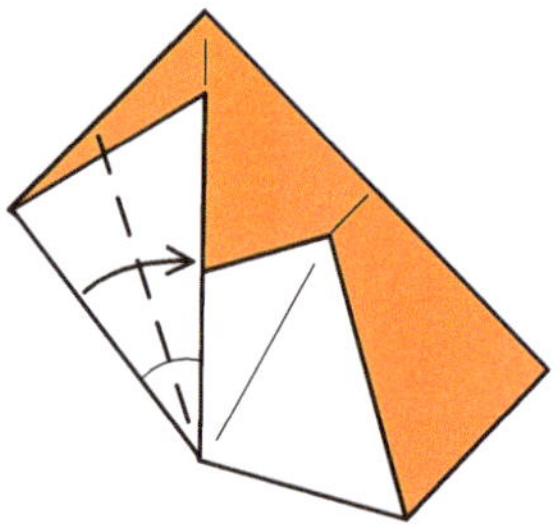

5

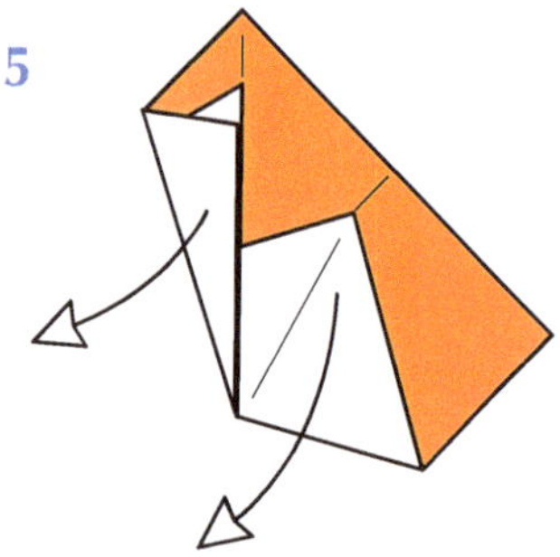

Unfold everything.

6

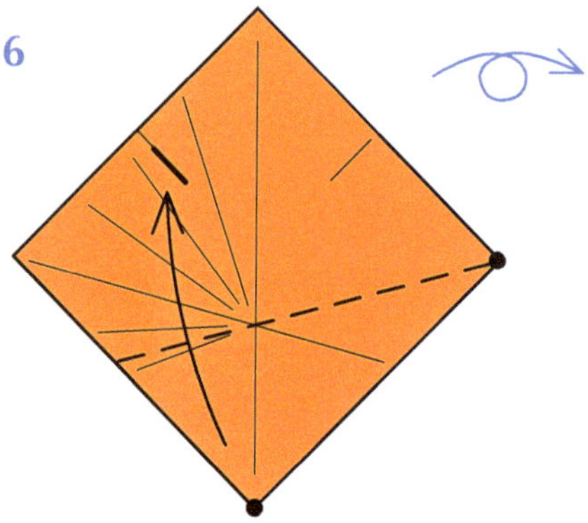

Repeat steps 2–5 in the opposite direction. Rotate 180°.

24 *Magical Origami Gnomes*

7

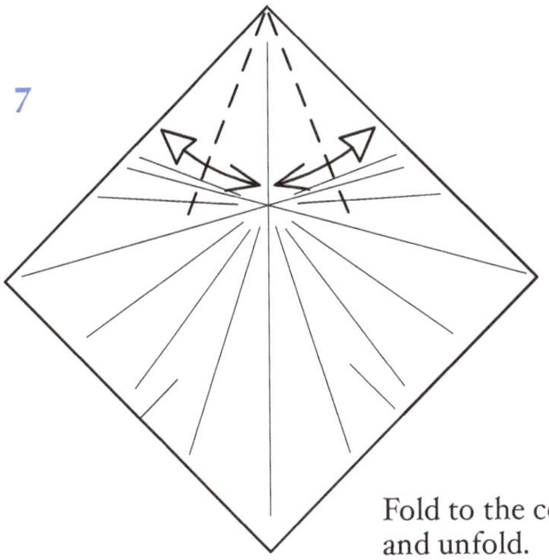

Fold to the center and unfold.

8

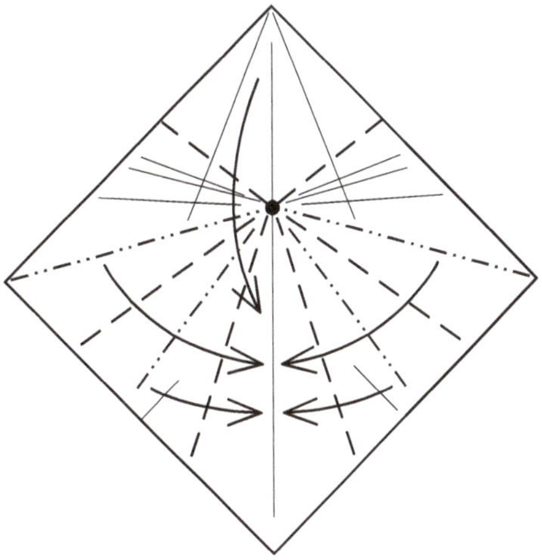

Push in at the dot, fold along the creases and flatten.

9

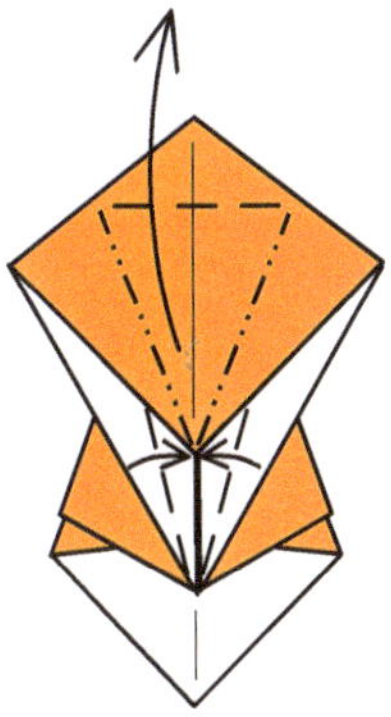

Petal-fold.

10

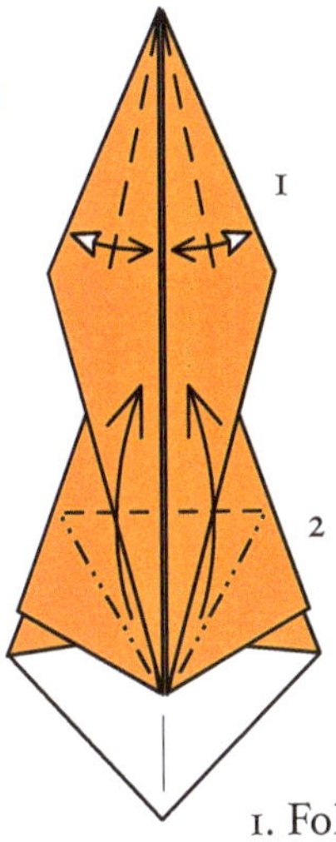

1. Fold and unfold.
2. Make squash folds.

11

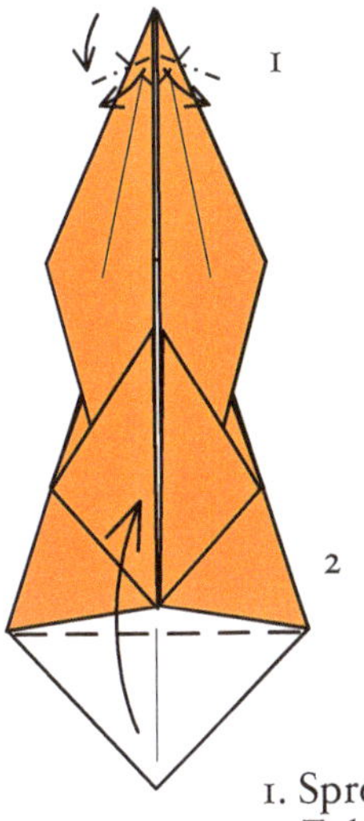

1. Spread the tip.
2. Fold up.

12

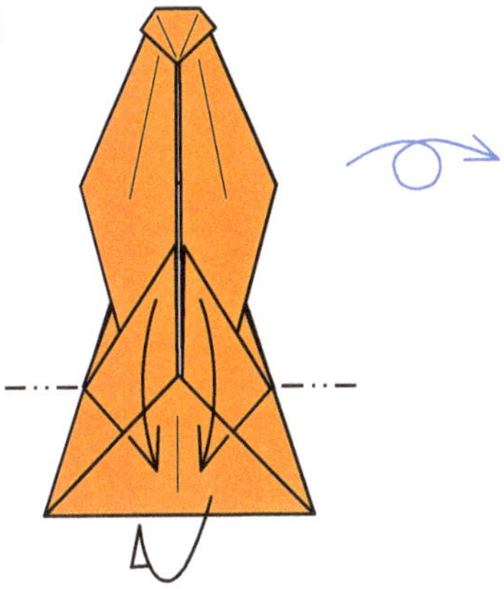

Fold behind and swing out from in front.

13

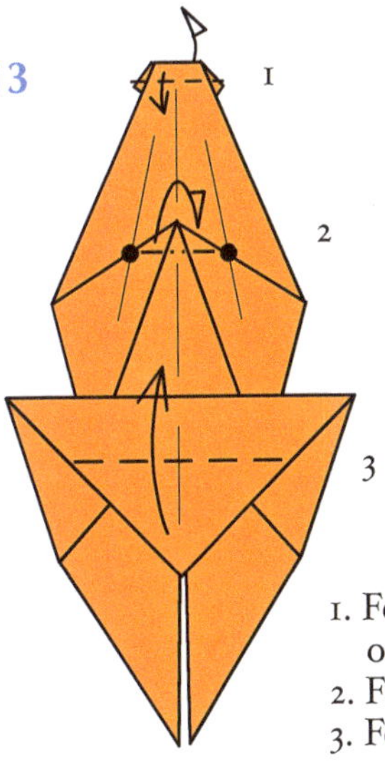

1. Fold down and swing out from behind.
2. Fold behind.
3. Fold up.

14

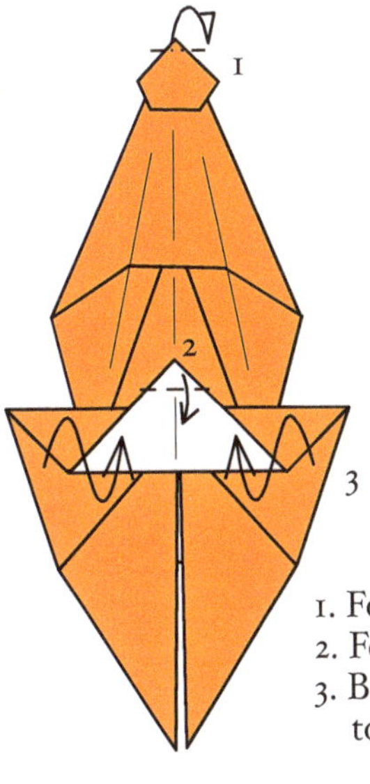

1. Fold behind.
2. Fold down.
3. Bring the layers to the front.

15

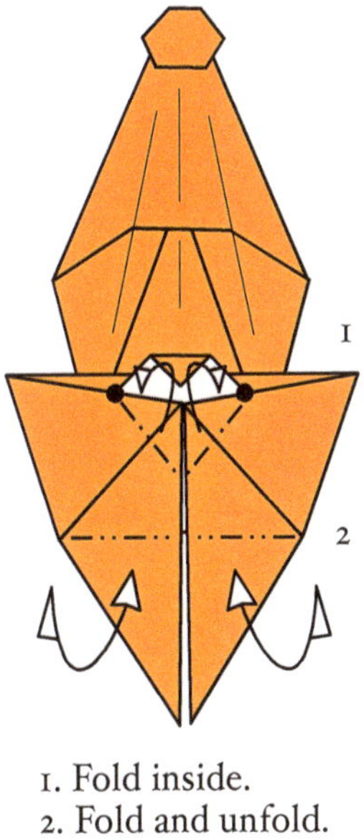

1. Fold inside.
2. Fold and unfold.

Dabble Rumpleburr 25

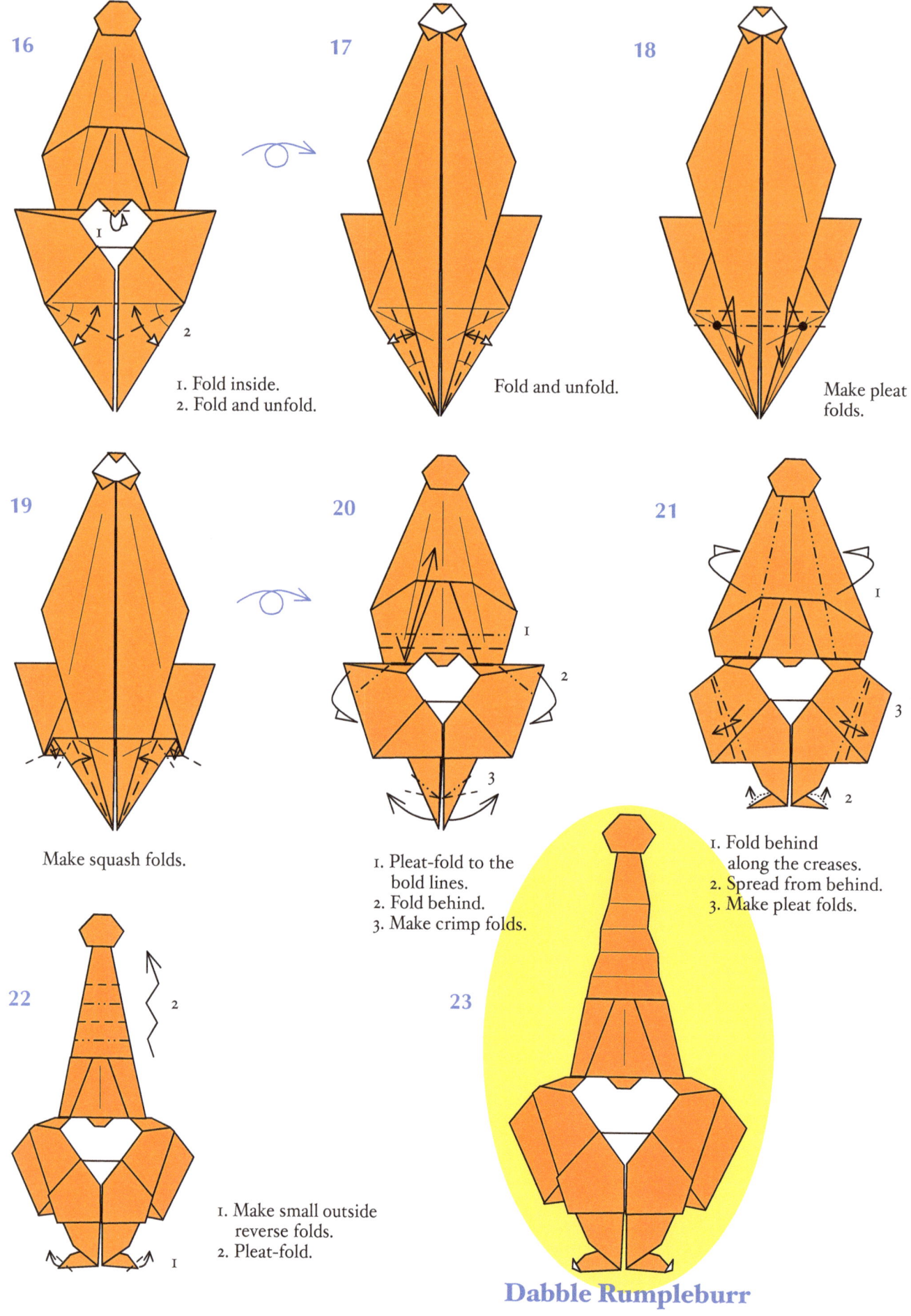

Dabble Rumpleburr

Hobb Tillerpot

This garden gnome invites you to join garden tasks, such as growing moss in intricate patterns, while telling stories. He will leave gift baskets of sun-dried oak leaves, overgrown blueberries, and fresh vines. With wind chimes and fountains nearby, he will teach you how to sleep with a ladybug on your nose. Follow the red mushrooms as you continue your journey.

1

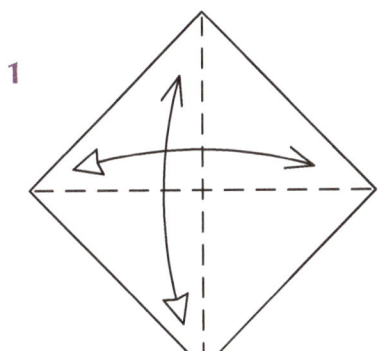

Fold and unfold.

2

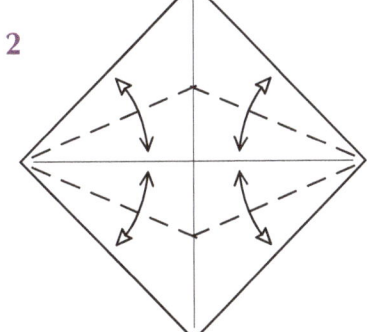

Fold to the center and unfold.

3

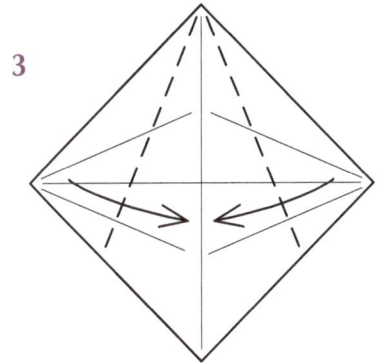

Fold to the center.

4

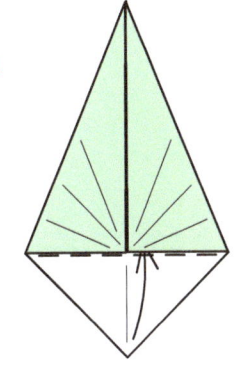

Tuck inside.

5

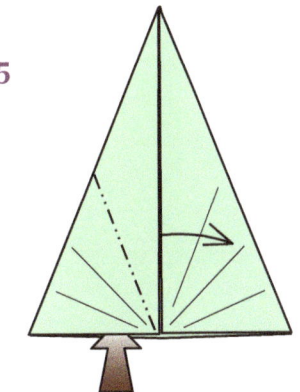

Reverse-fold.

6

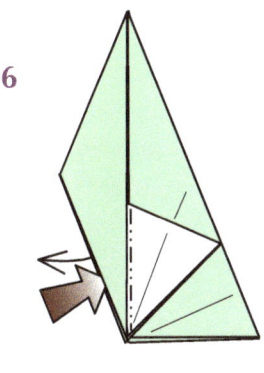

Reverse-fold.

Hobb Tillerpot 27

7
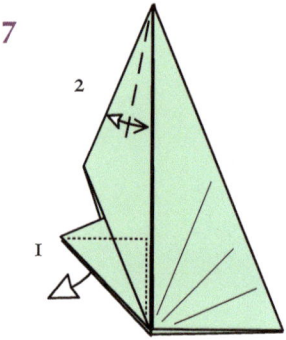

1. Pull out from inside.
2. Fold and unfold.

8
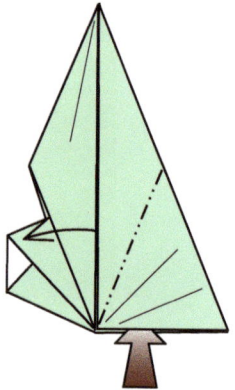

Repeat steps 5–7 on the right.

9
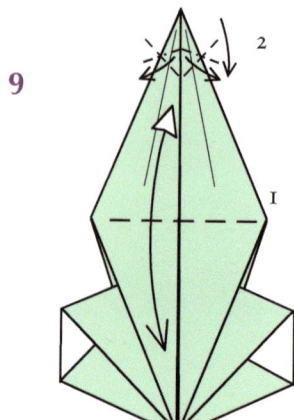

1. Fold and unfold.
2. Spread.

10
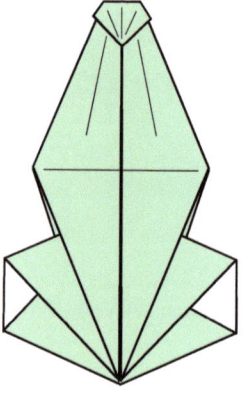

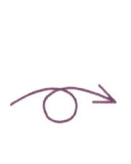

11
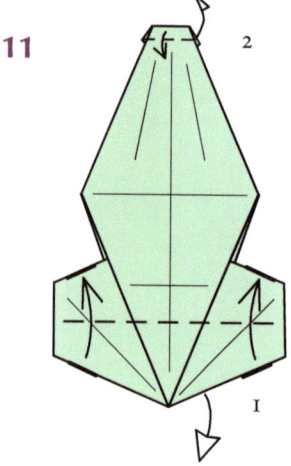

1. Fold up and swing out from behind.
2. Fold down and swing out from behind.

12
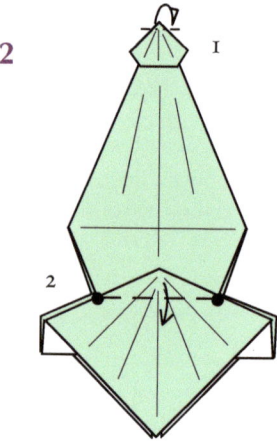

1. Fold behind.
2. Fold down.

13
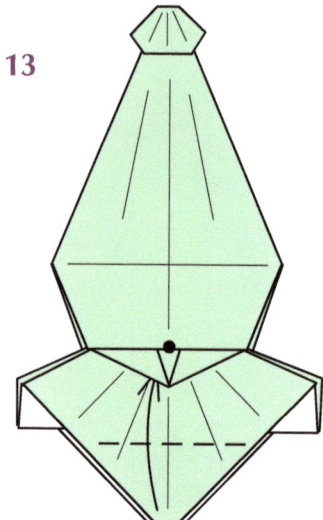

Tuck inside. The dots will meet.

14
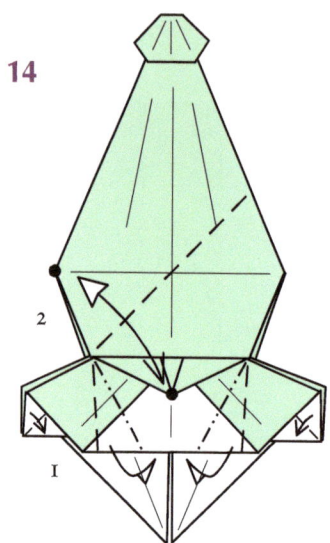

1. Fold inside on the left and right.
2. Fold and unfold.

15
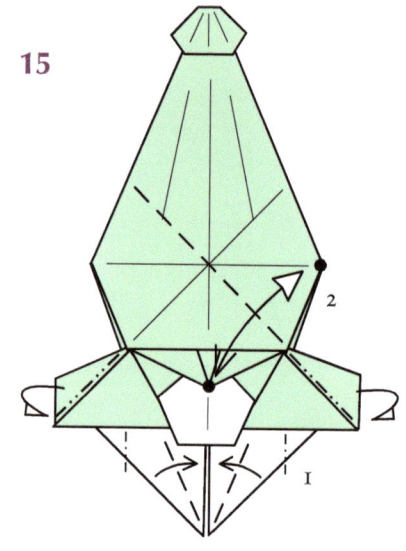

1. Fold inside on the left and right.
2. Fold and unfold.

28 *Magical Origami Gnomes*

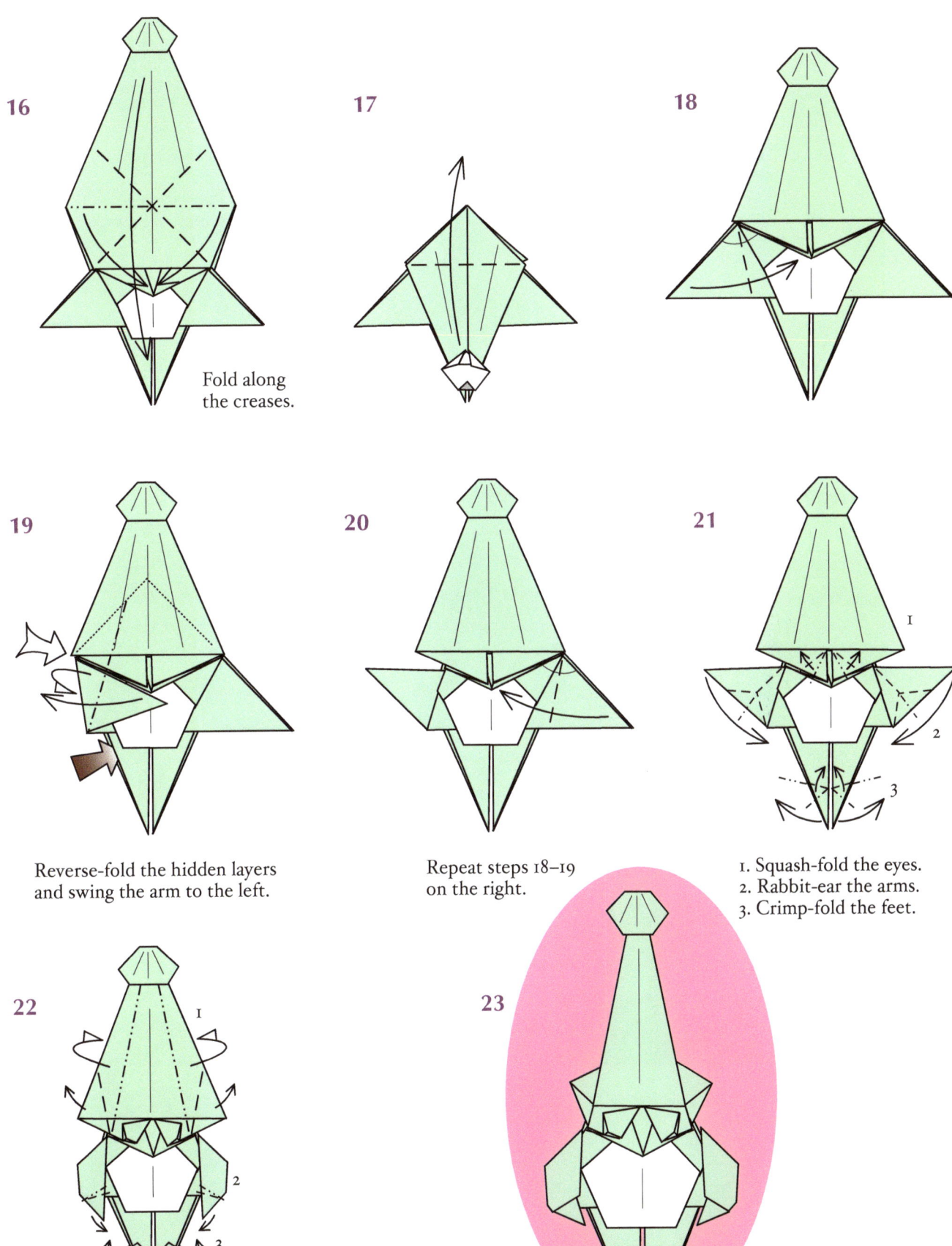

Hobb Tillerpot

Mountain Gnomes of the East

The cold mountains in the East are filled with caves. Mountain Gnomes have found the way to these caves that ramble on like mazes. These gnomes mine precious metals and guard their hidden treasures. By hiding their legs and arms, they resemble the surrounding rocks and can speak to them. They craft intricate jewelry.

Varnic Thunderforge

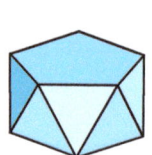

This gnome is skillful at combining magic with stone-shaping, known as "geomancy". He keeps a carved stone in each corner of the cave. When cracks appear in the cave, he fixes them with gnome improvement tools.

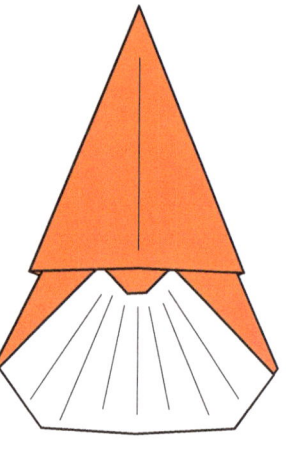

1

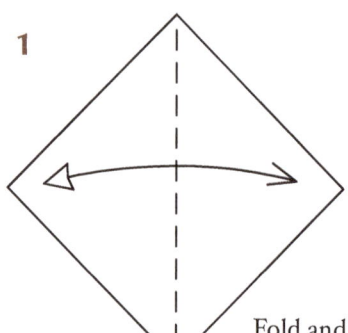

Fold and unfold.

2

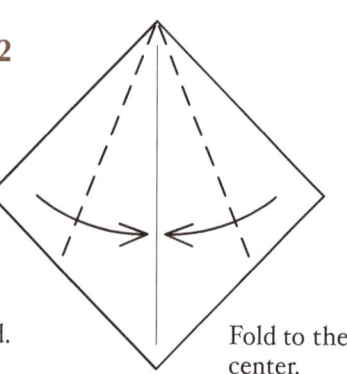

Fold to the center.

3

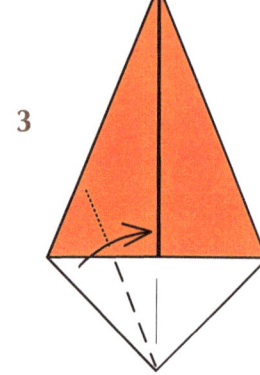

Crease on the bottom part.

4

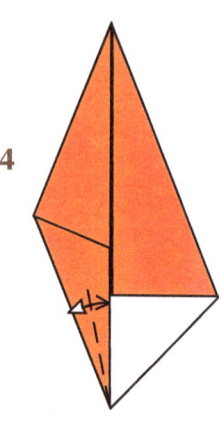

Fold and unfold all the layers.

30   *Magical Origami Gnomes*

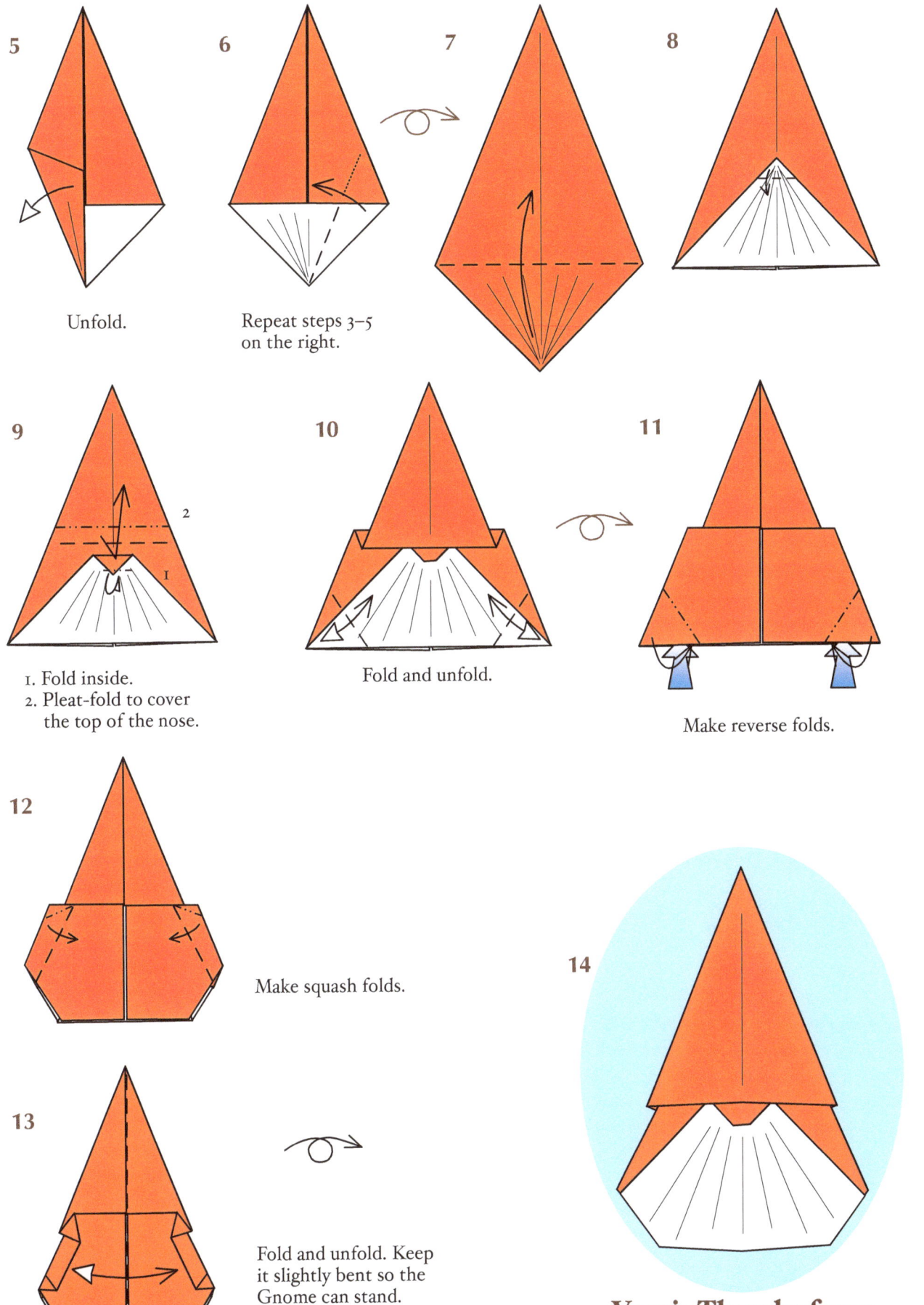

Varnic Thunderforge

Brindle Copperknot

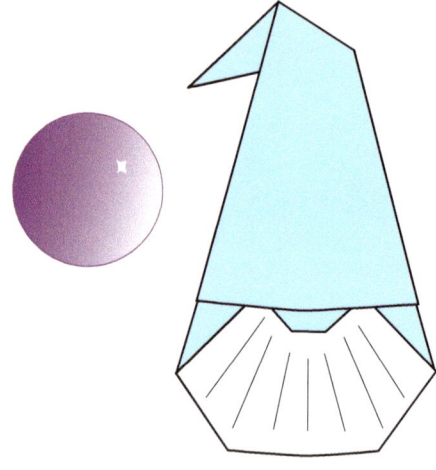

Mining rare gems, Brindle Copperknot is surrounded by beautiful gems. He creates colorful lutes with his gems. On rainy days he stays in his cave. Sunny days, too. He likes his cave.

1

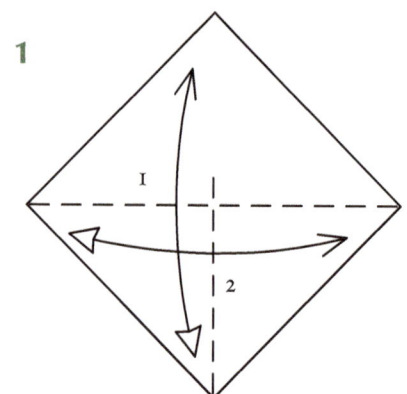

1. Fold and unfold.
2. Fold and unfold on the bottom half.

2

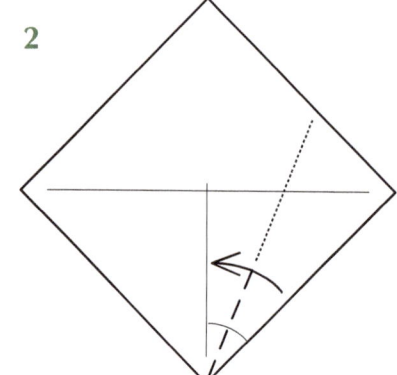

Fold to the center. Crease on the bottom.

3

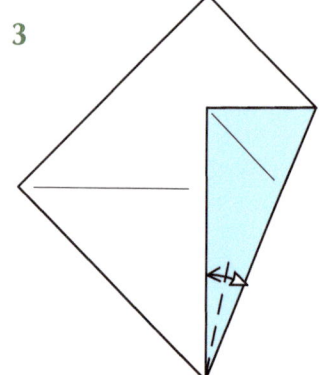

Fold and unfold all the layers.

4

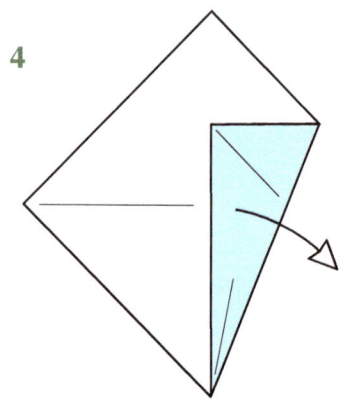

Unfold.

5

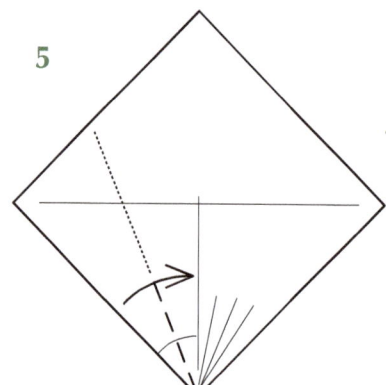

Repeat steps 2–4 on the left.

6

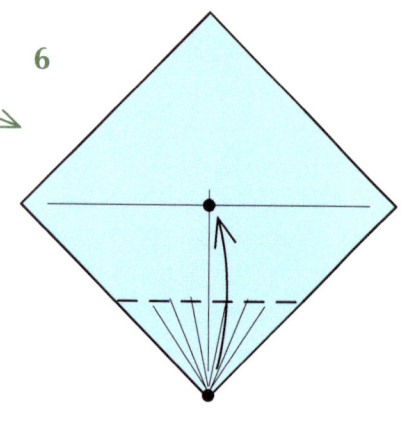

32 *Magical Origami Gnomes*

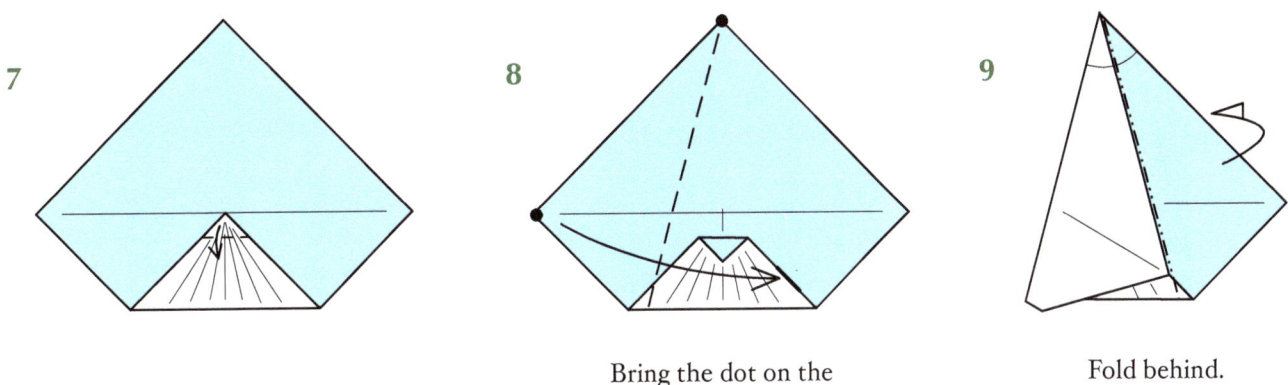

8. Bring the dot on the left to the bold line.

9. Fold behind.

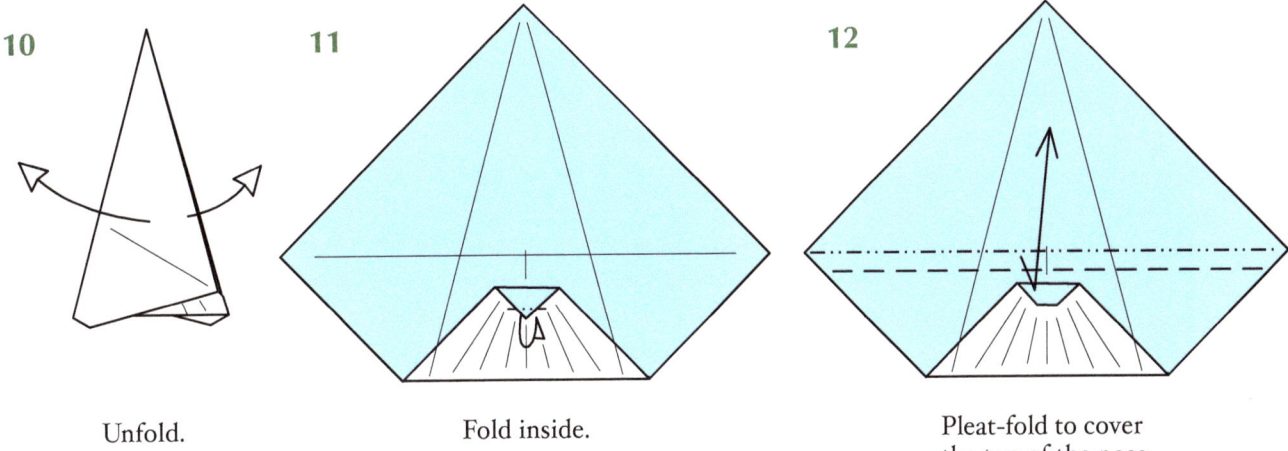

10. Unfold.

11. Fold inside.

12. Pleat-fold to cover the top of the nose.

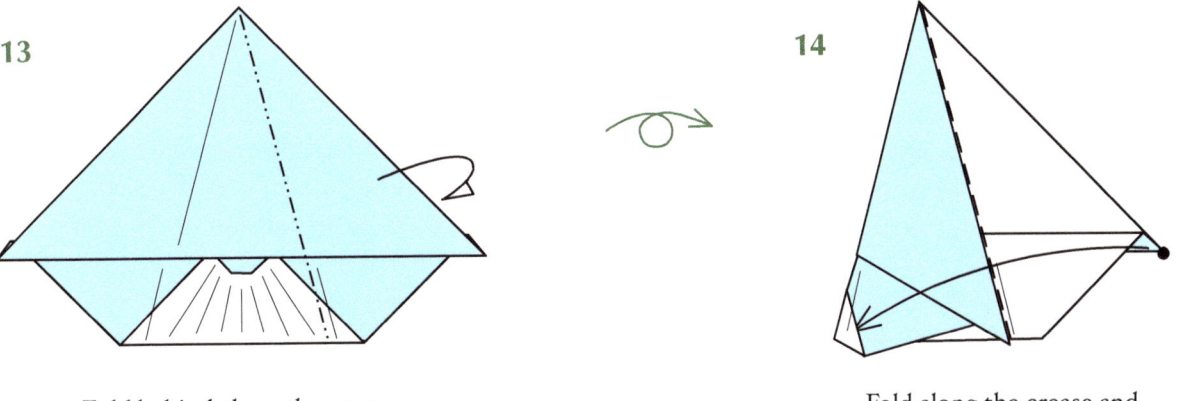

13. Fold behind along the crease.

14. Fold along the crease and tuck into the pocket.

Brindle Copperknot 33

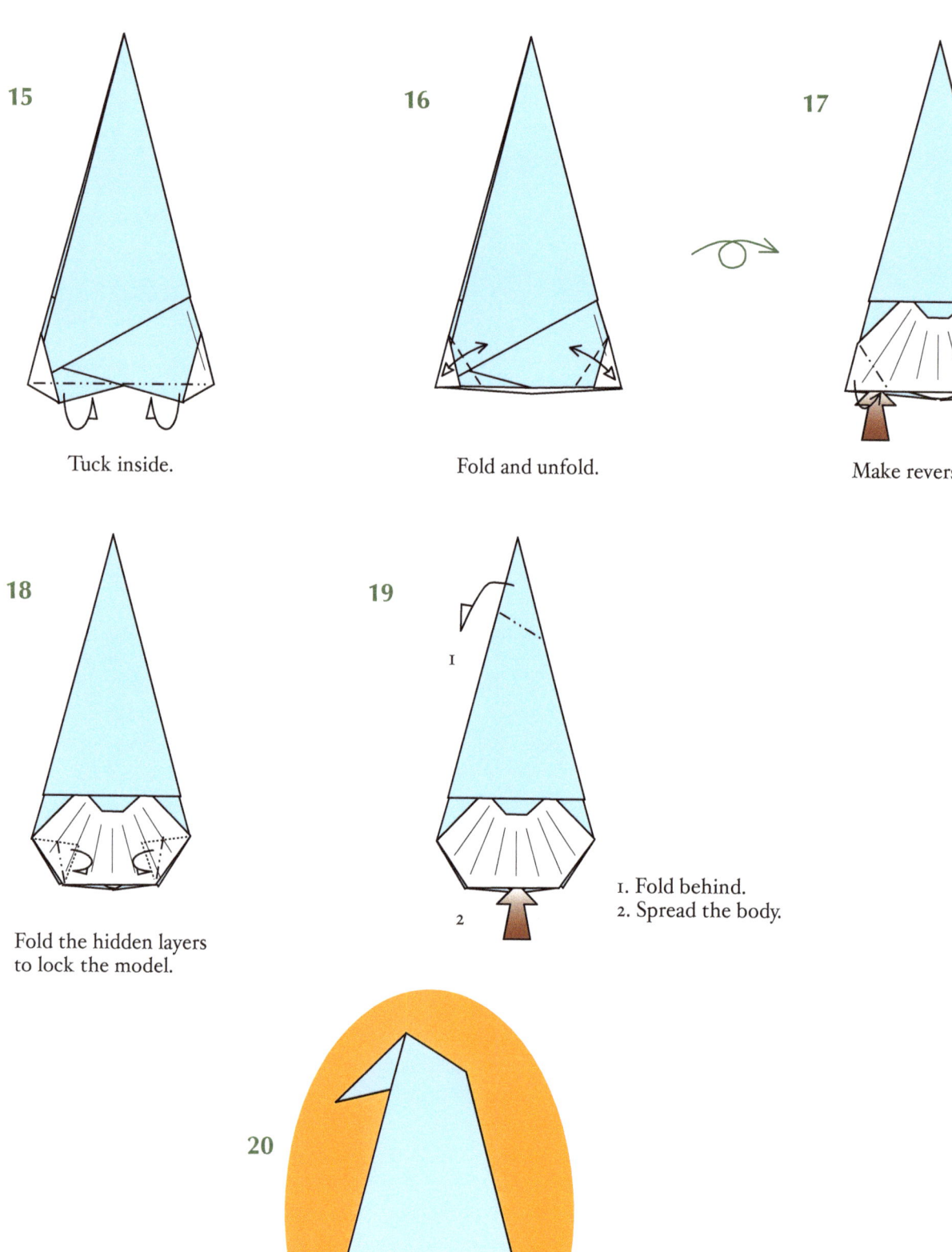

15 Tuck inside.

16 Fold and unfold.

17 Make reverse folds.

18 Fold the hidden layers to lock the model.

19
1. Fold behind.
2. Spread the body.

20

Brindle Copperknot

MountainCliffer

MountainCliffer likes to explore the deepest caves because they hold the brightest crystals. He walks barefoot ever since a stone in his shoe told him "walk barefoot". On outings in the rugged terrain, when crossing deep streams, he summons the stones to be his stepping stones.

1

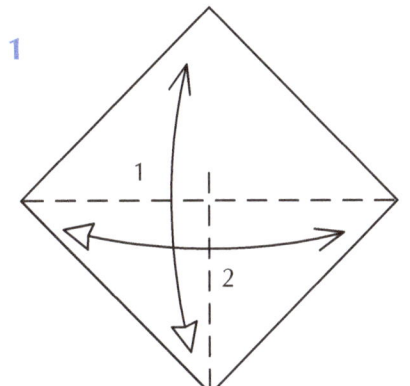

1. Fold and unfold.
2. Fold and unfold on the bottom half.

2

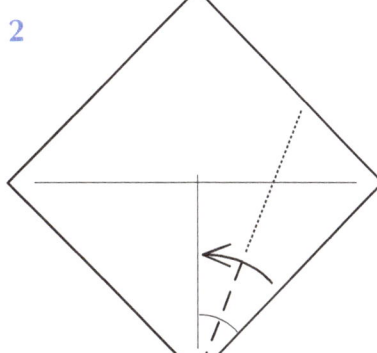

Fold to the center. Crease on the bottom.

3

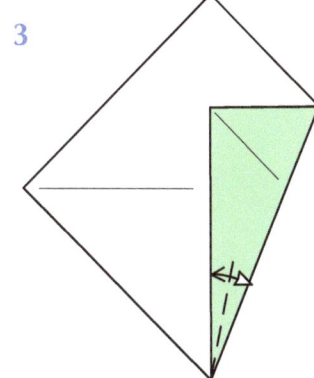

Fold and unfold all the layers.

4

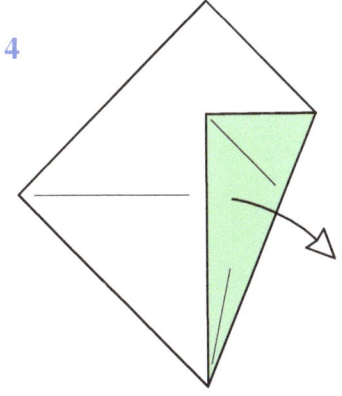

Unfold.

5

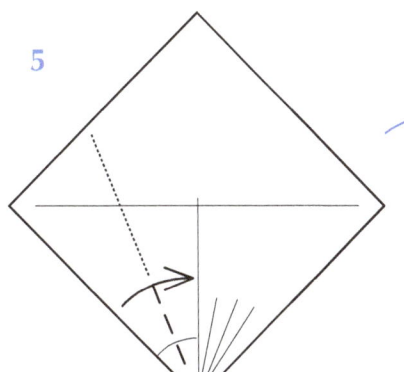

Repeat steps 2–4 on the left.

6

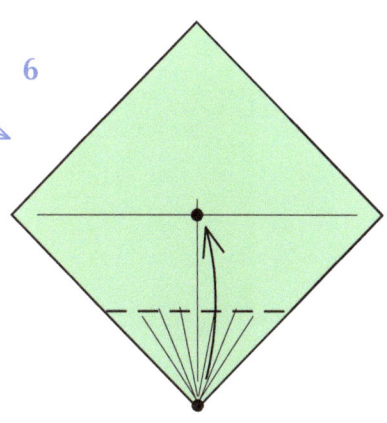

MountainCliffer 35

7

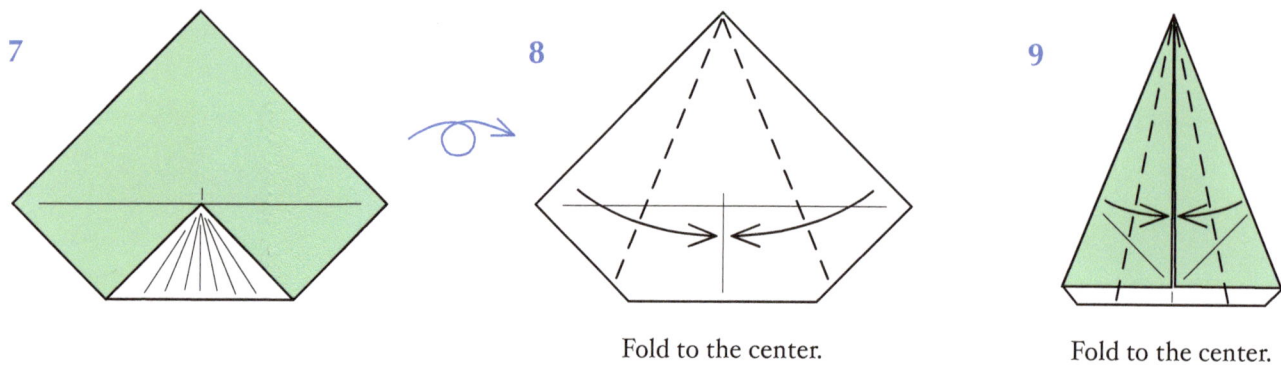

8

Fold to the center.

9

Fold to the center.

10

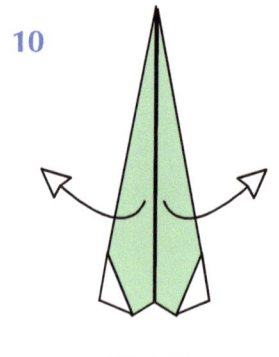

Unfold.

11

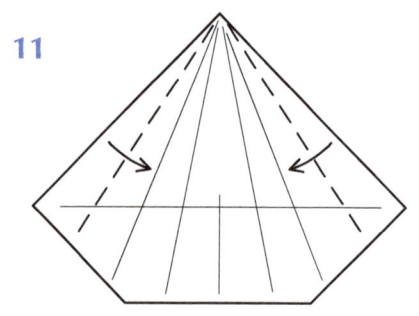

Fold along the creases.

12

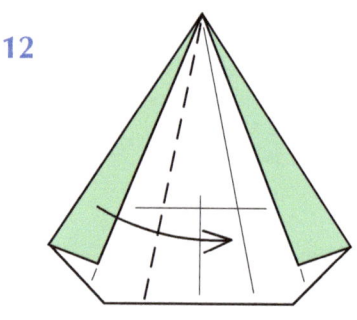

Fold along the crease.

13

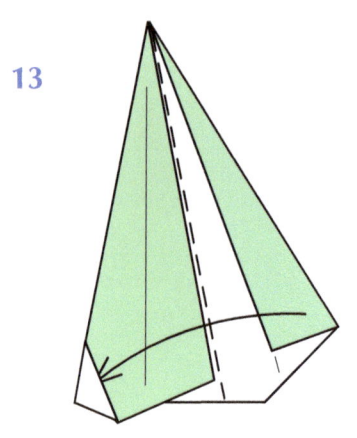

Tuck inside.

14

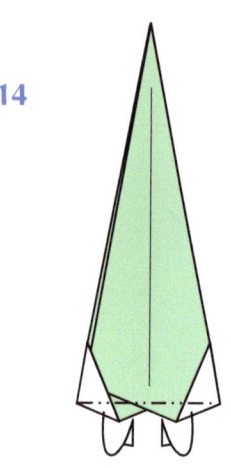

Tuck inside.

15

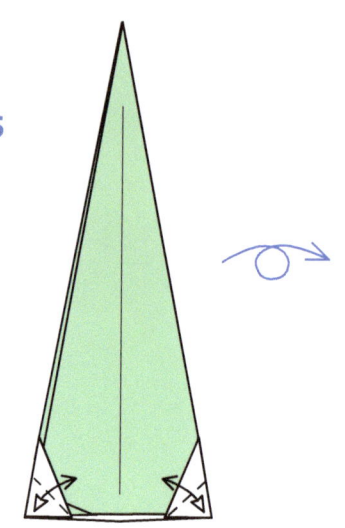

Fold and unfold.

36 *Magical Origami Gnomes*

16

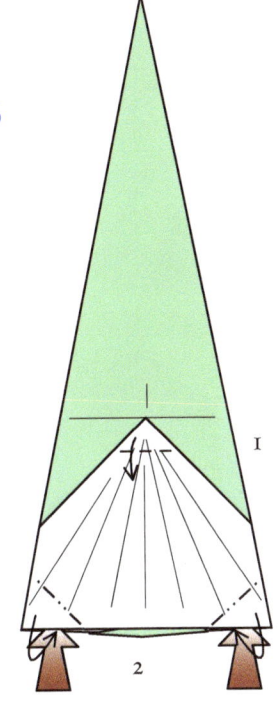

1. Fold down.
2. Make reverse folds.

17

1. Fold inside.
2. Pleat-fold to cover the top of the nose. Mountain-fold along the crease.

18

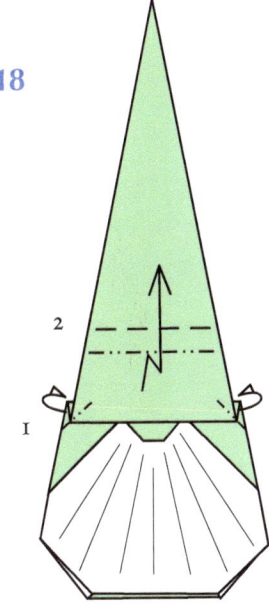

1. Fold behind.
2. Pleat-fold.

19

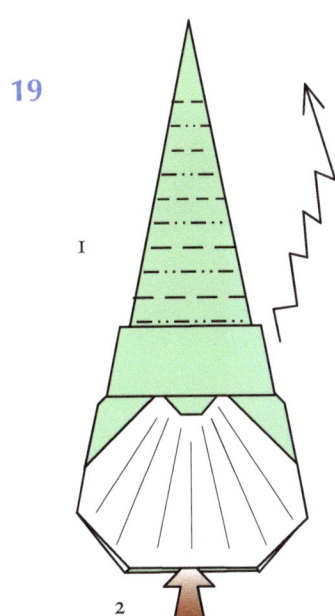

1. Continue with pleat folds for the hat. Then spread the hat.
2. Spread the body.

20

MountainCliffer

MountainCliffer 37

Crystalline Ironsprocket

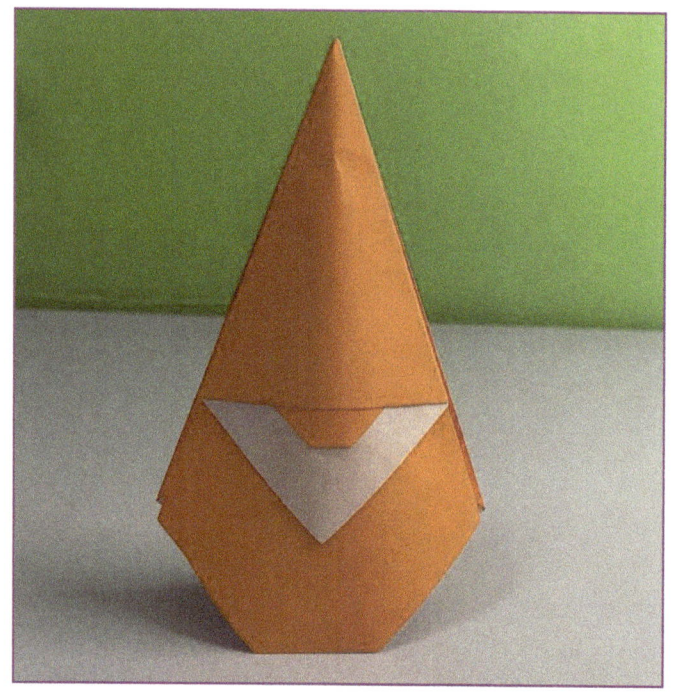

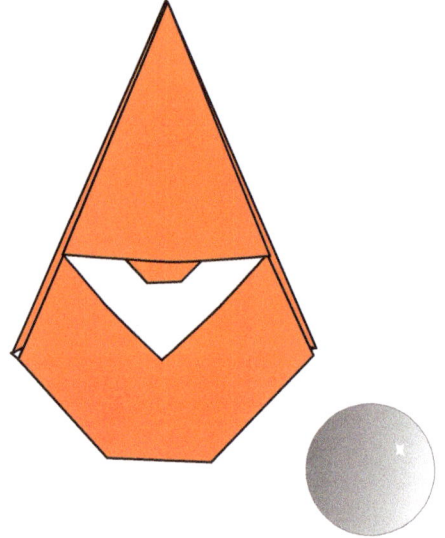

Crystalline Ironsprocket creates colorful crystals that make beautiful music. Listen carefully to these unearthly sounds and you will sleep like a rock.

1

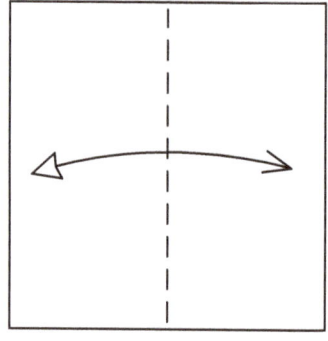

Fold and unfold.

2

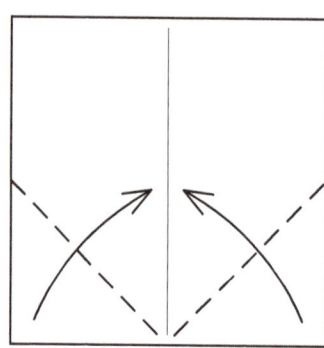

3

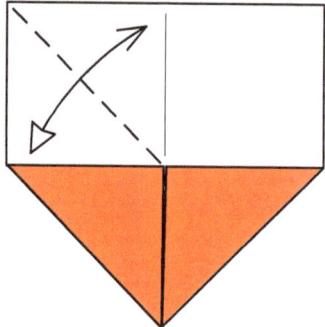

Fold and unfold.

4

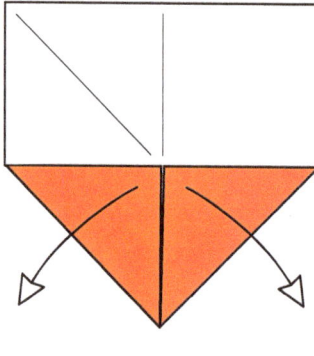

Unfold.

5

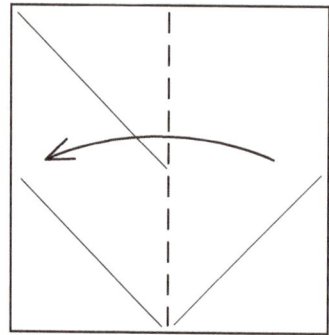

6

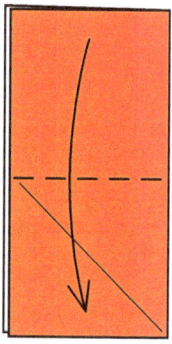

38   *Magical Origami Gnomes*

7

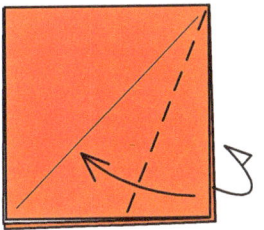

Fold the top flap and repeat behind.

8

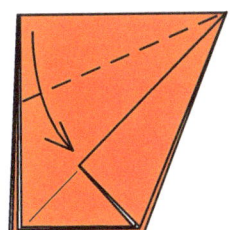

Fold all the layers.

9

Unfold everything.

10

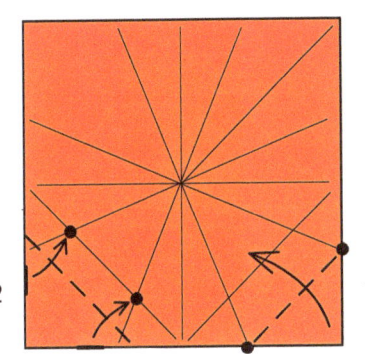

1. Valley-fold.
2. The edges will meet the dots.

11

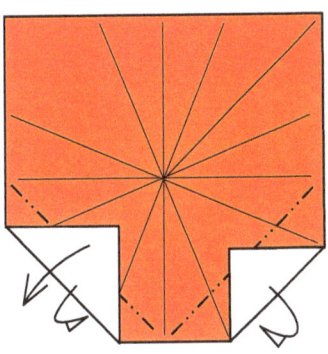

Mountain-fold along the creases.

12

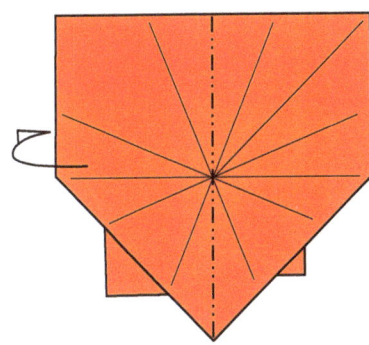

Fold along the crease and rotate 90°.

13

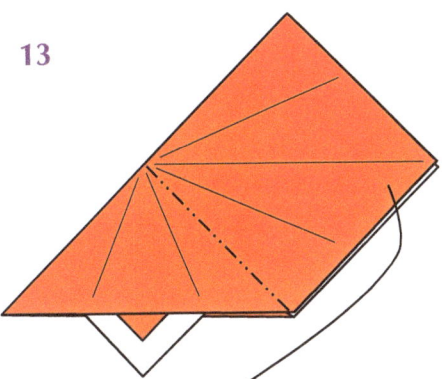

Mountain-fold along the crease.

14

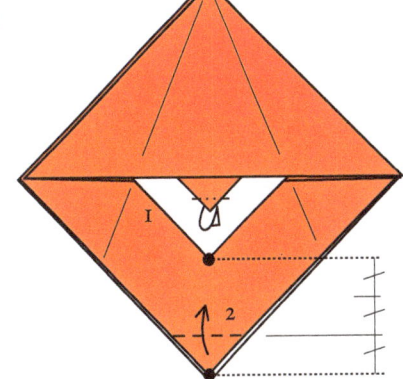

1. Fold behind.
2. Fold both layers up about 1/3 from the dots.

Crystalline Ironsprocket 39

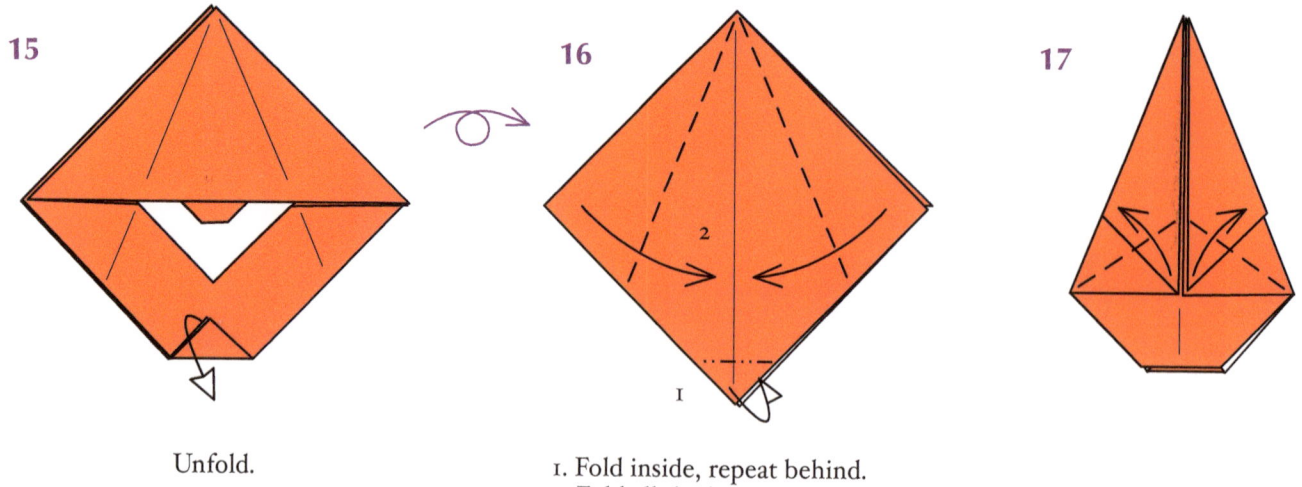

Unfold.

1. Fold inside, repeat behind.
2. Fold all the layers to the center.

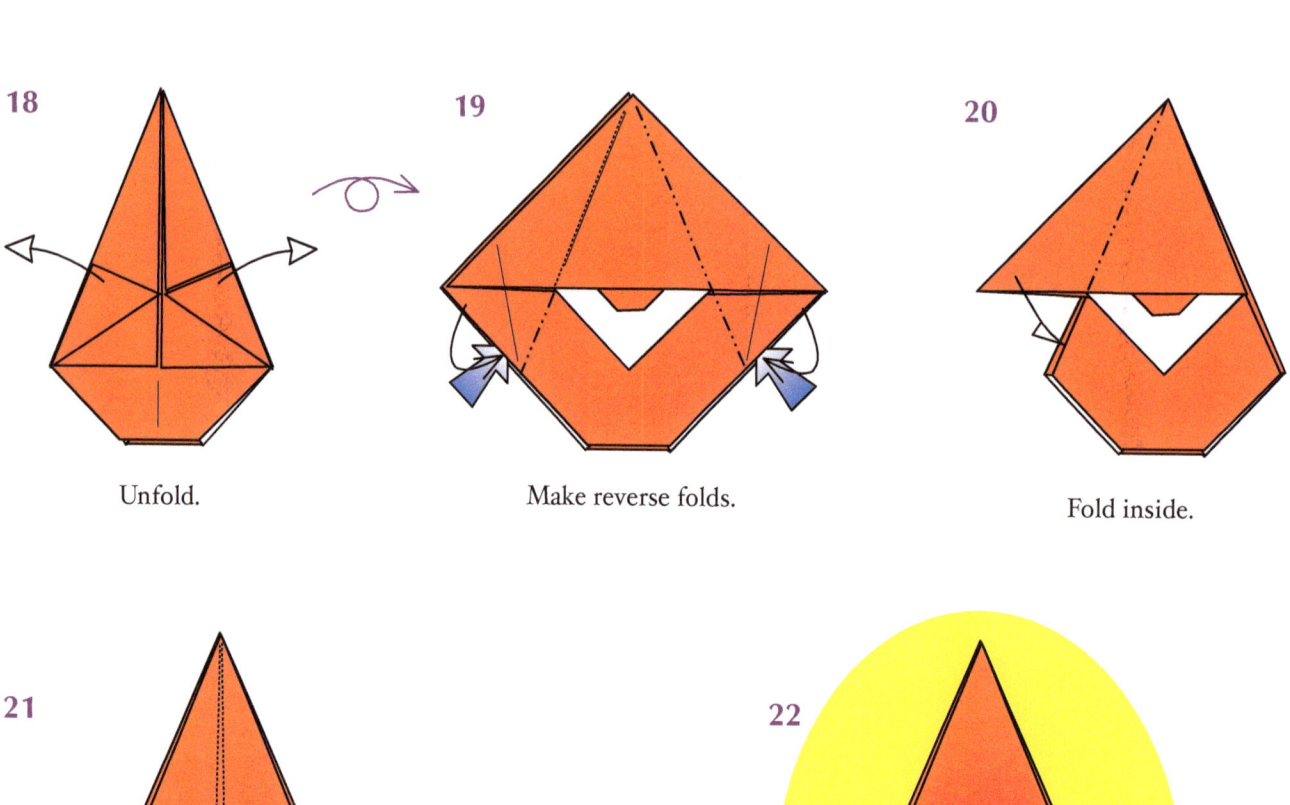

Unfold.

Make reverse folds.

Fold inside.

1. Fold the inside layers to lock the model.
2. Puff out to make the model round.

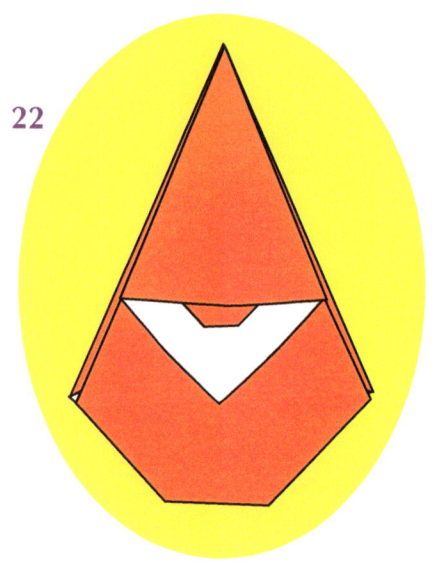

Crystalline Ironsprocket

40 *Magical Origami Gnomes*

Crystalline Flintcoil

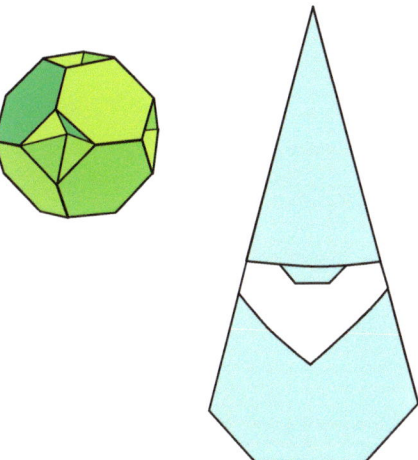

This gnome also creates crystals but at a higher musical range. Listen carefully and sing along with Crystalline Flintcoil. Crystalline snacks on rock candy, sweet and crunchy, but only on Gringleday... which is every other day. Gnomes keep their calendar simple.

1

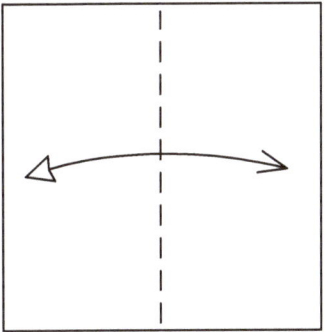

Fold and unfold.

2

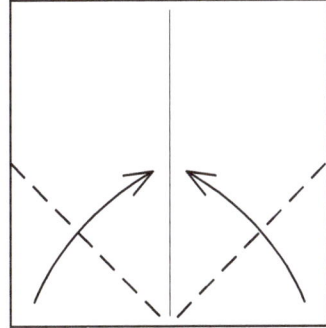

3

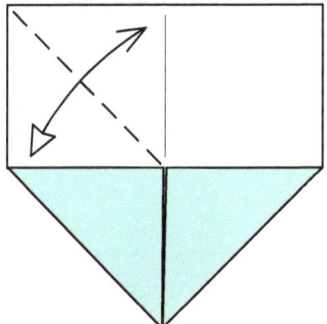

Fold and unfold.

4

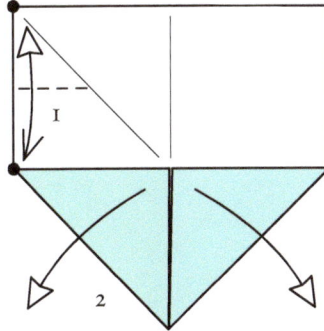

1. Fold and unfold.
2. Unfold.

5

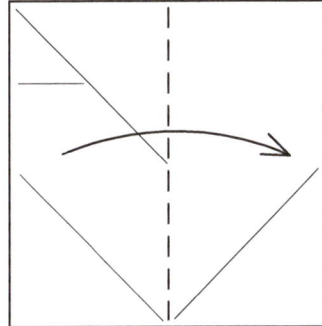

6

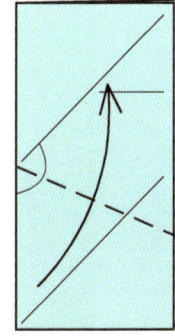

Crystalline Flintcoil 41

7

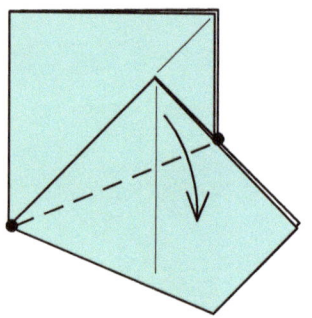

8

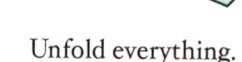

Unfold everything.

9

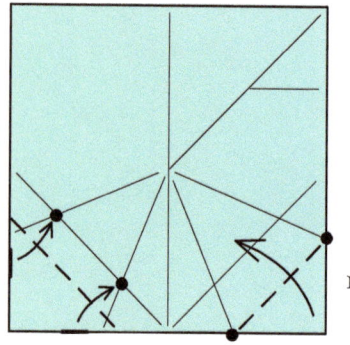

1. Valley-fold.
2. The edges will meet the dots.

10

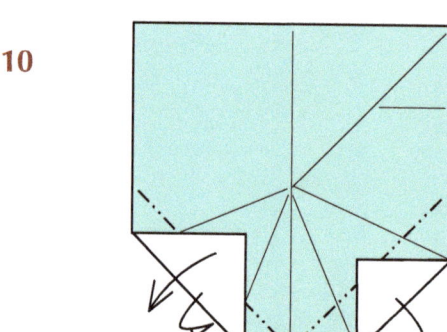

Mountain-fold along the creases.

11

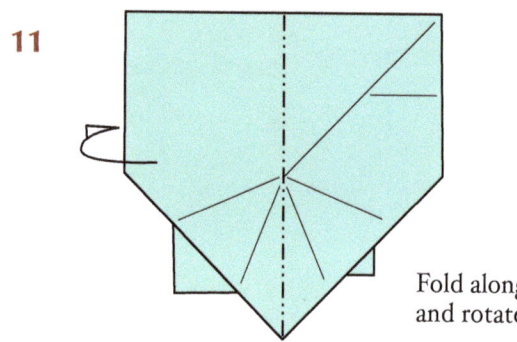

Fold along the crease and rotate 90°.

12

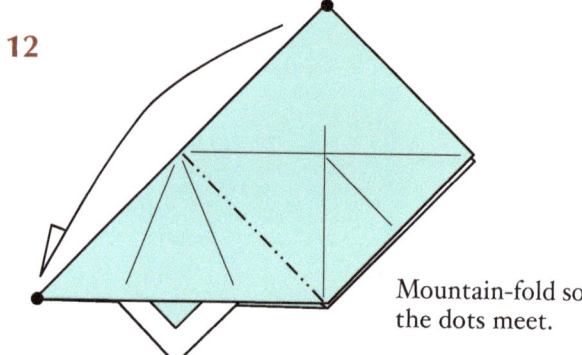

Mountain-fold so the dots meet.

13

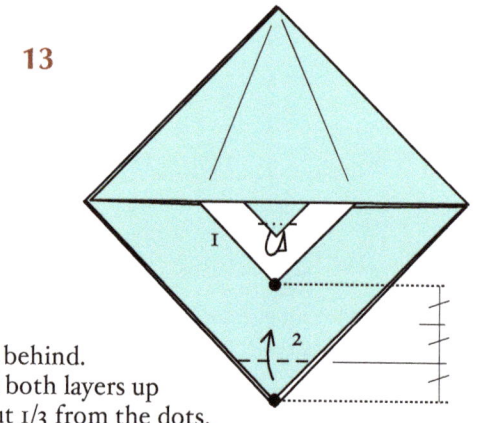

1. Fold behind.
2. Fold both layers up about 1/3 from the dots.

14

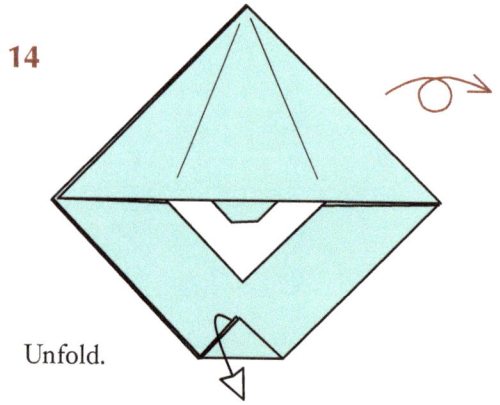

Unfold.

42 *Magical Origami Gnomes*

15

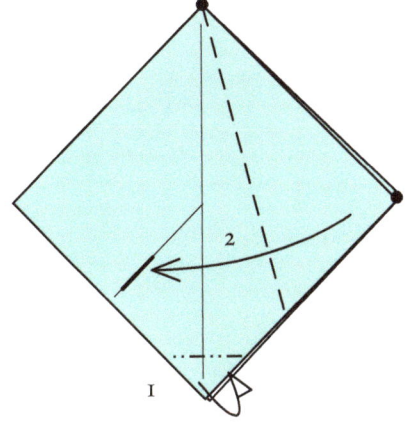

1. Fold inside, repeat behind.
2. Fold all the layers so the dot on the right meets the line.

16

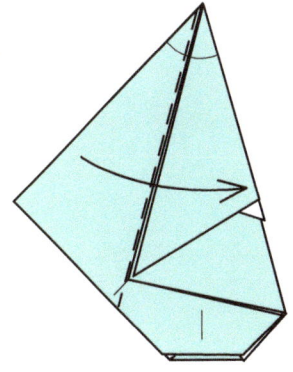

17

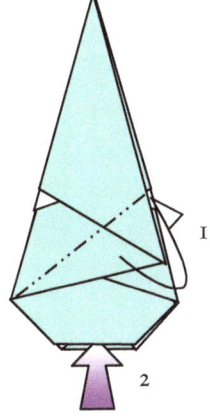

1. Tuck inside.
2. Puff out to make the model round.

18

Crystalline Flintcoil

Crystalline Flintcoil 43

Snowgnome

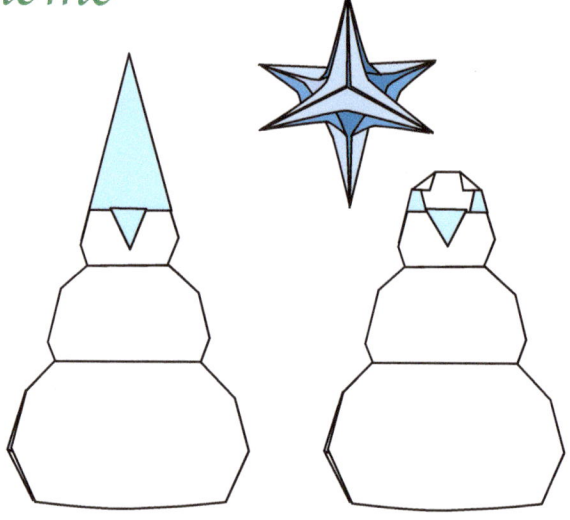

Snowgnomes are found in the snowy mountain caps. They thrive in the cold and can turn into snowmen with just a few folds. To keep the mountains cold they can scare away warmer weather.

1

Fold in half.

2

Fold and unfold the top layer.

3

Bring the dot on the left to the line.

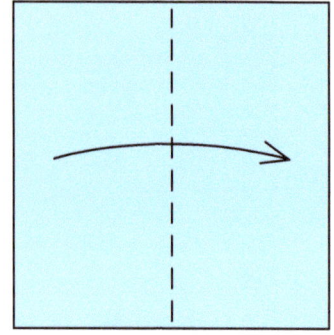

4

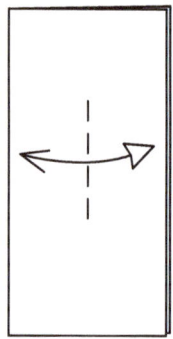

5

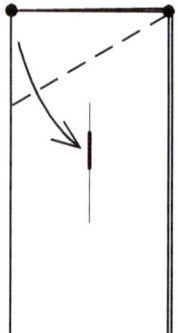

6

44 *Magical Origami Gnomes*

7

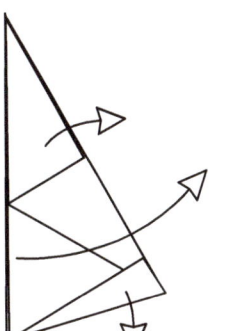

Unfold everything.

8

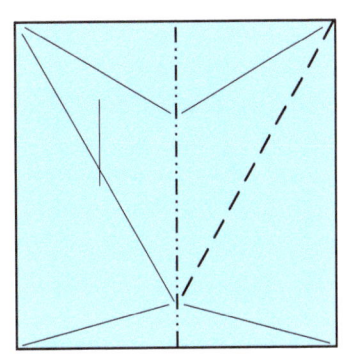

Fold and unfold along the creases.

9

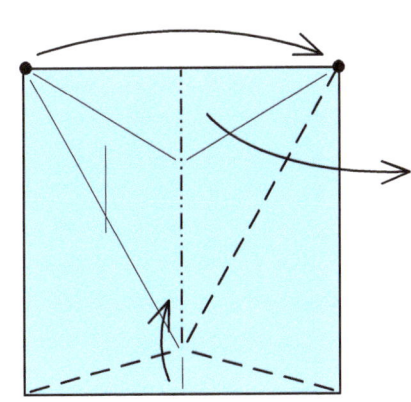

Fold along the creases so the dots meet.

10

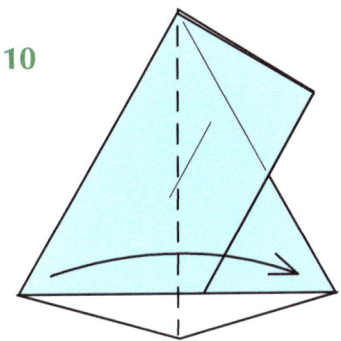

11

Reverse-fold.

12

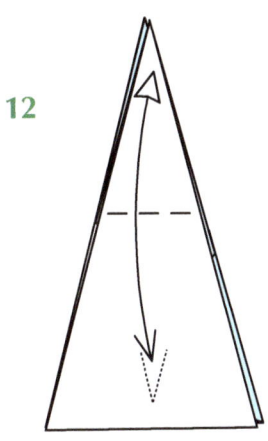

Fold and unfold all the layers, so it goes above the bottom line.

13

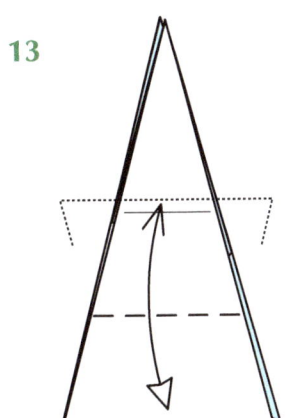

Fold and unfold all the layers, so the bottom goes slightly above the crease.

14

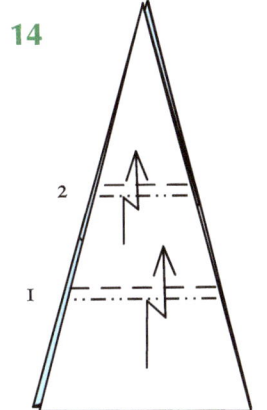

Pleat-fold all the layers at 1 and 2. Mountain-fold along the creases.

15

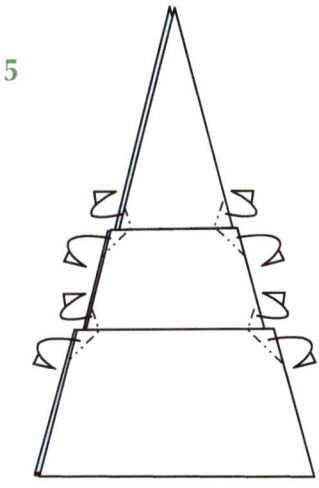

These form small squash folds behind. Fold all the layers.

Snowgnome 45

16

1. Fold and unfold.
2. Fold and unfold.
3. Fold inside, repeat behind.
4. Reverse-fold.

17

Pleat-fold the top flap.

18

1. Fold out.
2. Spread at the bttom so the model can stand.

19

Snowgnome

20

Tuck inside so the edges meet the left and right sides of the nose. Note the nose is facing forward.

21

22

Snowman

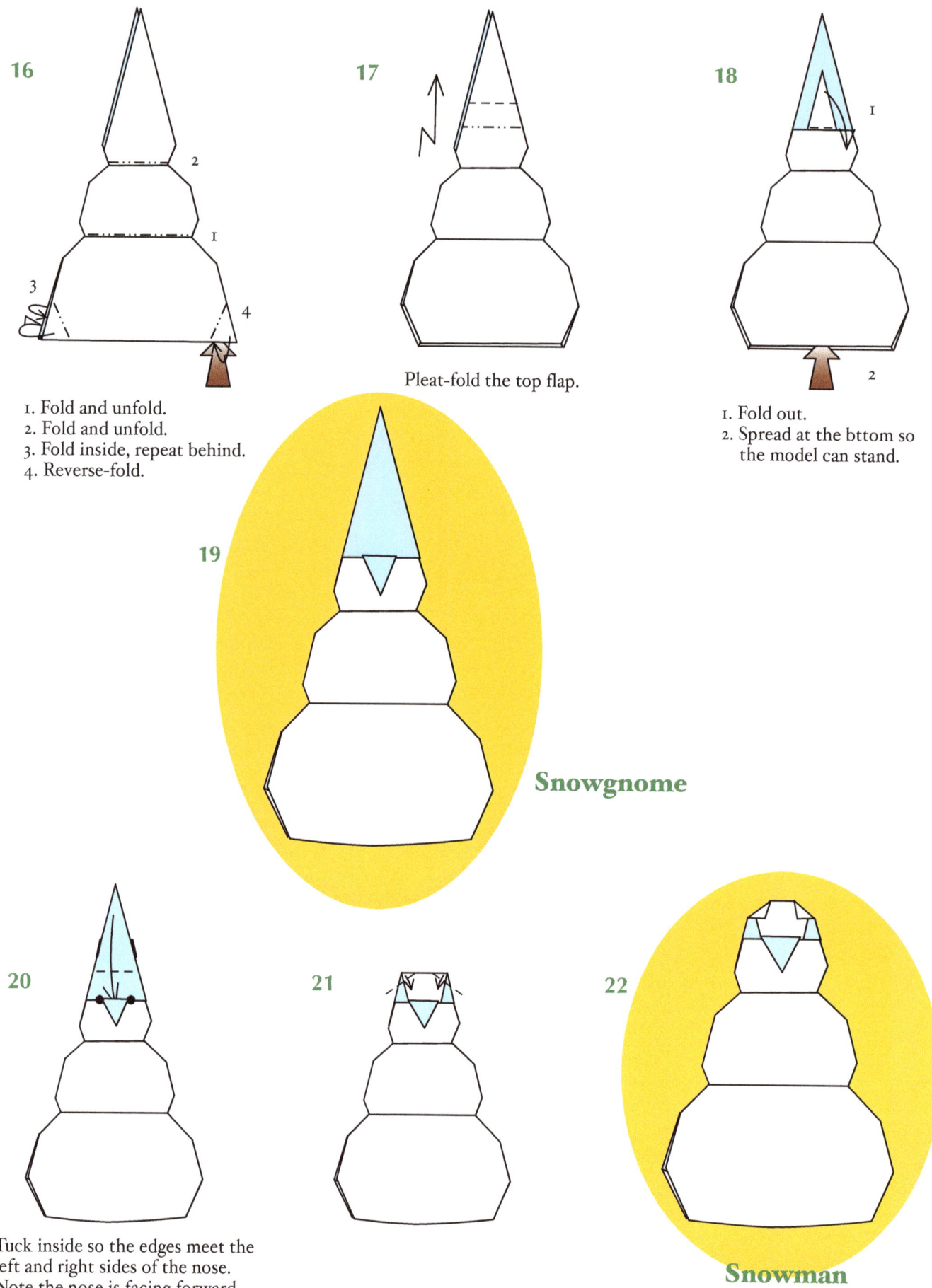

46   *Magical Origami Gnomes*

Brindle Deepdelver

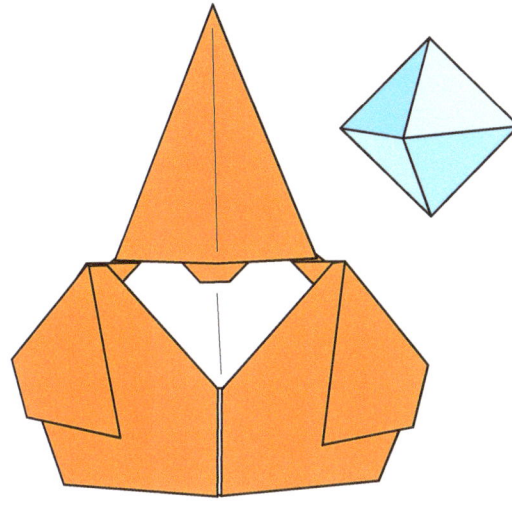

This gnome wields a stone hammer and defends the mountain passes from giants and trolls. He brings snacks into his cave because even rocks get hungry after a long day.

1
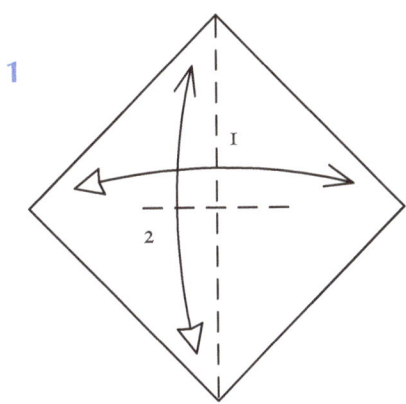

1. Fold and unfold.
2. Fold and unfold in the center.

2
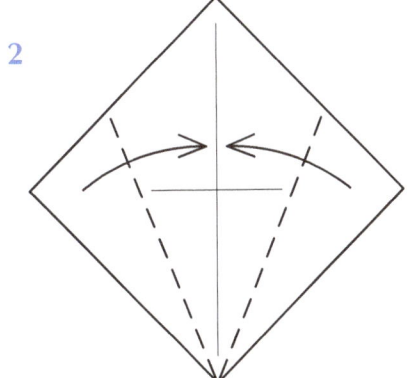

Fold to the center.

3
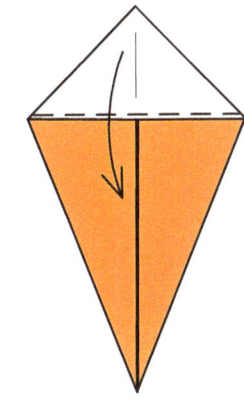

4
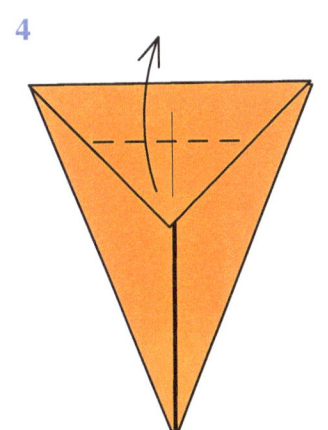

5
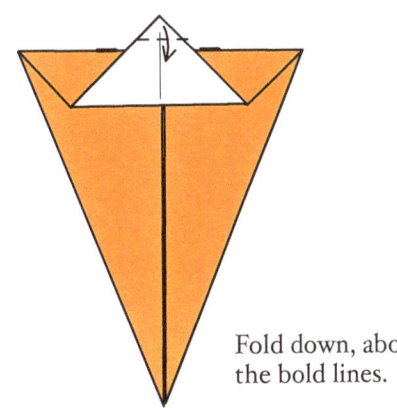

Fold down, above the bold lines.

6
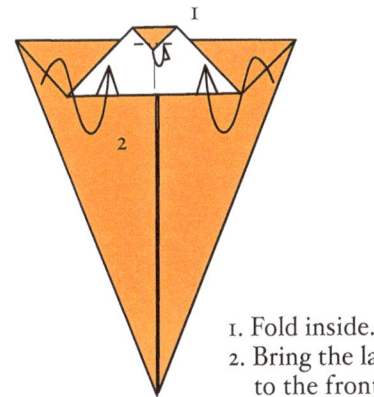

1. Fold inside.
2. Bring the layers to the front.

Brindle Deepdelver 47

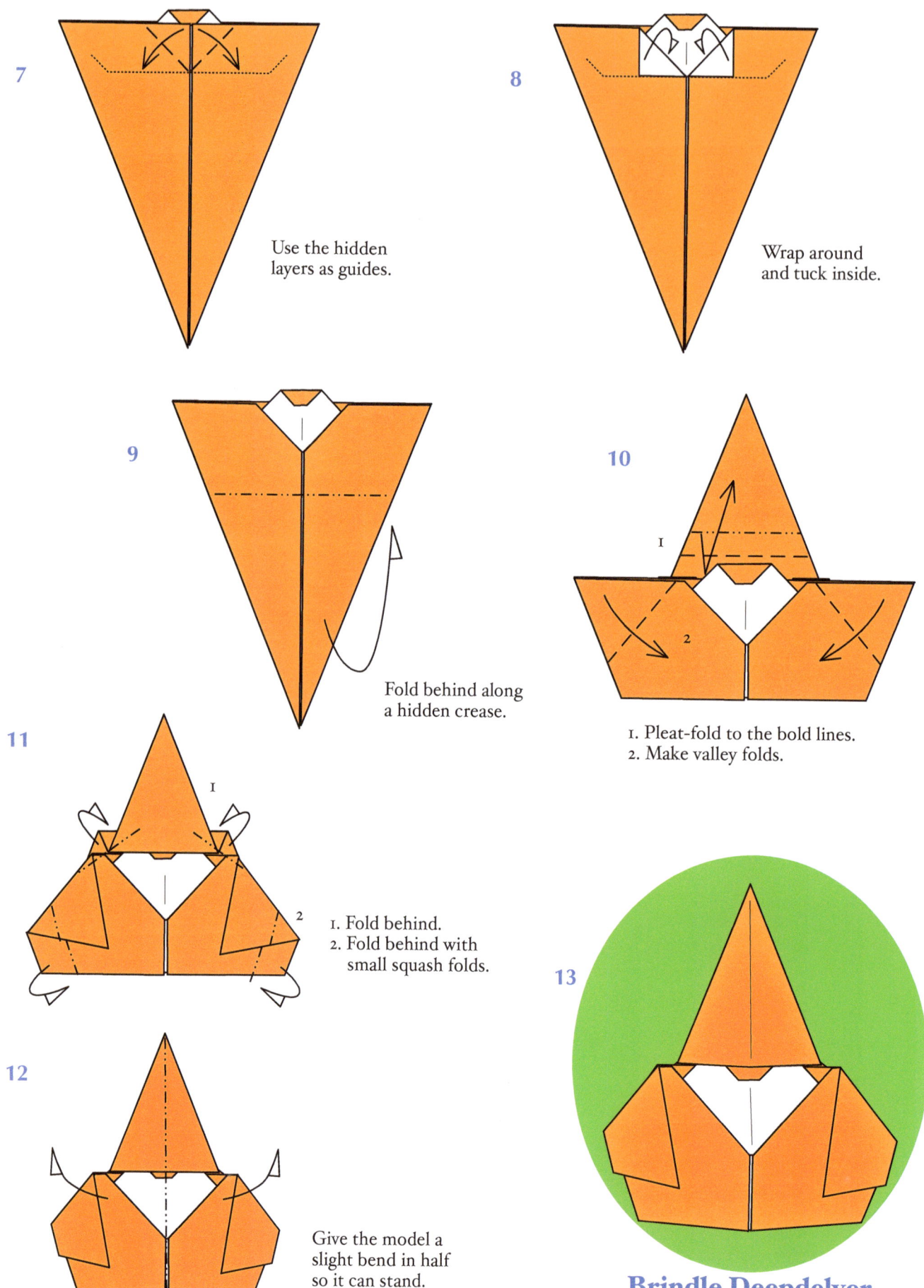

48 *Magical Origami Gnomes*

MetalCrafter

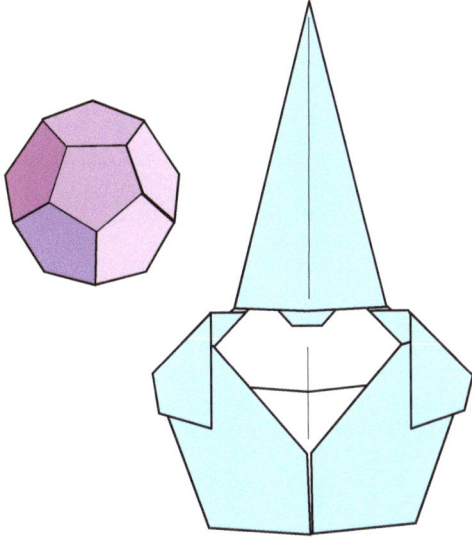
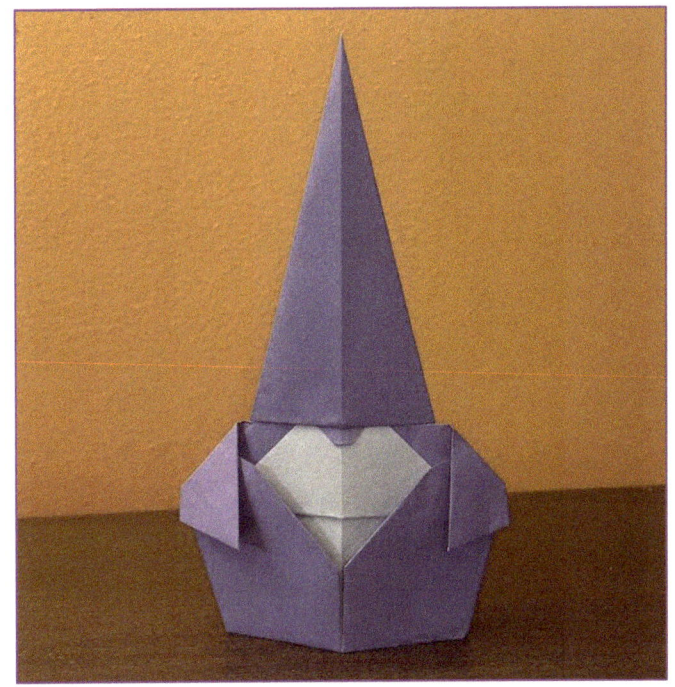

Taking the metal from the mountain mines, MetalCrafter can shape it into intricate sculptures, like dragons and mermaids. If something is worth doing, it's worth doing slowly and with snacks.

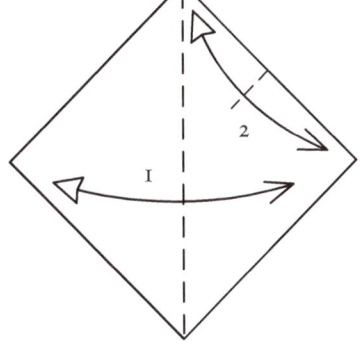

1. Fold and unfold.
2. Fold and unfold on the edge.

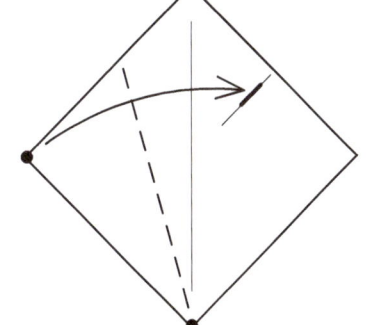

Bring the corner to the line.

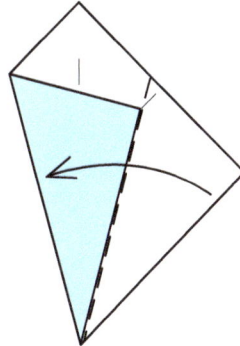

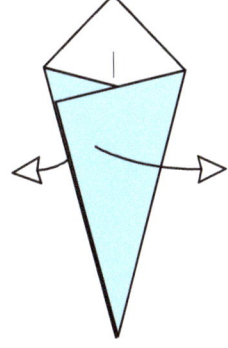

Unfold.

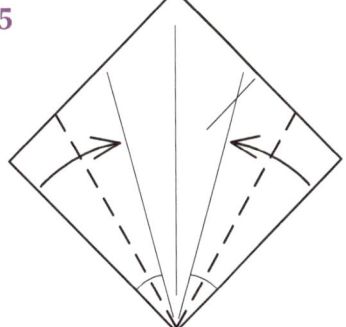

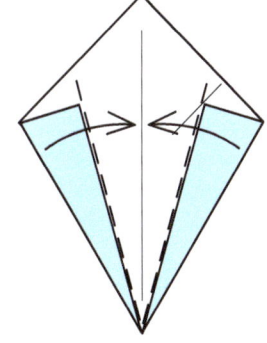

Fold to the center.

MetalCrafter 49

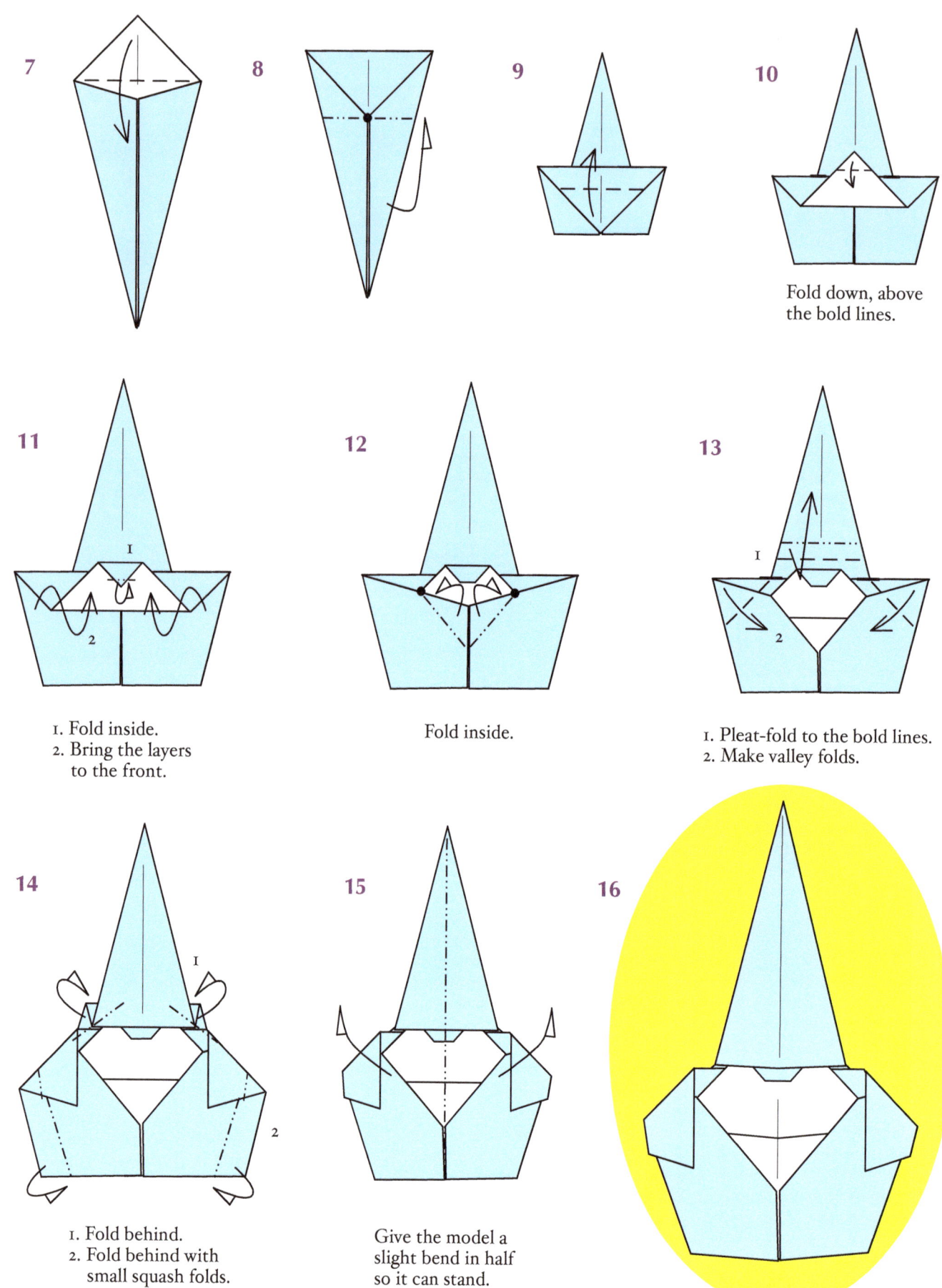

MetalCrafter

50 *Magical Origami Gnomes*

Tinker Gnomes of the South

Meet the TinkerBlinker family. These Tinker Gnomes enjoy creating all kinds of whimsical machinery. Living by a Gnome Mill, Mr. and Mrs. TinkerBlinker house their four sons, an uncle, and grandfather. Every day, they try to outdo each other with their inventions, knowing that the one who makes the best is treated to dandelion stew and warm tulip tarts with a red rose on top.

Mr. LaberDaber TinkerBlinker

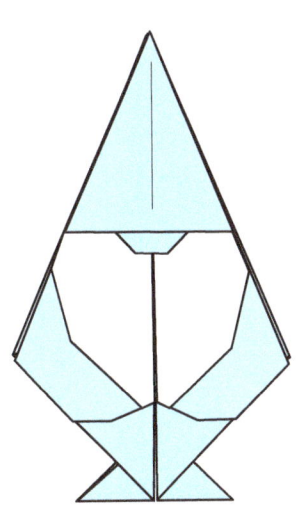

Mr. LaberDaber TinkerBlinker owns the family workshop. The ceiling is mounted with tracks of little buckets zooming around, delivering tools that seem to drop everywhere. He insists everyone in the family does their part to make the best mess, as proof of productivity.

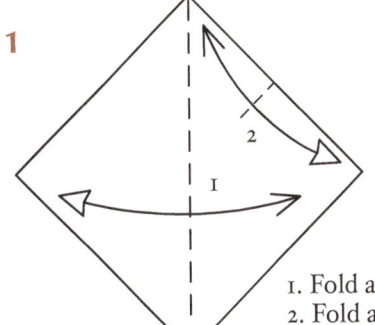

1. Fold and unfold.
2. Fold and unfold on the edge.

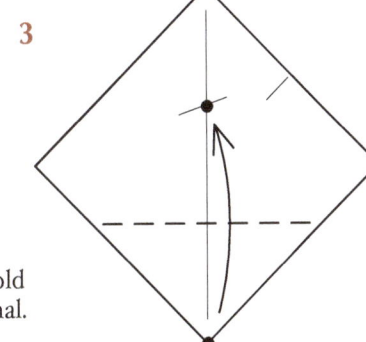

Fold and unfold on the diagonal.

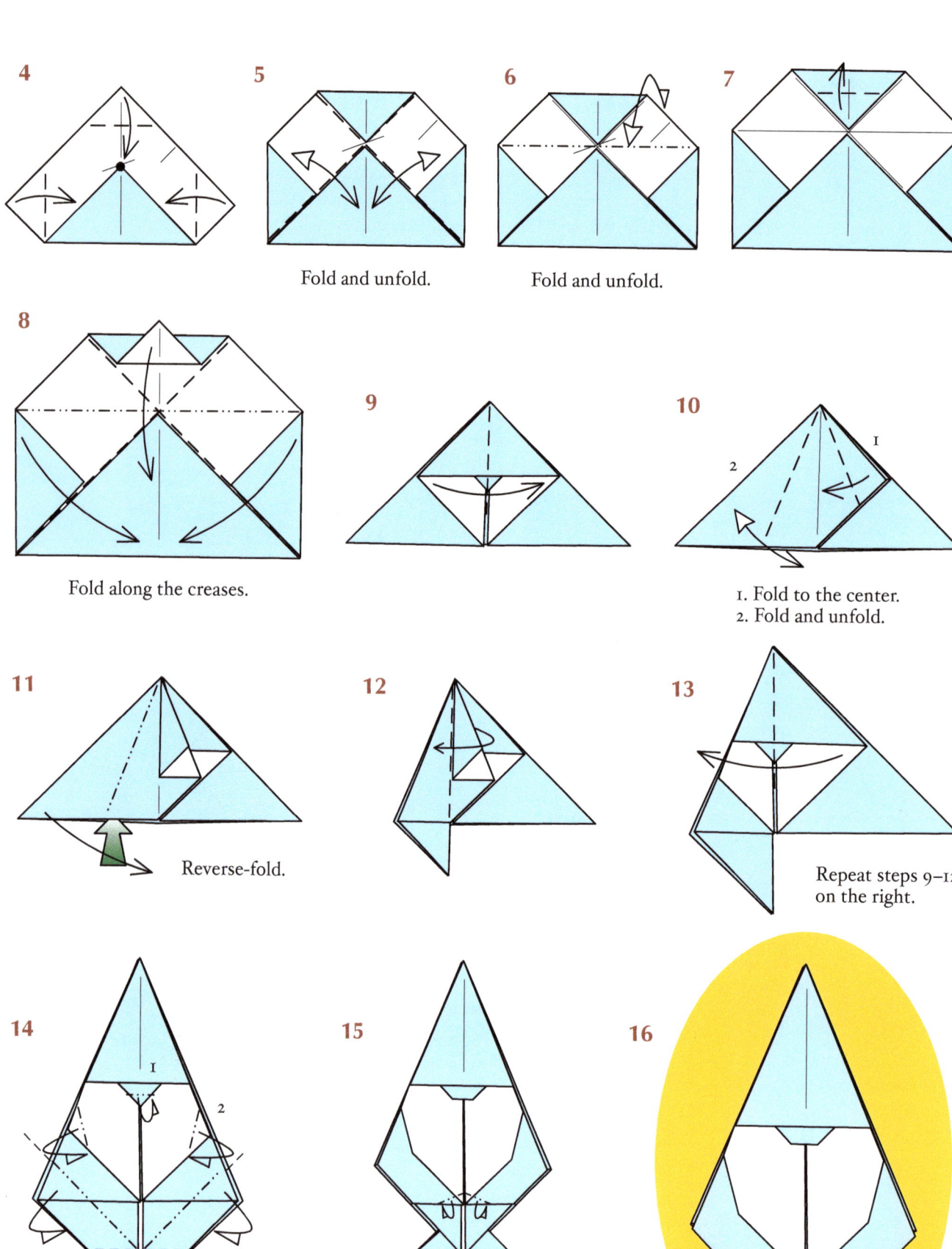

Mr. LaberDaber TinkerBlinker

52 *Magical Origami Gnomes*

Mrs. GearWhirl TinkerBlinker

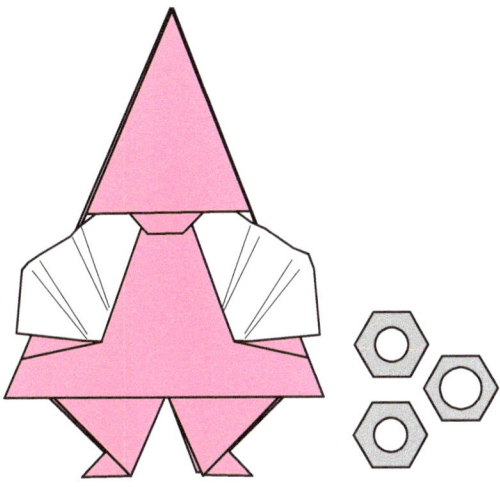

Mrs. GearWhirl TinkerBlinker is working on a perpetual teacup maker, using a spinning wheel and mosquito helpers. She is also tasked to handle the messes in the the lab. A female gnome is a gnomess (perfect for handling messes). Her motto is: if it works the first time, you probably forgot something.

1

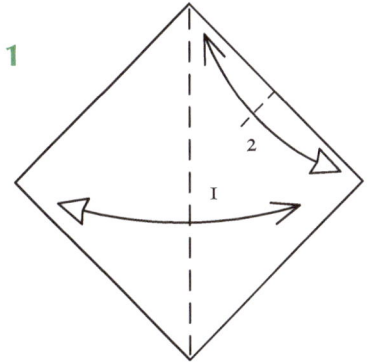

1. Fold and unfold.
2. Fold and unfold on the edge.

2

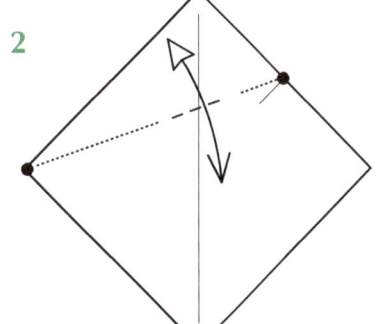

Fold and unfold on the diagonal.

3

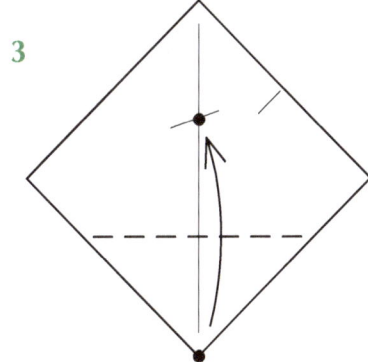

4

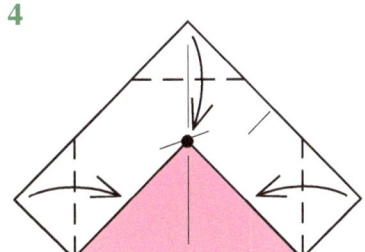

5

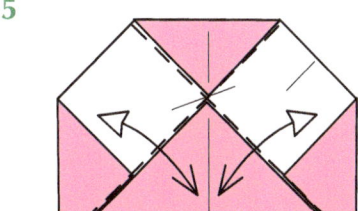

Fold and unfold.

6

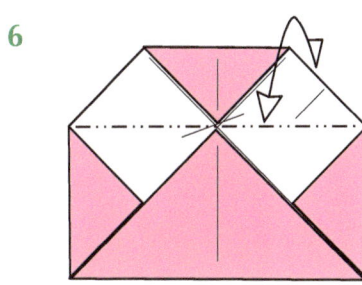

Fold and unfold.

Mrs. GearWhirl TinkerBlinker 53

7

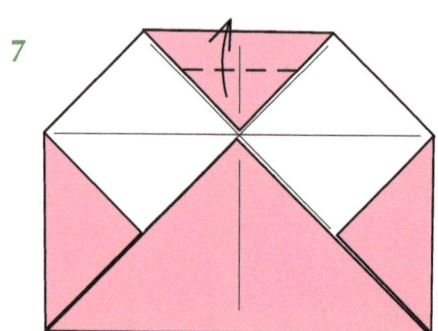

8

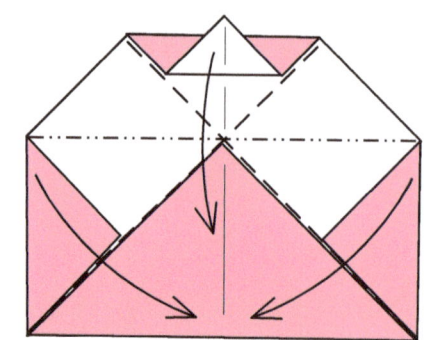

Fold along the creases.

9

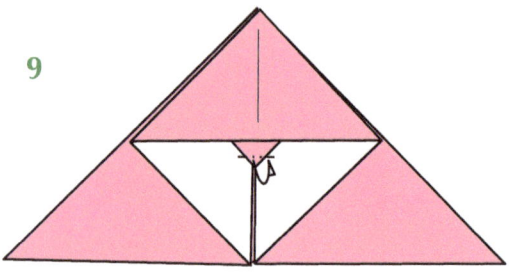

Fold inside.

10

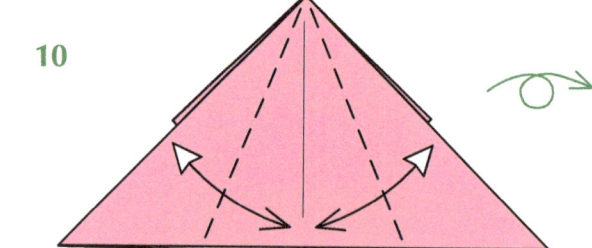

Fold and unfold all the layers.

11

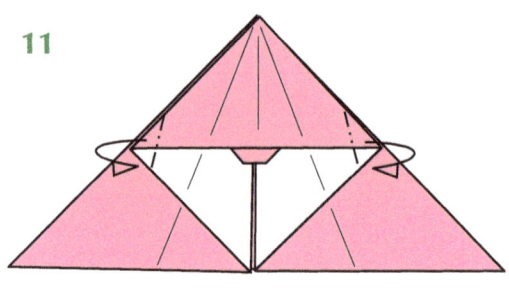

Fold inside.

12

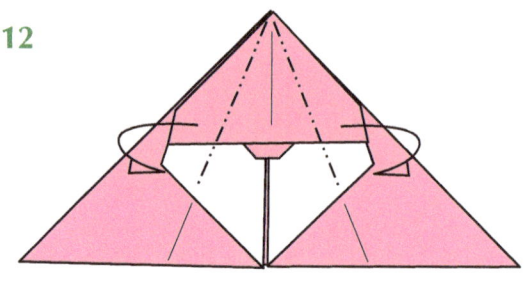

Fold inside.

13

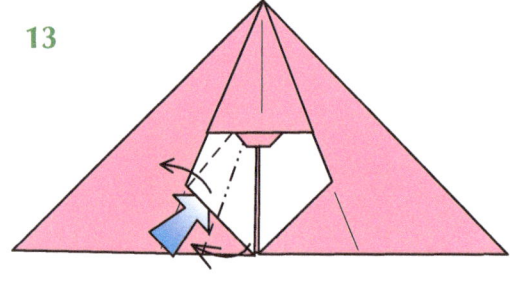

Squash-fold.

14

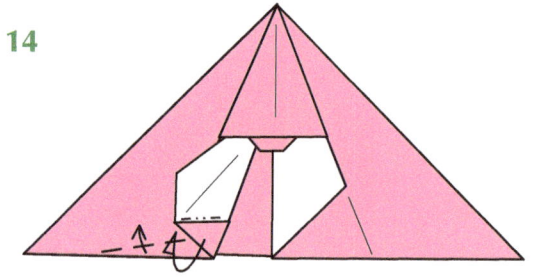

Reverse-fold.

54 *Magical Origami Gnomes*

15

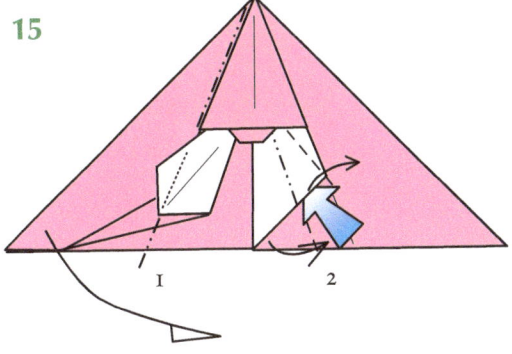

1. Fold behind.
2. Repeat steps 13–15 on the right.

16

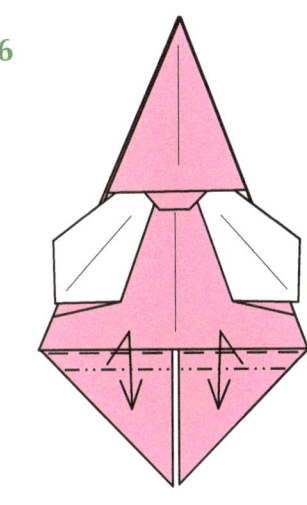

Make pleat folds.

17

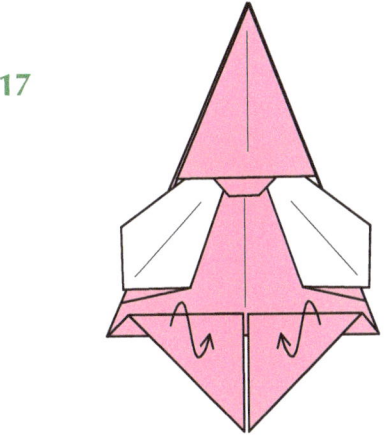

Tuck inside.

18

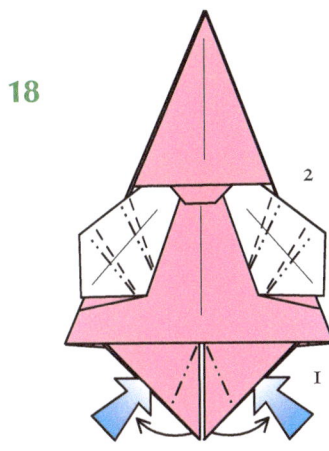

1. Make reverse folds.
2. Make pleat folds.

19

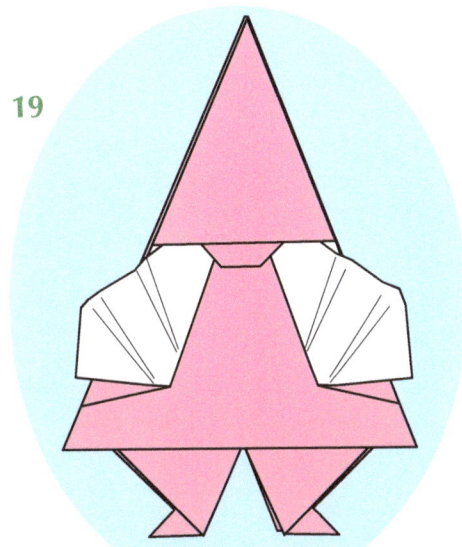

Mrs. GearWhirl TinkerBlinker

Fribbin TinkerBlinker

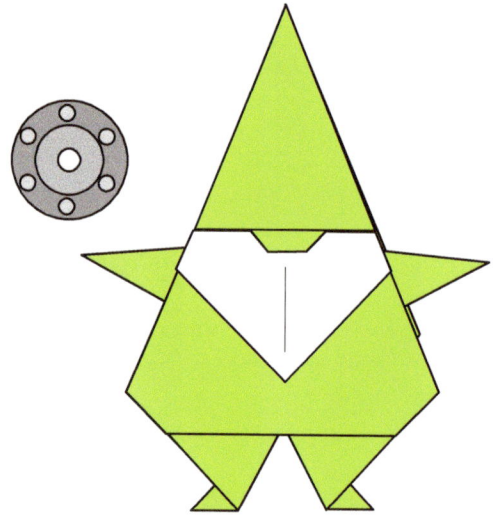

Son Fribbin TinkerBlinker makes a web of crisscrossing hammocks so he can escape and rest from all the heavy work. He would have preferred to take a vacation but the last time he did, the lab built a second lab.

1

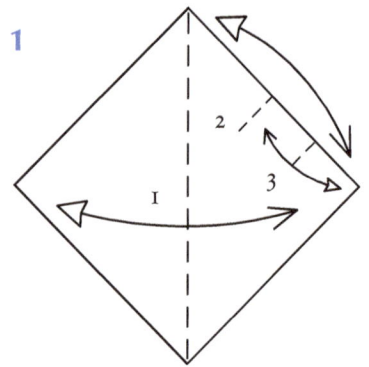

1. Fold and unfold.
2, 3. Fold and unfold on the edge.

2

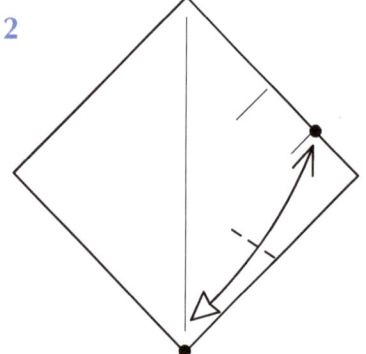

Fold and unfold on the edge so the dots meet.

3

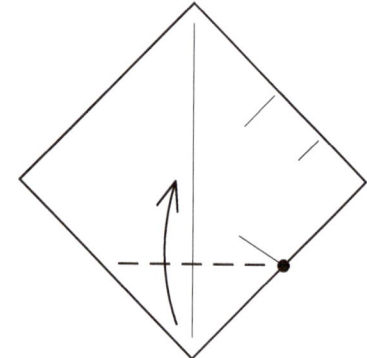

4

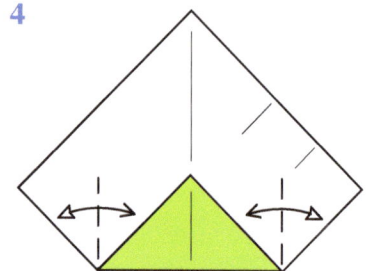

Fold and unfold on the lower part.

5

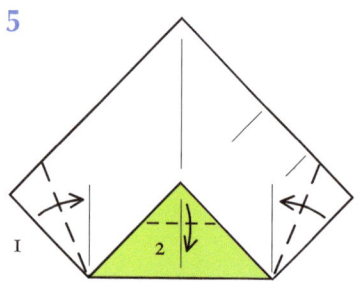

1. Fold on the left and right.
2. Fold down near the bottom.

6

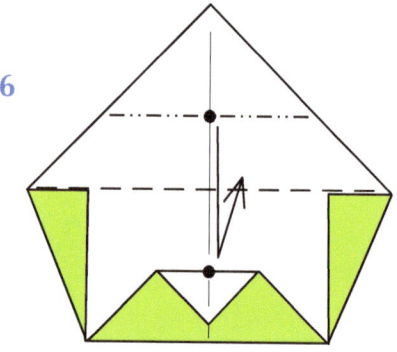

Pleat-fold so the dots meet.

56   *Magical Origami Gnomes*

7

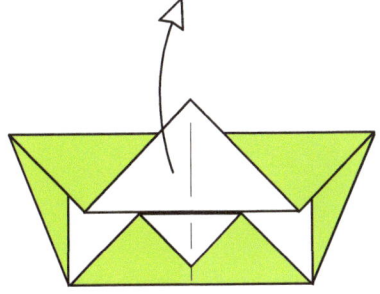

Unfold.

8

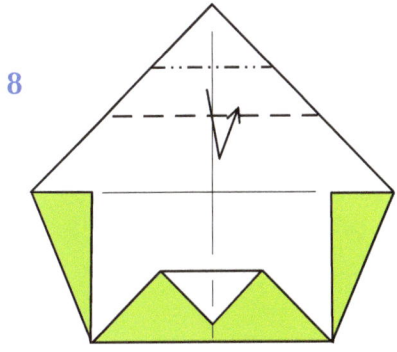

Valley-fold along the crease for this pleat fold.

9

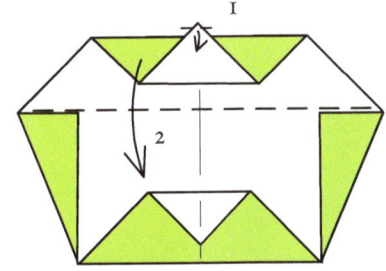

1. Fold down.
2. Fold along the crease.

10

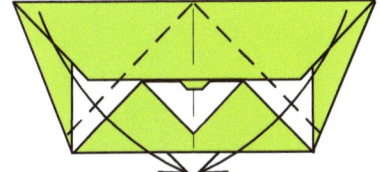

11

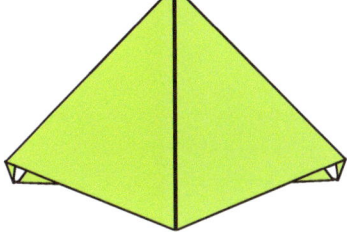

12

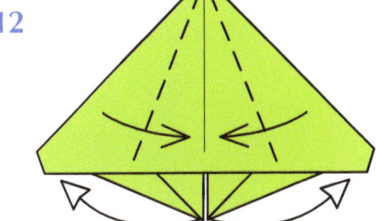

Fold to the center and swing out from behind.

13

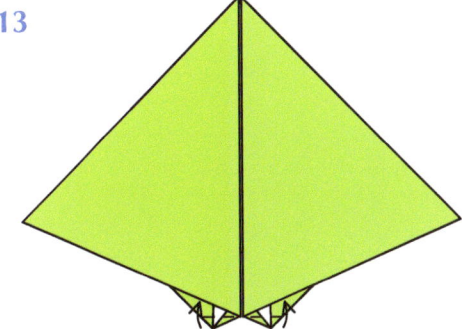

Fold up.

14

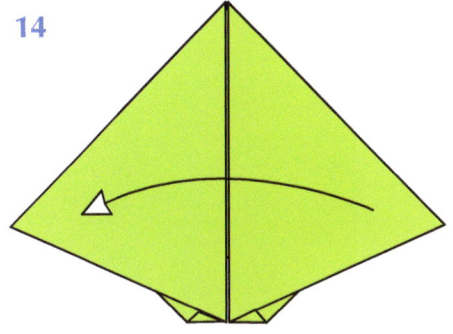

Unfold.

Fribbin TinkerBlinker 57

15

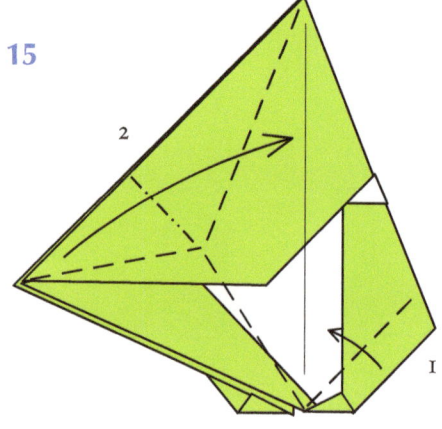

1. Fold a thin strip.
2. Rabbit-ear.

16

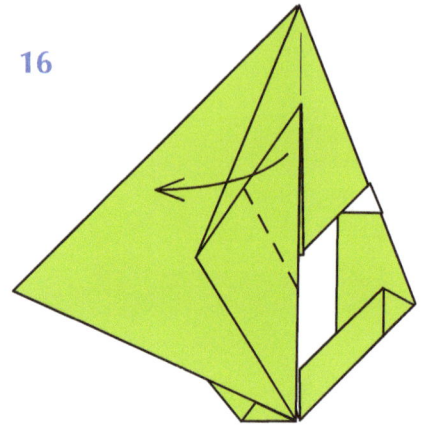

Spread-squash-fold.

17

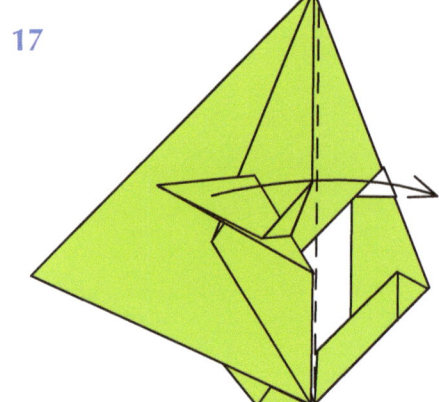

18

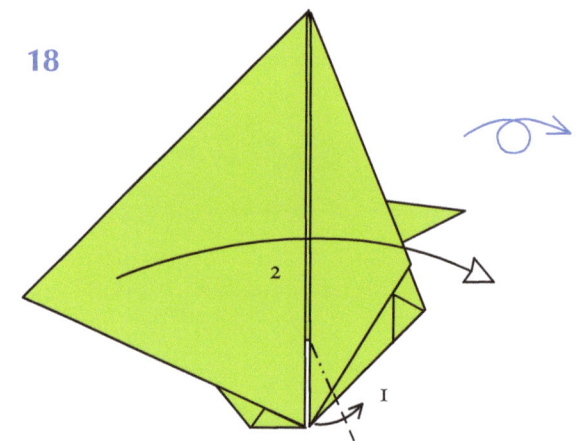

1. Reverse-fold.
2. Repeat steps 14–18 in the opposite direction.

19

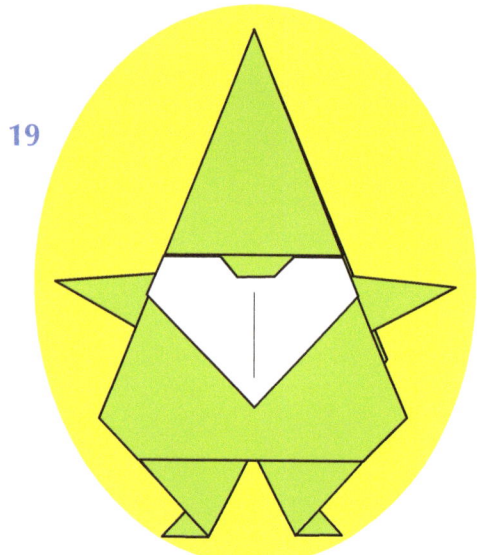

Fribbin TinkerBlinker

58   *Magical Origami Gnomes*

Glimmer TinkerBlinker

Glimmer TinkerBlinker created a self opening umbrella that fits snuggly on his hat. When it rains it pops open and starts singing out of key. His motto is: always have a second plan, and hide it in your hat.

1

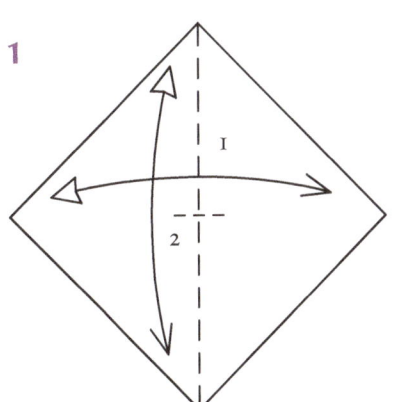

1. Fold and unfold.
2. Fold and unfold in the center

2

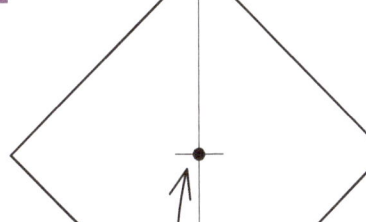

1. Fold and unfold.
2. Fold and unfold.

3

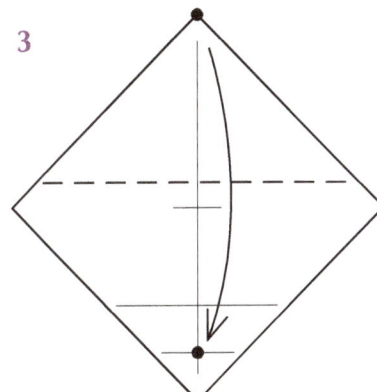

The dots will meet.

4

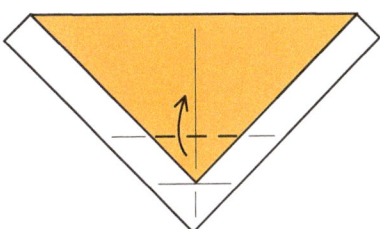

Fold up along the hidden crease.

5

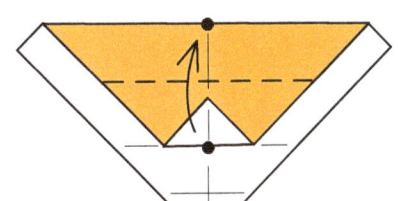

6

Fold along the crease.

Glimmer TinkerBlinker 59

7

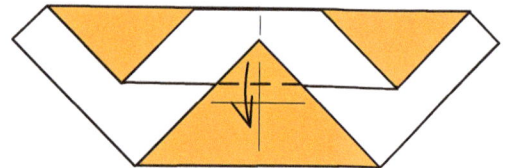

Fold along the hidden edge.

8

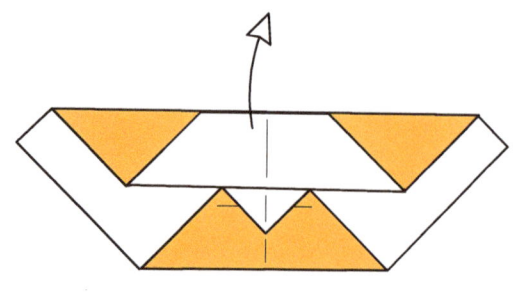

Unfold.

9

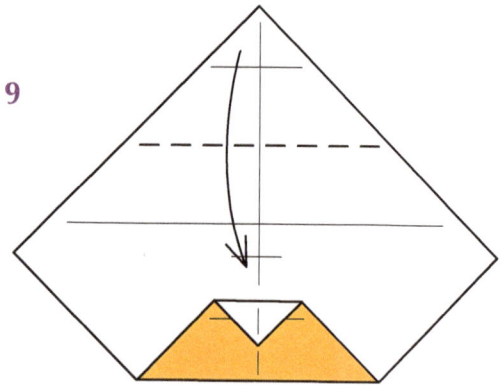

Fold along the crease.

10

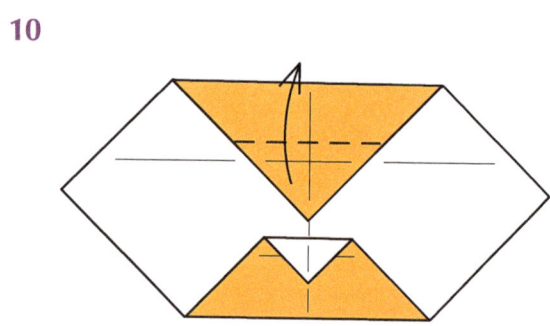

11

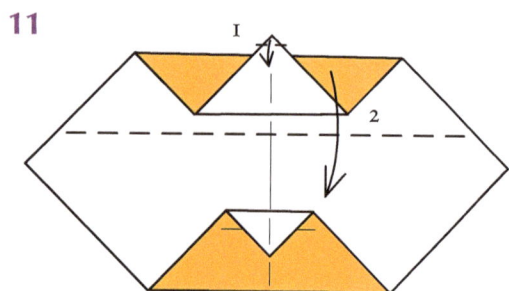

1. Fold down.
2. Fold along the crease.

12

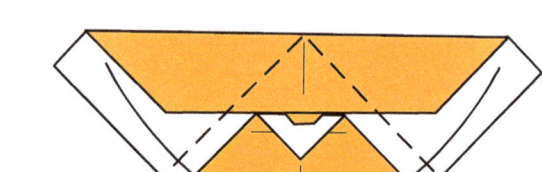

Fold to the center.

13

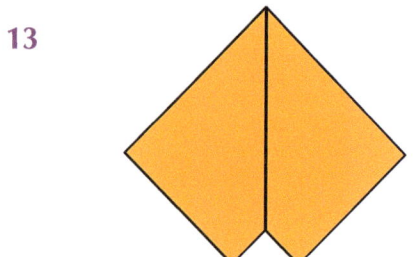

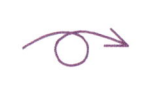

14

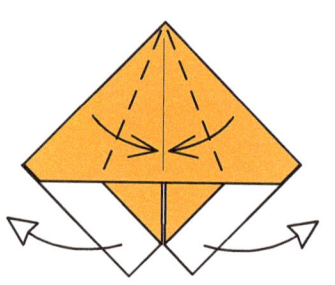

Fold to the center and swing out from behind.

60 *Magical Origami Gnomes*

15

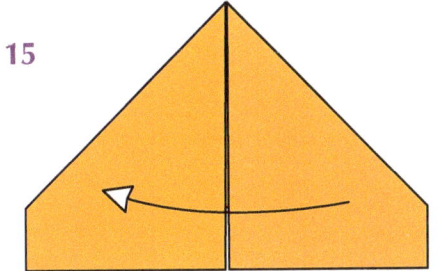

Unfold.

16

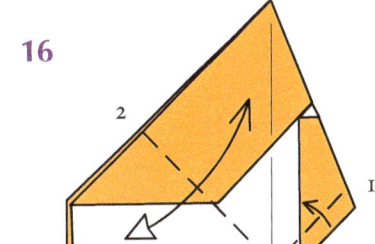

1. Fold a thin strip.
2. Fold and unfold.

17

18

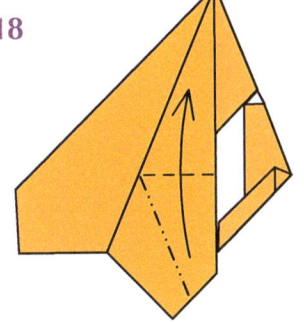

Squash-fold.

19

20

21

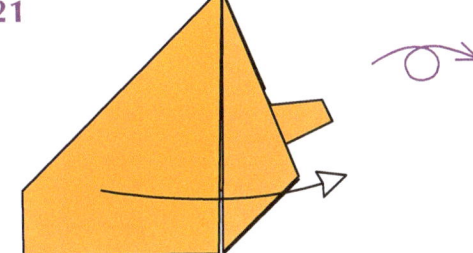

Repeat steps 15–20 in the opposite direction.

22

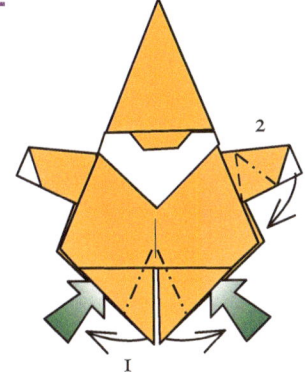

1. Make reverse folds.
2. Pleat-fold.

23

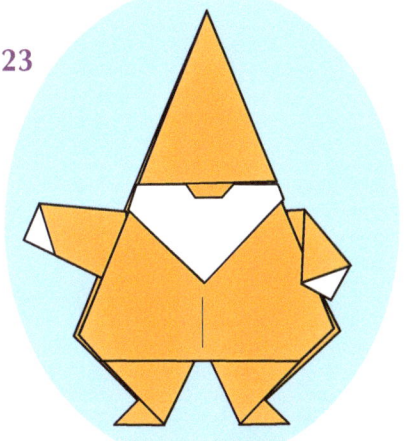

Glimmer TinkerBlinker

CoggleJam TinkerBlinker

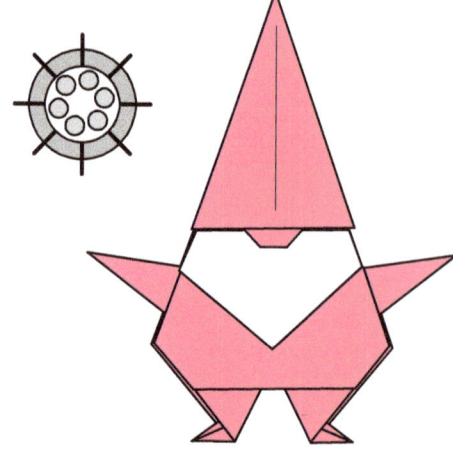

CoggleJam TinkerBlinker built a breakfast machine complete with gears, fire explosions, and whirling buckets. When the machine splattered milk everywhere, he cried over spilt milk. Luckily, the machine broke after that, or he would have been scrambled, fried, and slightly roasted. Gnomes are all about making mistakes. They just hope to be around to make another one.

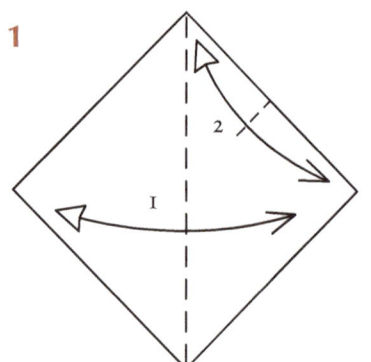

1. Fold and unfold.
2. Fold and unfold on the edge.

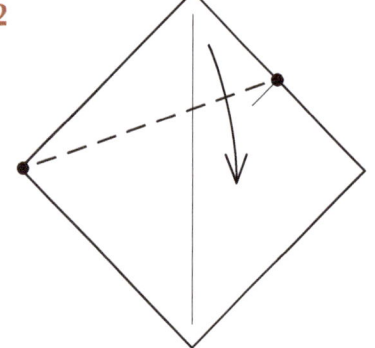

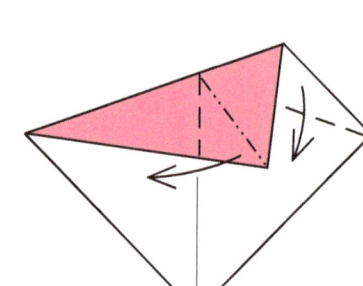

Squash-fold.

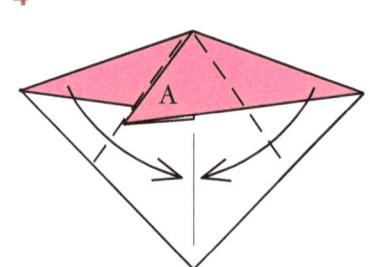

Keep flap A on top while folding to the center.

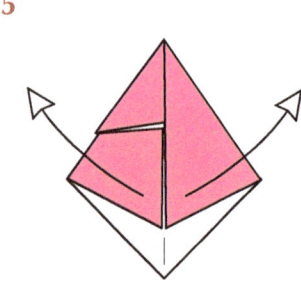

Unfold.

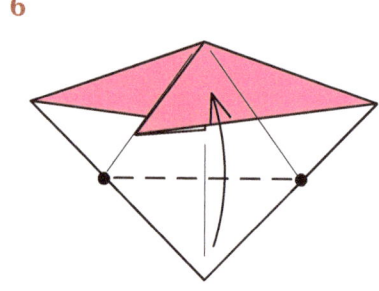

62 *Magical Origami Gnomes*

7

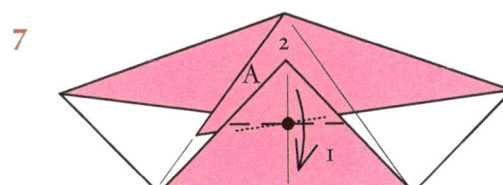

1. Fold down along a hidden line.
2. Bring flap A to the front.

8

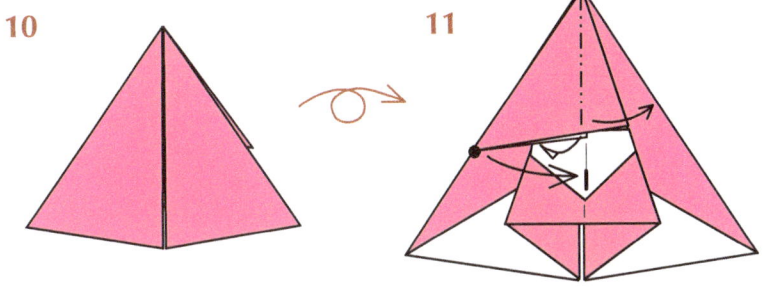

9

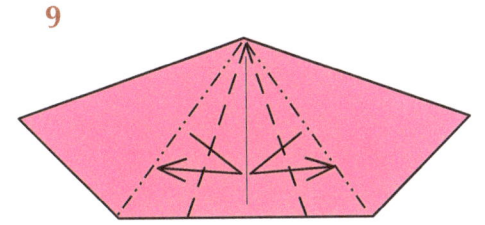

Pleat-fold to the center. Do not fold the hidden flap, shown as A in step 7.

10

11

Spread and squash fold.

12

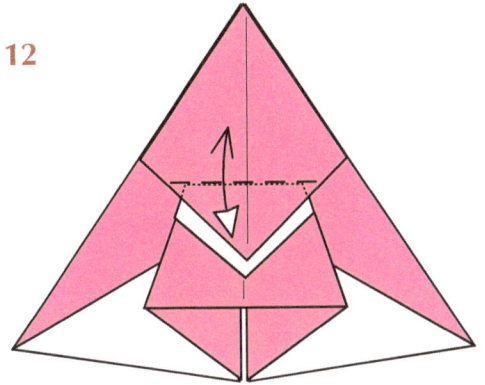

Fold and unfold along the hidden edge.

13

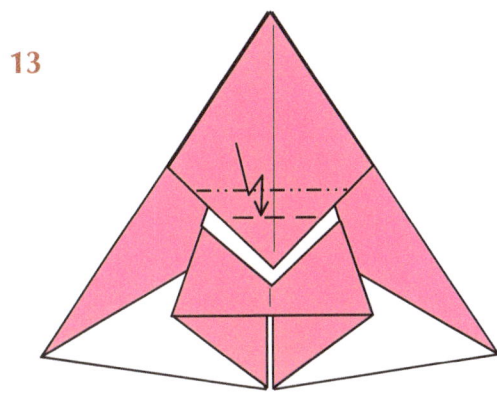

Mountain-fold along the crease for this pleat fold.

14

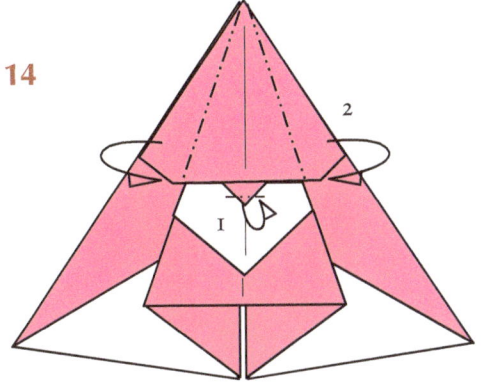

1. Fold inside.
2. Fold inside.

15

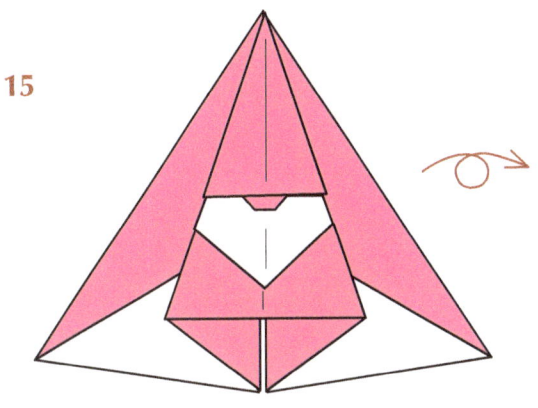

CoggleJam TinkerBlinker 63

16

Unfold.

17

Rabbit-ear.

18

Spread-squash-fold.

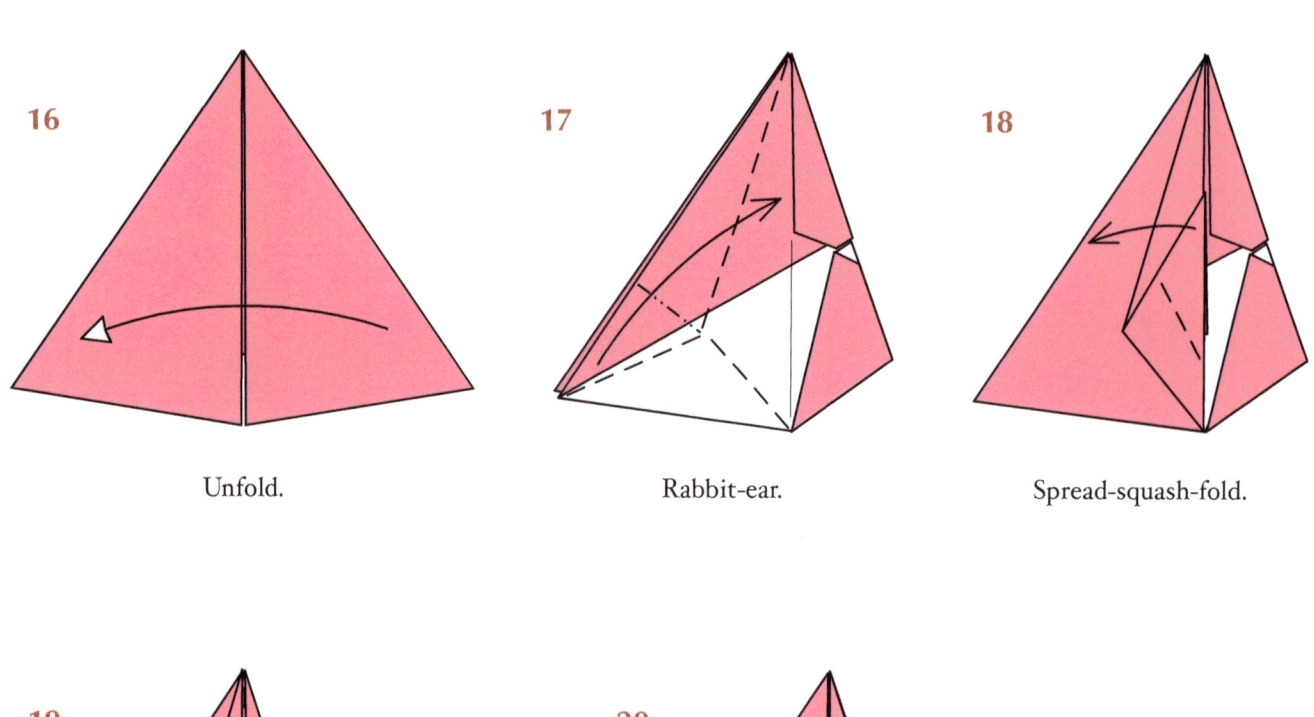

19

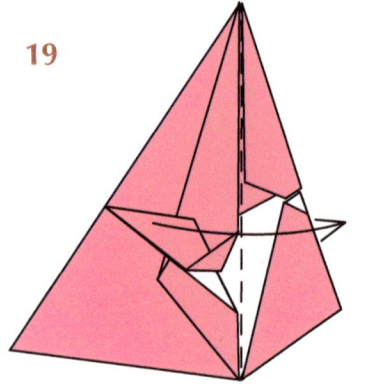

20

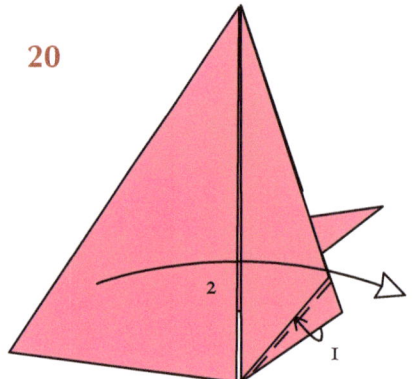

1. Fold inside.
2. Repeat steps 16–20 in the opposite direction.

21

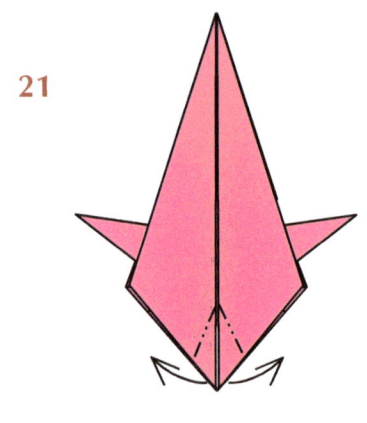

Make reverse folds.

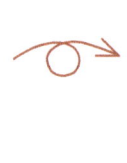

22

CoggleJam TinkerBlinker

64   *Magical Origami Gnomes*

PlanetGranite TinkerBlinker

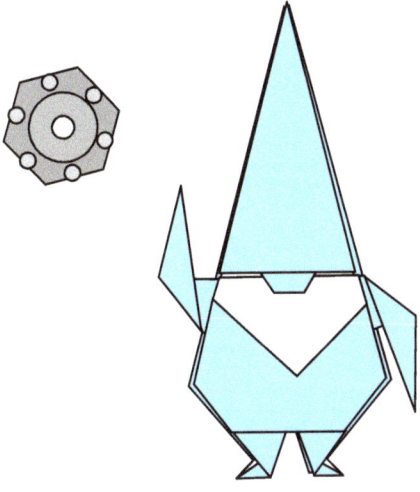

PlanetGranite TinkerBlinker is the most intelligent gnome of all. Doing experiments on earth and, with the help of gnomes in distant galaxies, he discovered his formula works everywhere, all the time, in any space or volume: $E = mc^3$. E is for excellence, mc is for more chocolate, thus the more chocolates cubed, the more excellent.

1

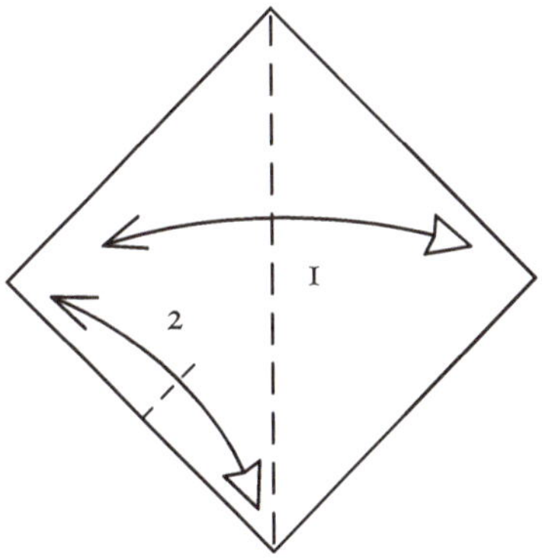

1. Fold and unfold.
2. Fold and unfold on the edge.

2

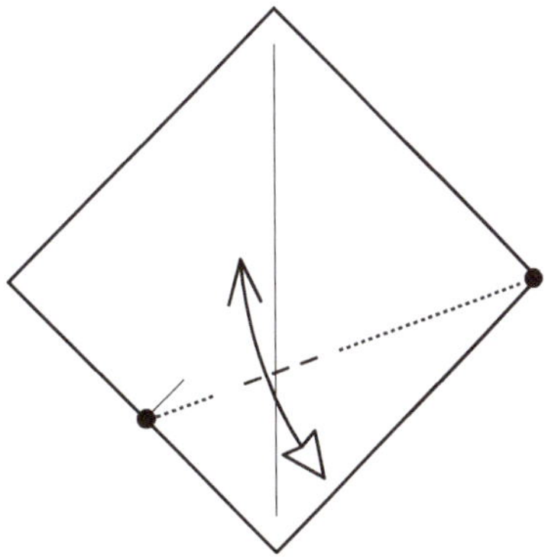

Fold and unfold on the diagonal.

3

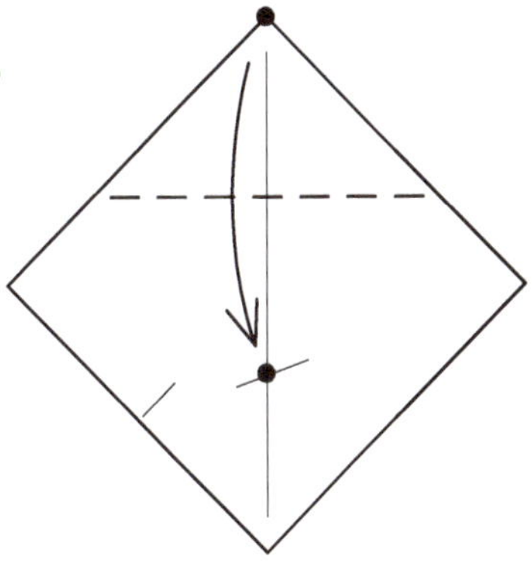

4

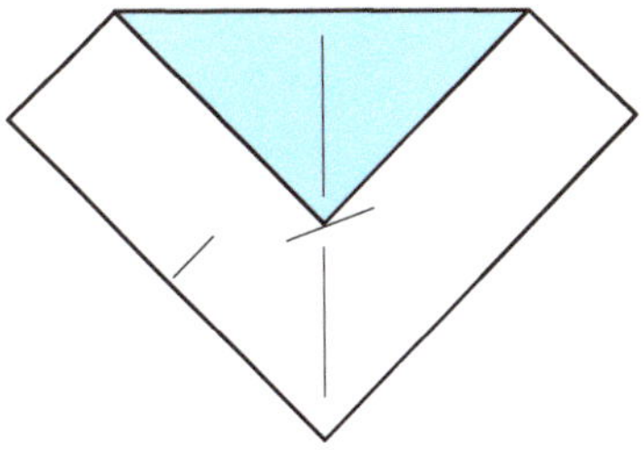

5

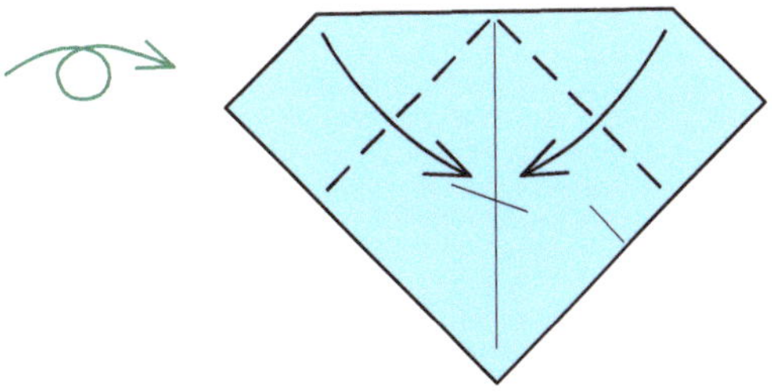

Fold to the center.

6

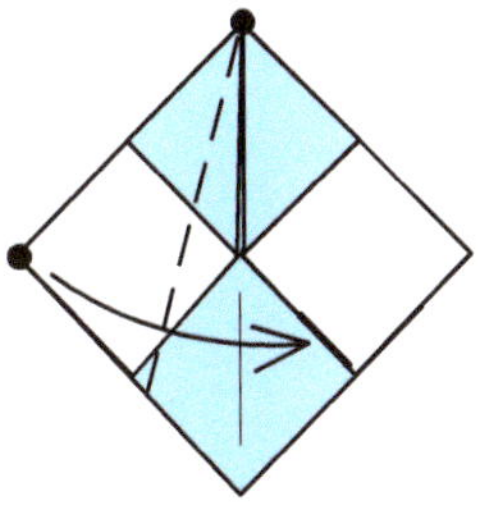

Bring the lower dot to the bold line.

PlanetGranite TinkerBlinker 65

7

8

9

10

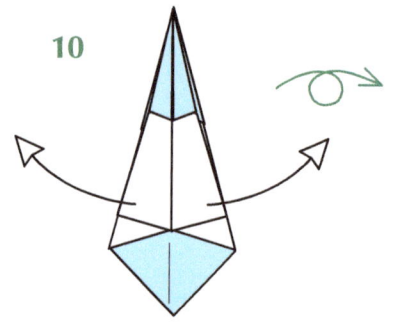

Unfold everything.

11

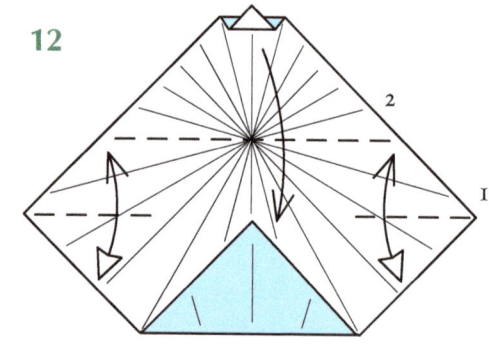

1. Pleat-fold.
2. Fold up.

12

1. Fold and unfold at the corners.
2. Fold along the crease.

13

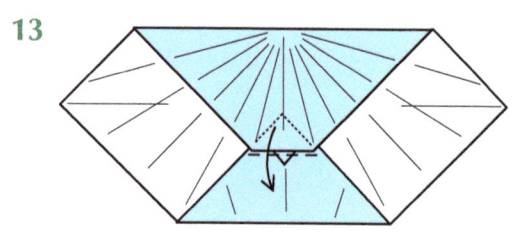

Fold down.

14

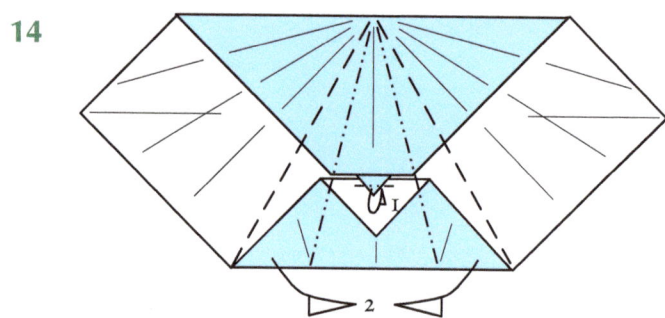

1. Fold behind.
2. Pleat-fold along the creases.

15

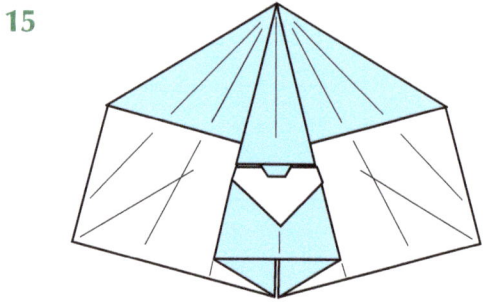

16

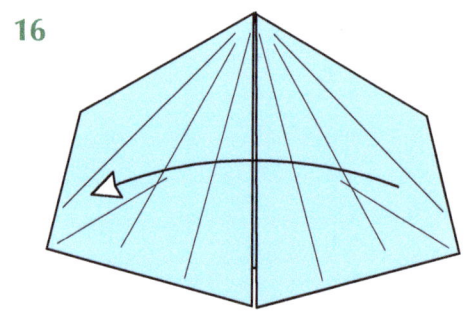

Unfold.

66 *Magical Origami Gnomes*

17

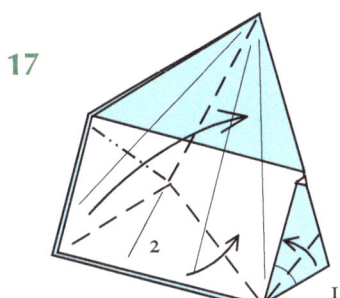

1. Valley-fold.
2. Rabbit-ear. Valley-fold along some of the creases.

18

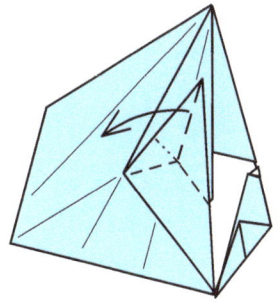

Rabbit-ear.

19

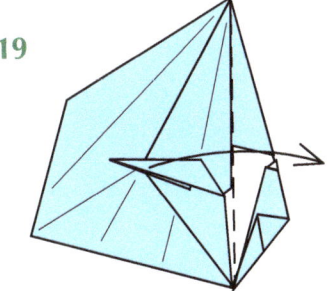

20

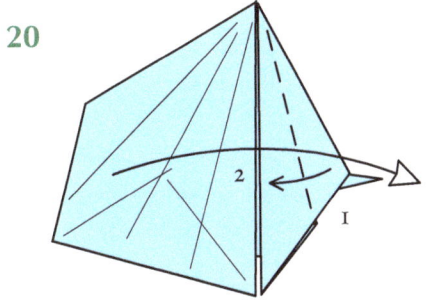

1. Fold along the crease.
2. Repeat steps 16–20 in the opposite direction.

21

22

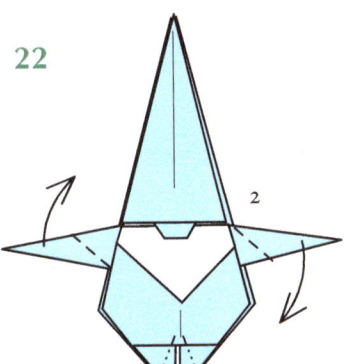

1. Make reverse folds.
2. Fold the arms.

23

PlanetGranite TinkerBlinker

PlanetGranite TinkerBlinker 67

Wizzle TinkerBlinker

Uncle Wizzle TinkerBlinker is obsessed with football. Using gears and rubber gloves, he invented a line of footballs in the shape of feet, guaranteed to make the game more entertaining. He always wins because he kicks into high gear.

1

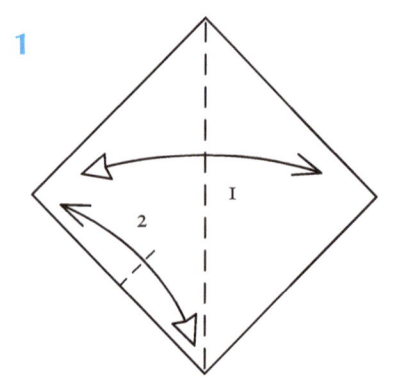

1. Fold and unfold.
2. Fold and unfold on the edge.

2

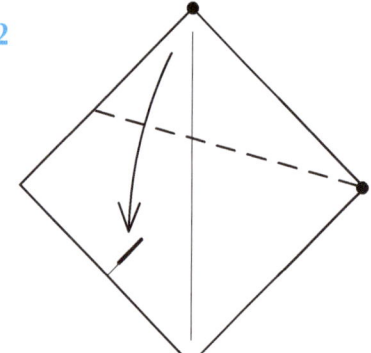

Bring the upper dot to the bold line.

3

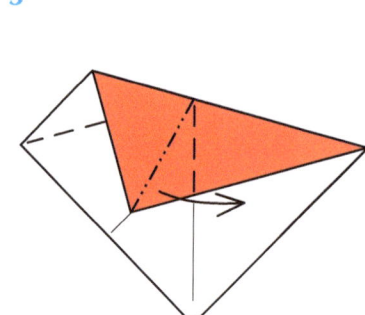

Squash-fold.

4

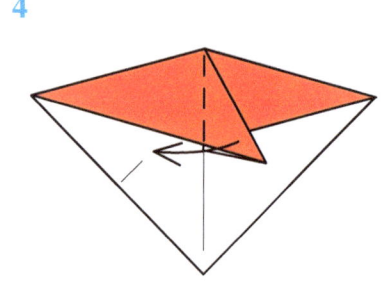

5

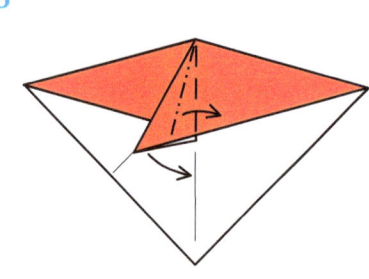

Squash-fold.

6

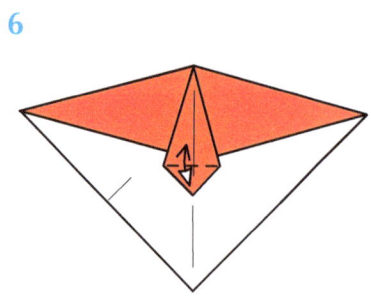

Fold and unfold.

68 *Magical Origami Gnomes*

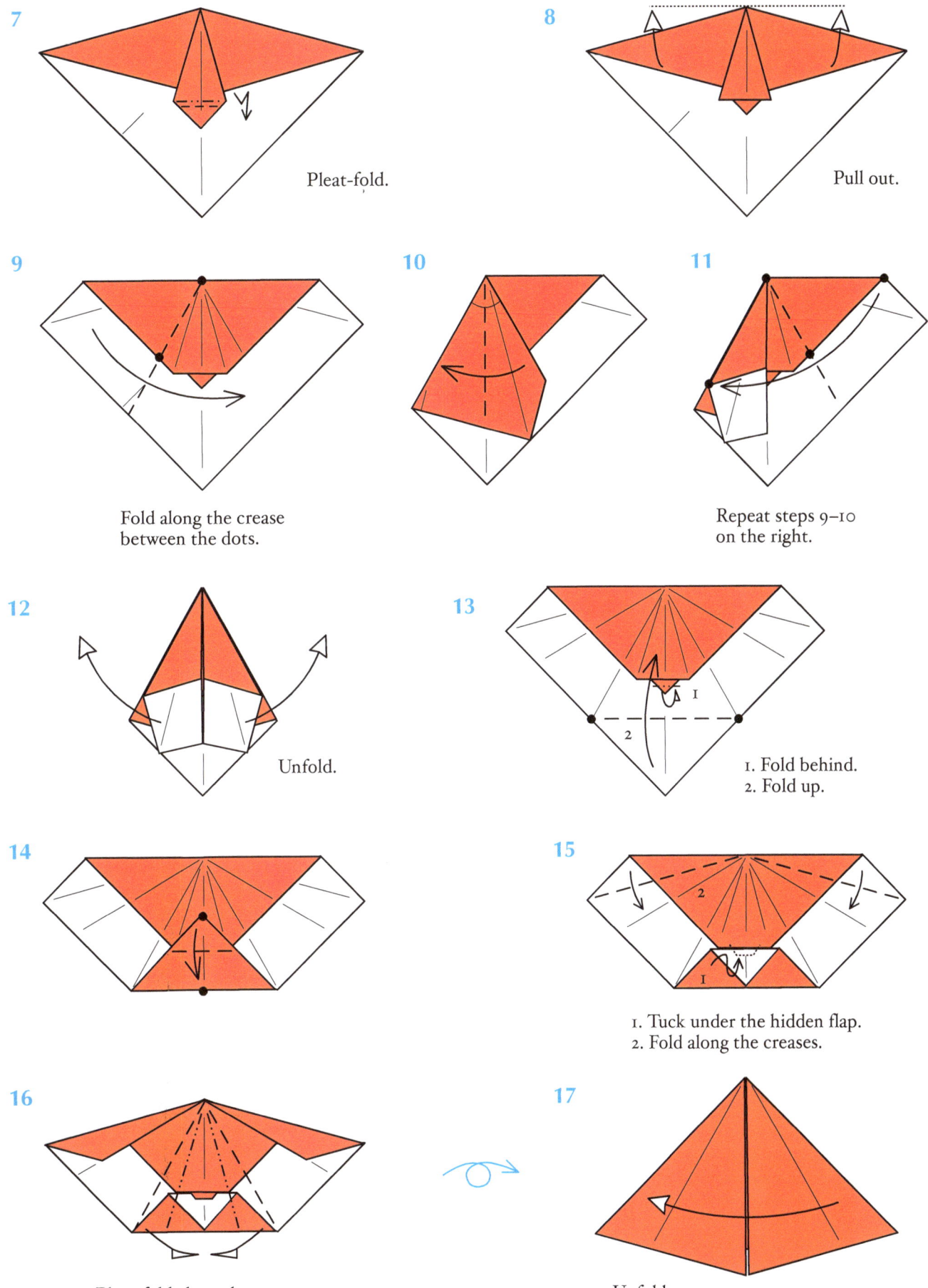

Wizzle TinkerBlinker 69

18

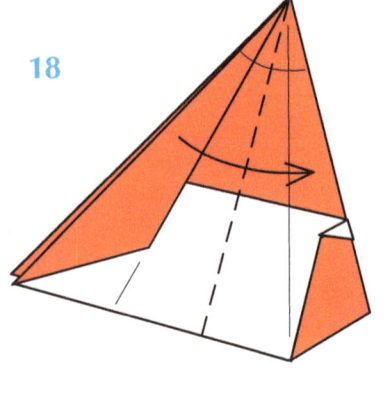

19

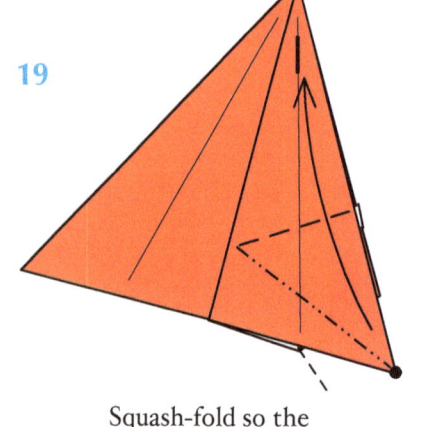

Squash-fold so the dot meets the line.

20

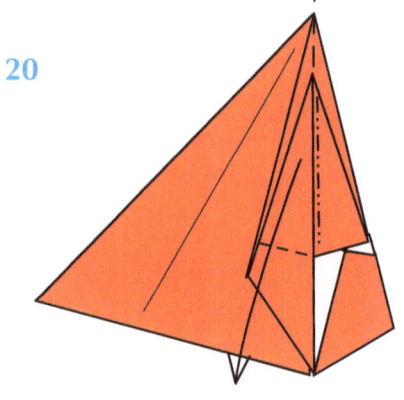

Squash-fold.

21

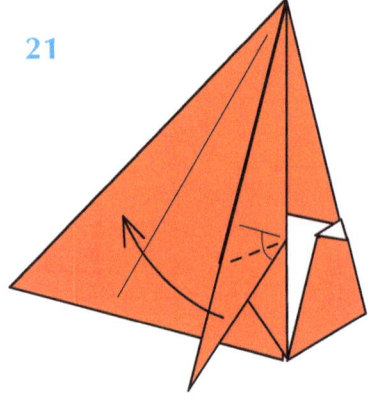

22

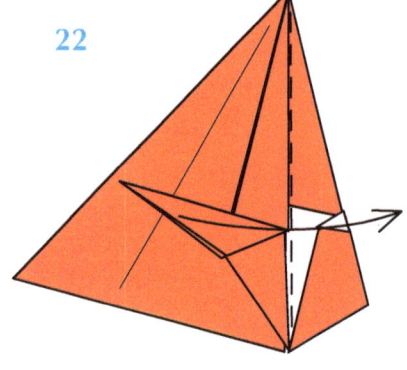

23

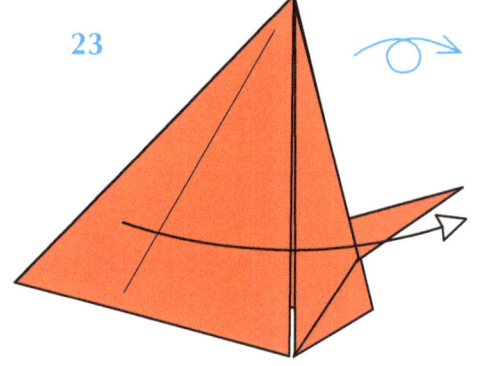

Repeat steps 17–22 in the opposite direction.

24

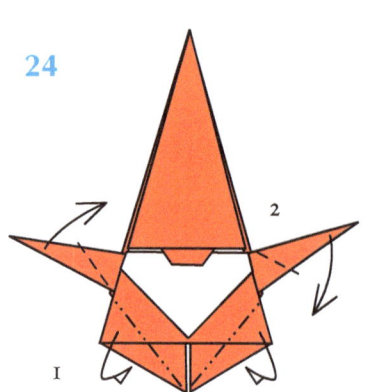

1. Fold inside.
2. Valley-fold the arms.

25

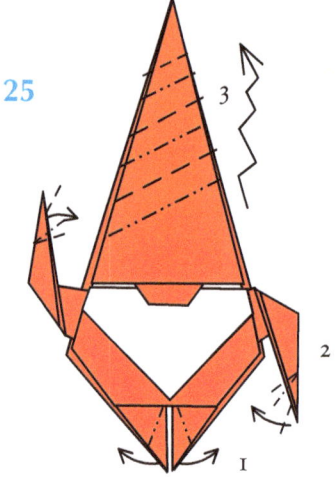

1. Make reverse folds.
2. Make squash folds.
3. Pleat-fold at an angle and unfold.

26

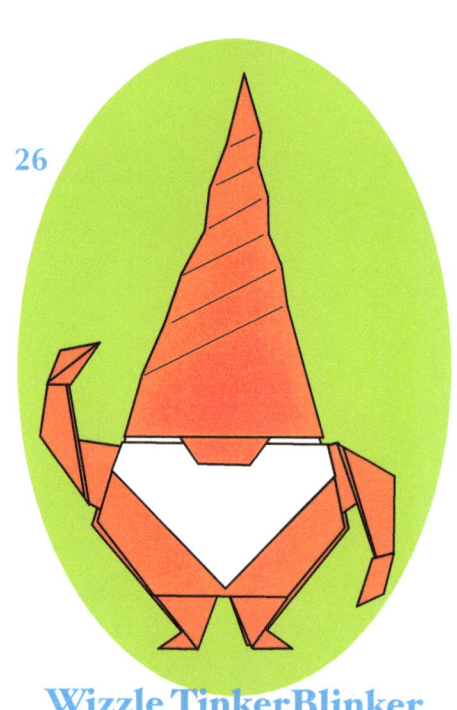

Wizzle TinkerBlinker

70 *Magical Origami Gnomes*

Bizzle TinkerBlinker

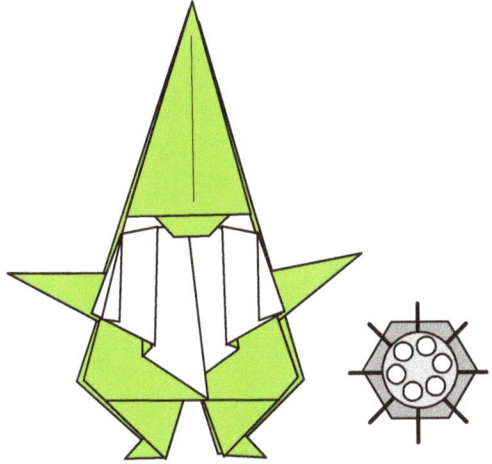

Grandfather Bizzle TinkerBlinker wants stop time. Using intricate gears along with high-quality molasses, he invented a clock that can stop time. By watching his stuckgearful clock, no matter how long you look at it, time does not change. Grandfather Gnome knows best: If it ain't broke... add more gears until it is.

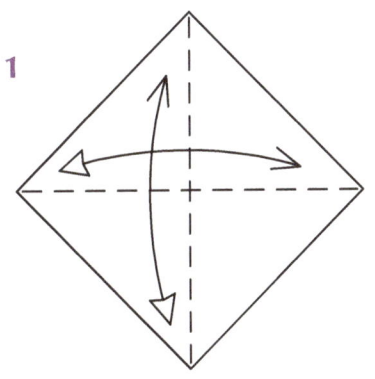

1

Fold and unfold.

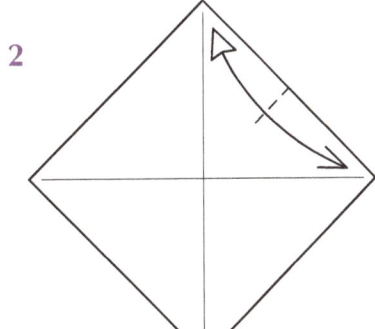

2

Fold and unfold on the edge.

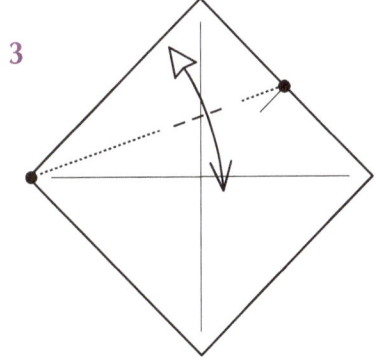

3

Fold and unfold on the diagonal.

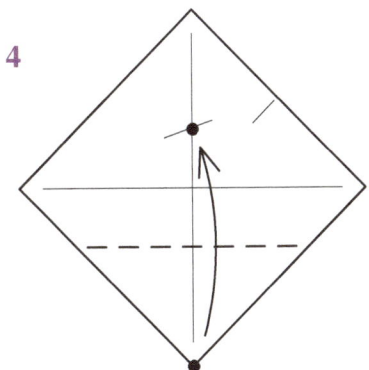

4

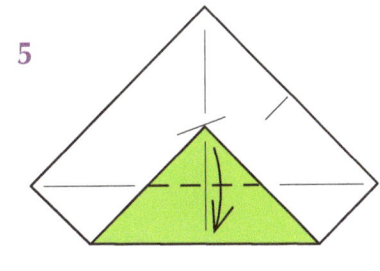

5

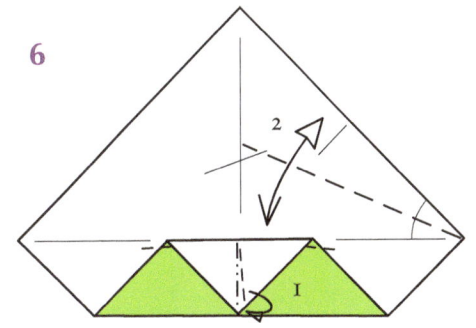

6

1. This is similar to a pleat fold.
2. Fold and unfold.

Bizzle TinkerBlinker 71

7

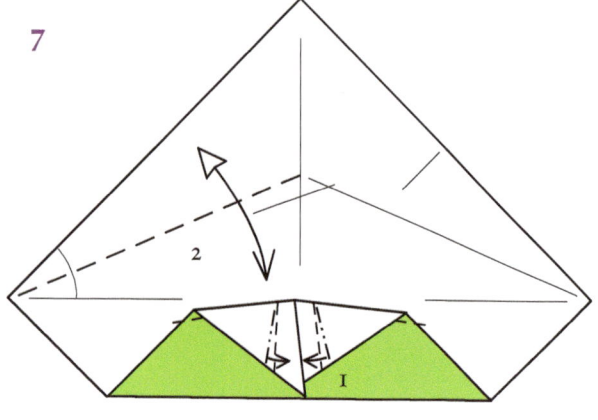

1. Make pleat folds.
2. Fold and unfold.

8

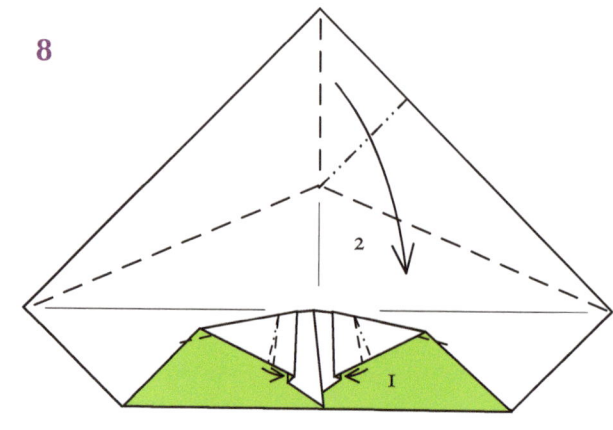

1. Make pleat folds.
2. Rabbit-ear.

9

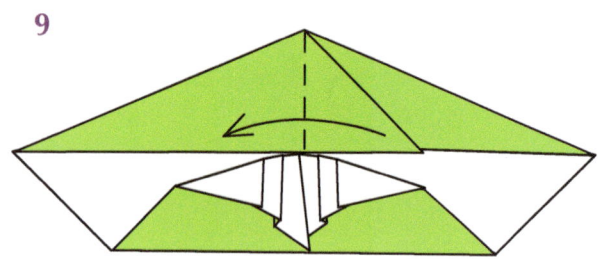

10

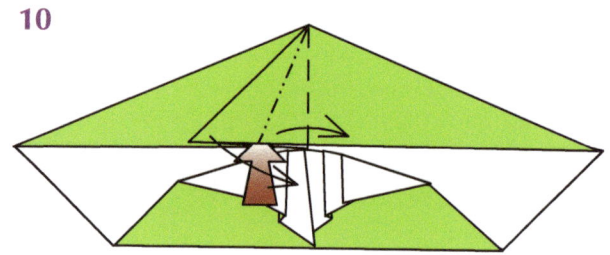

Squash-fold.

11

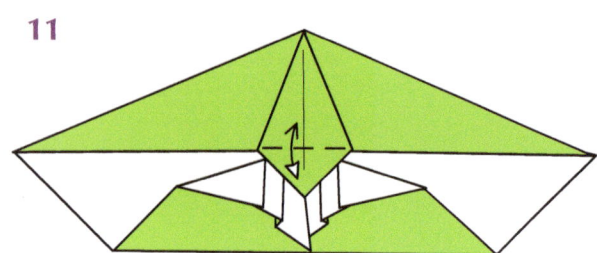

Fold and unfold.

12

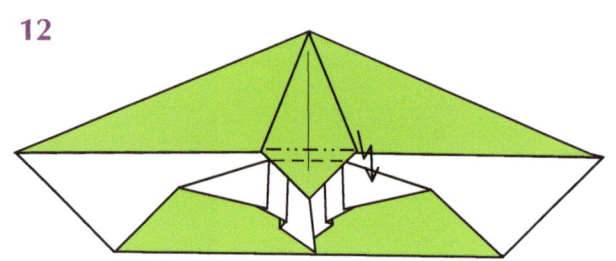

Fold inside for this pleat fold.

13

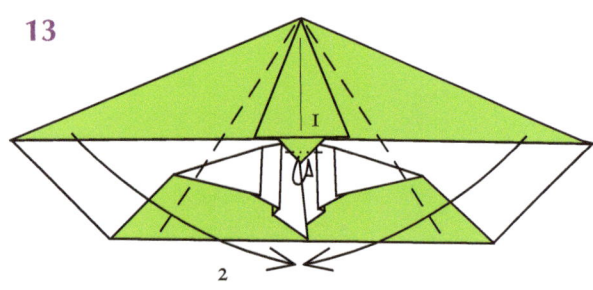

1. Fold behind.
2. Fold to the center.

14 15

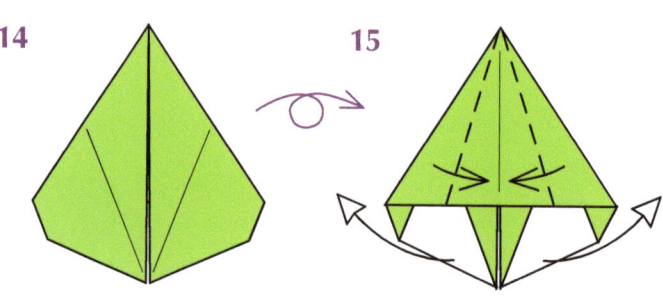

Fold to the center and swing out from behind. Do not fold the layers from the head.

72 *Magical Origami Gnomes*

16

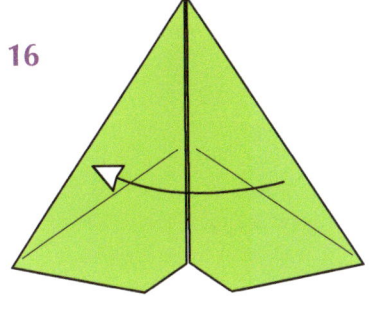

Unfold.

17

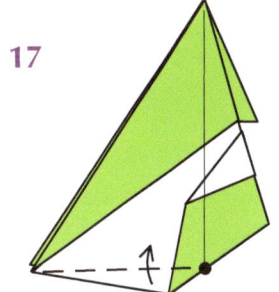

18

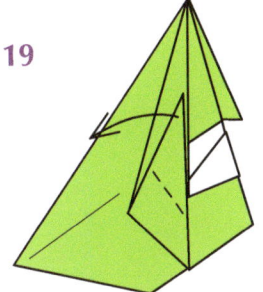

Rabbit-ear.

19

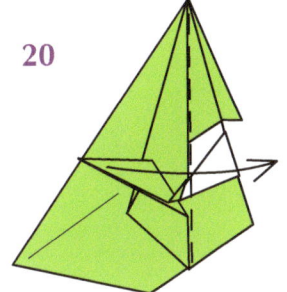

Spread-squash-fold.

20

21

Repeat steps 16–20 in the opposite direction.

22

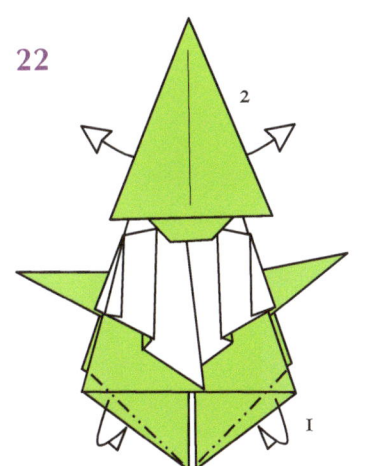

1. Fold inside.
2. Spread the paper.

23

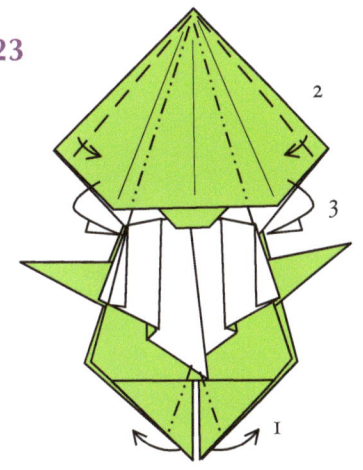

1. Make reverse folds.
2. Fold thin strips.
3. Fold inside.

24

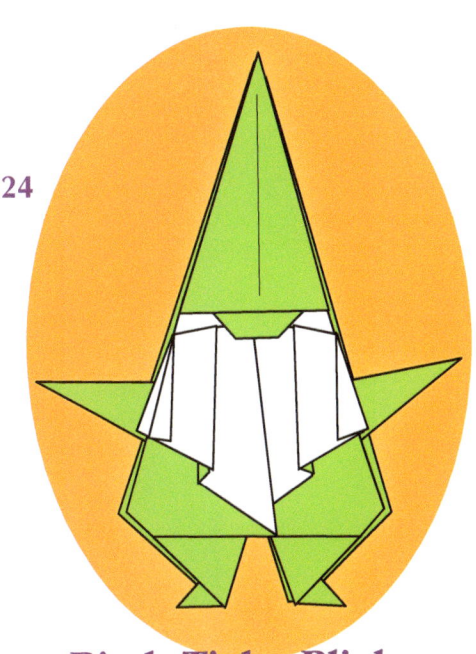

Bizzle TinkerBlinker

Bizzle TinkerBlinker 73

Forest Gnomes of the West

The West is filled with deep forests inhabited by Forest Gnomes. These gnomes live in harmony with the animals and plants. They are invisible to the outside world, and if they suspect they will be viewed, they will summon the mist to make them disappear. Since you are holding this book of gnomes, they will let you enter, but beware of the wild animals.

Wizard

To enter the forest, the Wizard will teach you some magic to protect you as you wander around. He will teach you how to speak to small forest creatures and how to summon insects of your choice to protect you from wild beasts. With his magic knowledge, you will be able to make mushrooms sing. The Wizard will show you how to fly into rainbows. If you can't fly, buzz.

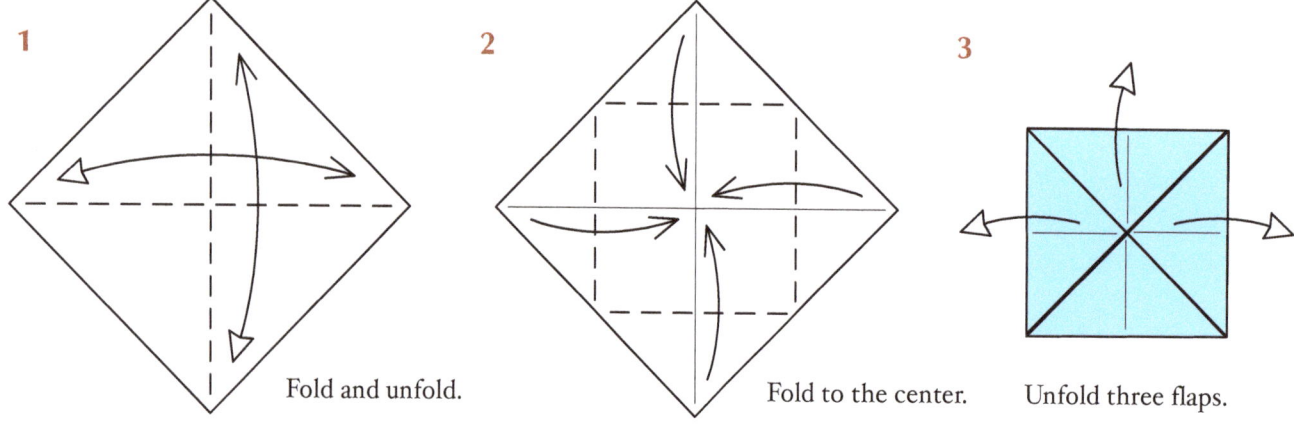

1. Fold and unfold.
2. Fold to the center.
3. Unfold three flaps.

74 *Magical Origami Gnomes*

4

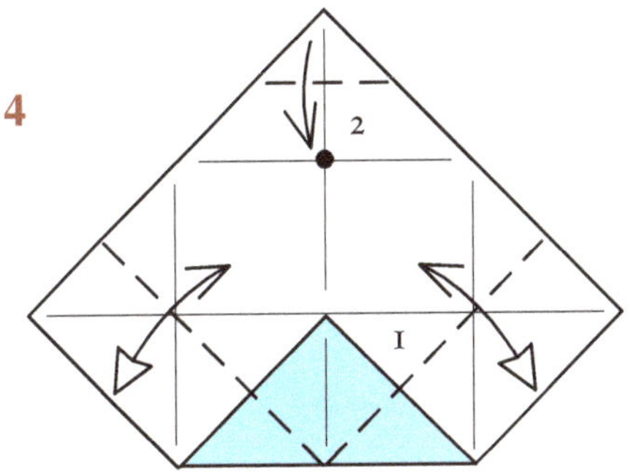

1. Fold and unfold.
2. Fold down.

5

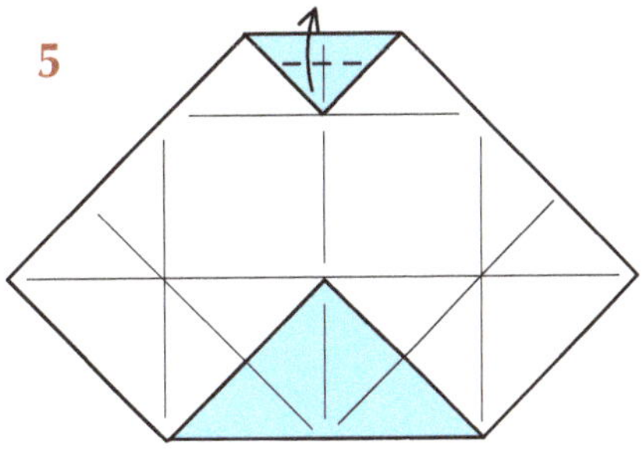

6

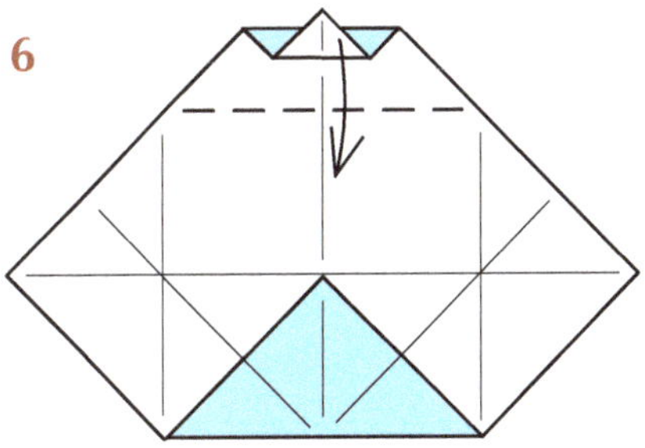

Fold along the crease.

7

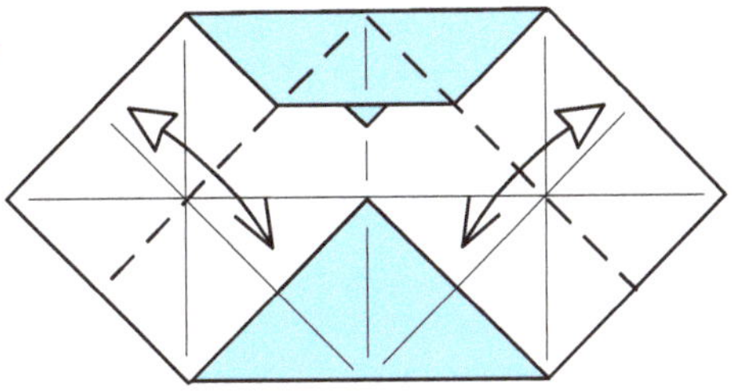

Fold and unfold.

8

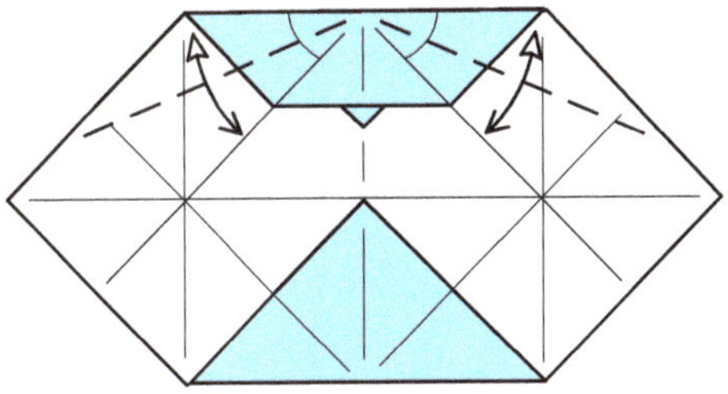

Fold and unfold.

9

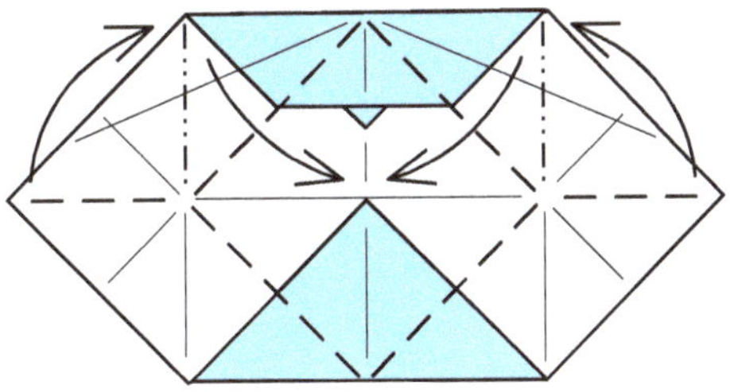

Make rabbit ears.

10

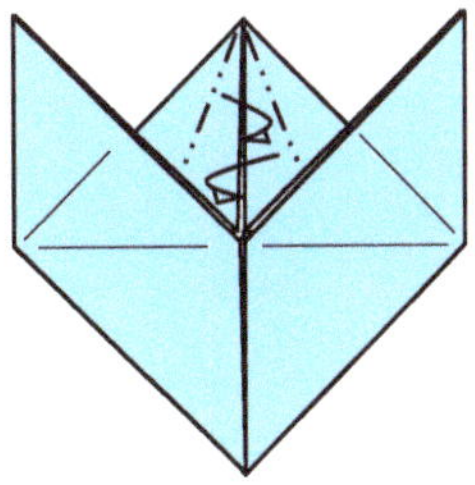

Fold inside along the creases.

11

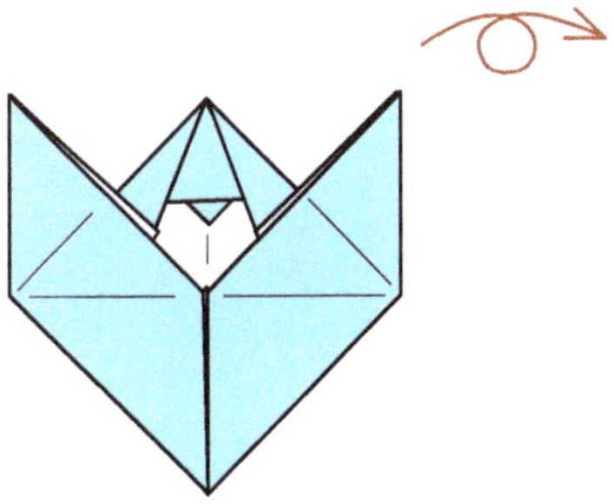

12

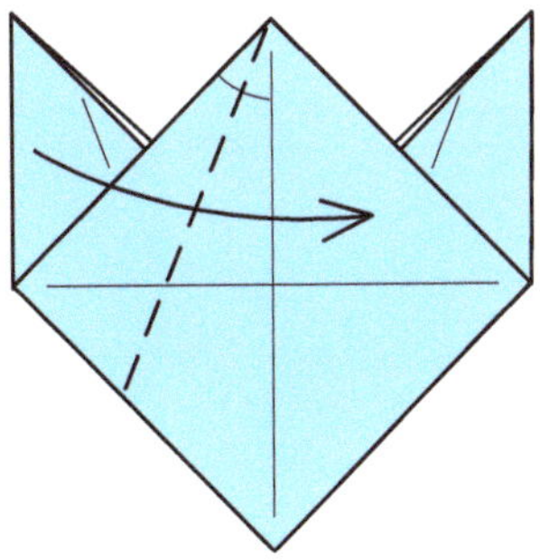

13

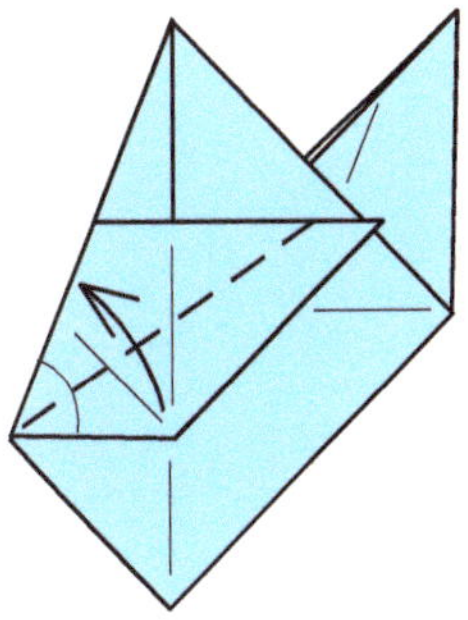

Wizard

14

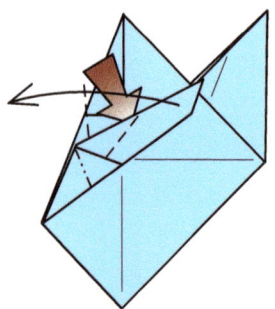

Reverse-fold.

15

1. Repeat steps 12–14 on the right.
2. Fold up.

16

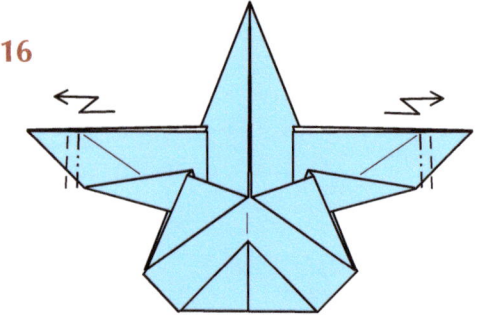

Make crimp folds.

17

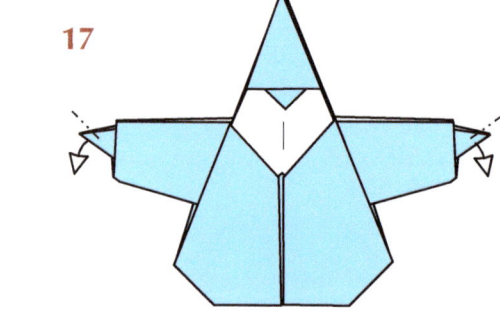

Spread the hands.

18

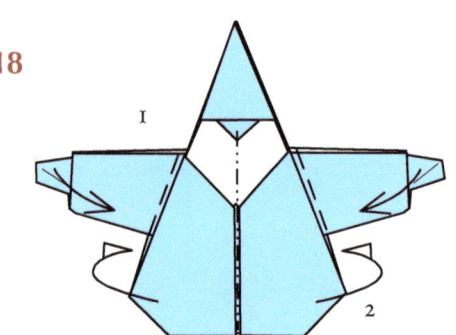

1. Bend the arms.
2. Bend slightly in half so the Wizard can stand.

19

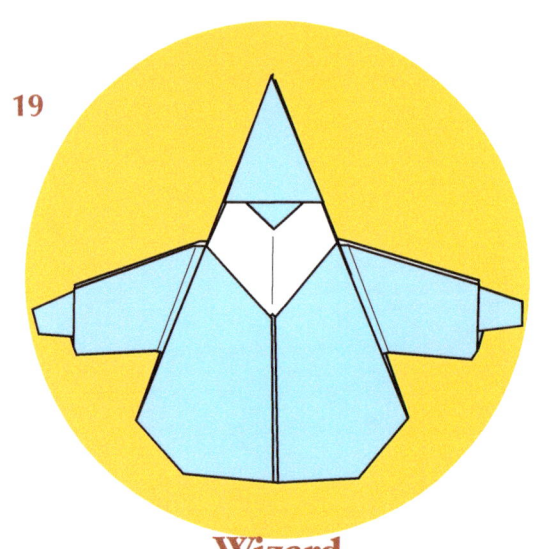

Wizard

76   *Magical Origami Gnomes*

Tinket Greenwhistle

Tinket Greenwhistle is a caretaker of owls and old trees. He likes to follow butterflies because they take the scenic route.

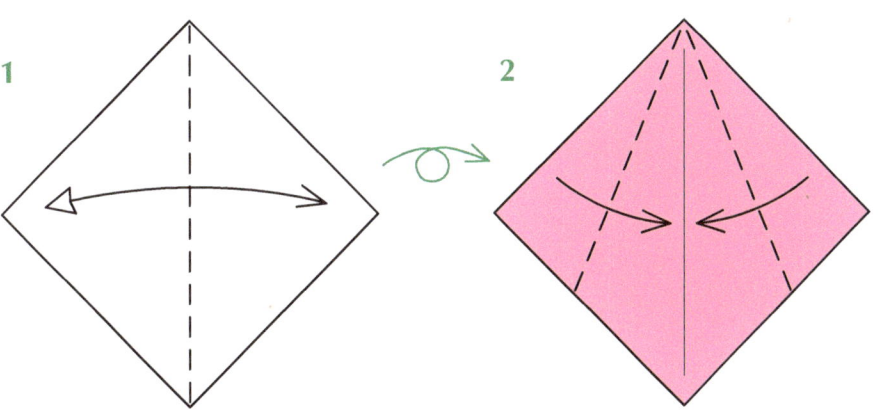

1. Fold and unfold.

2. Fold to the center.

3.

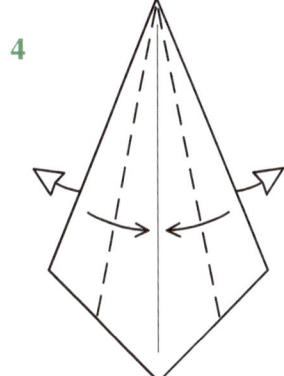
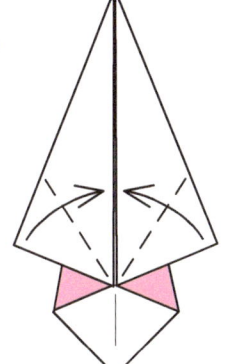
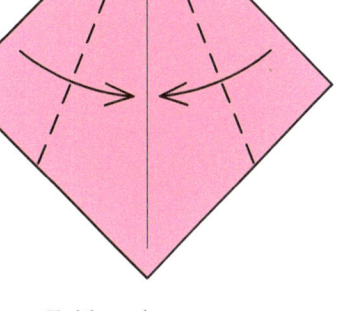
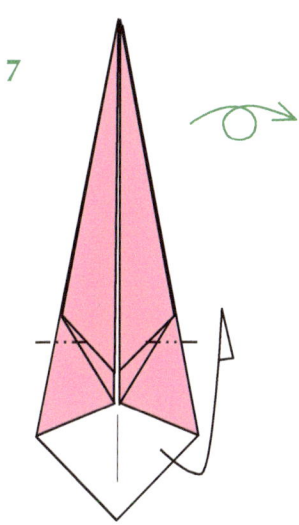

4. Fold to the center and swing out from behind.

5.

6. Make squash folds.

7.

Tinket Greenwhistle 77

8

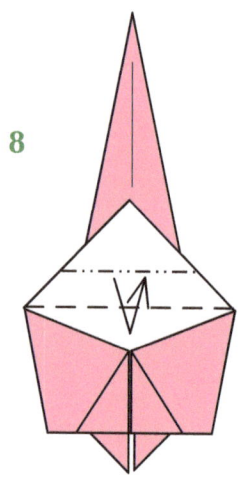

Pleat-fold.

9

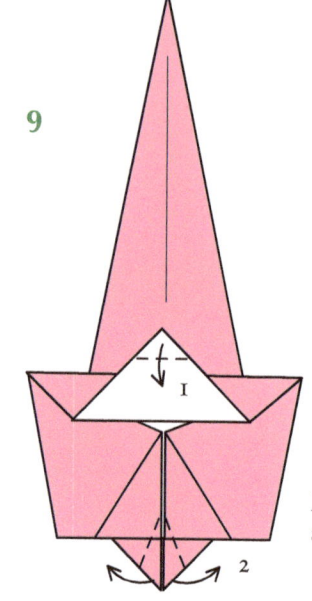

Make valley folds at 1 and 2.

10

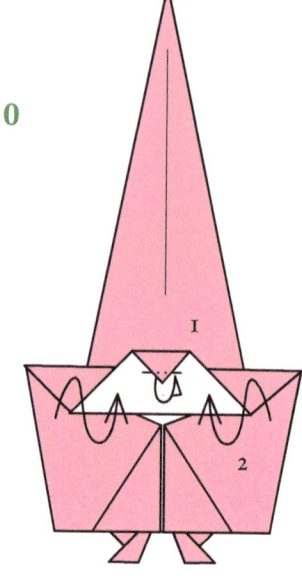

1. Fold inside.
2. Bring the layers to the front.

11

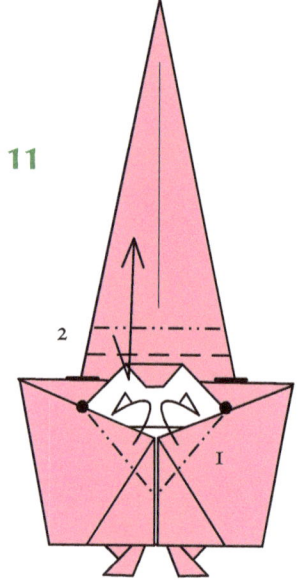

1. Fold inside.
2. Pleat-fold to the bold lines.

12

1. Fold behind.
2. Make squash folds.

13

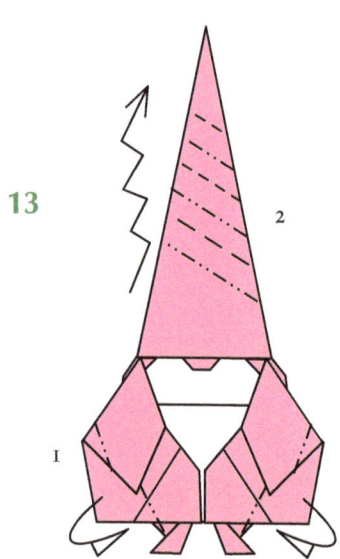

1. Fold behind with small squash folds.
2. Pleat-fold the hat and spread.

14

Tinket Greenwhistle

78 *Magical Origami Gnomes*

Bibble Thistlebrush

Bibble Thistlebrush lives in a mushroom house under a hollow oak. Using peanuts, he calls squirrels to his house and takes rides on them to reach treetops. On weekdays, he rides rabbits to work, using the express lane.

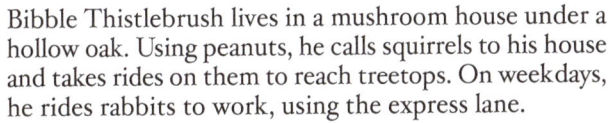

1. 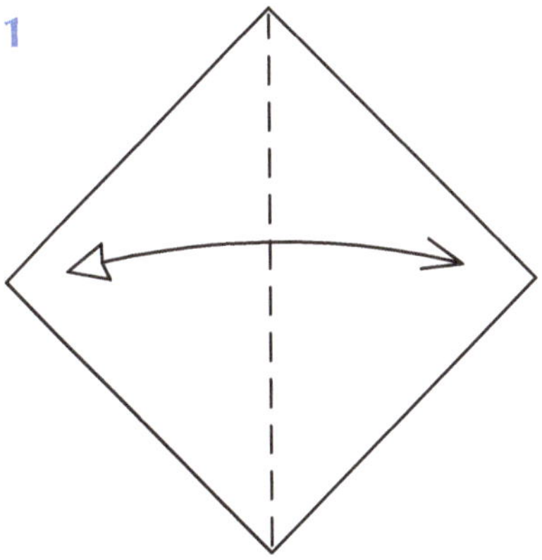 Fold and unfold.
2. Fold to the center and unfold.
3. Fold to the center.
4. Fold and unfold the top layer.
5. Fold to the center and swing out from behind.
6. Fold and unfold.

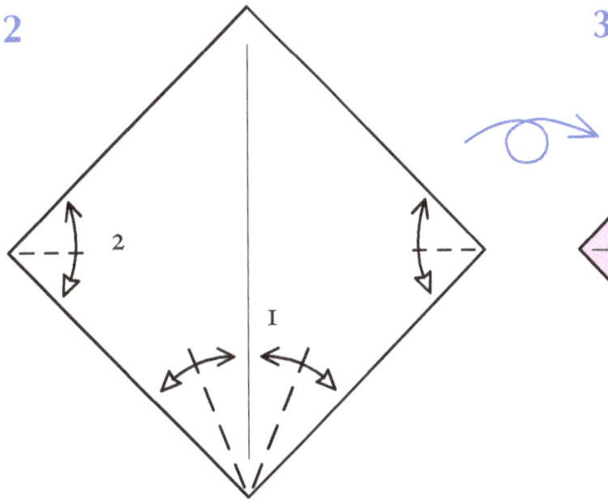

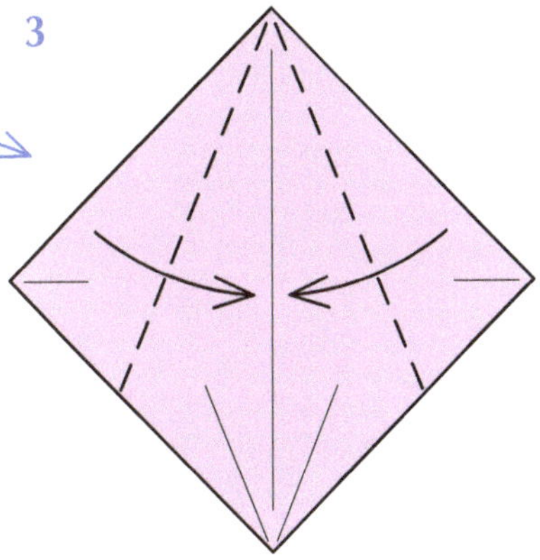

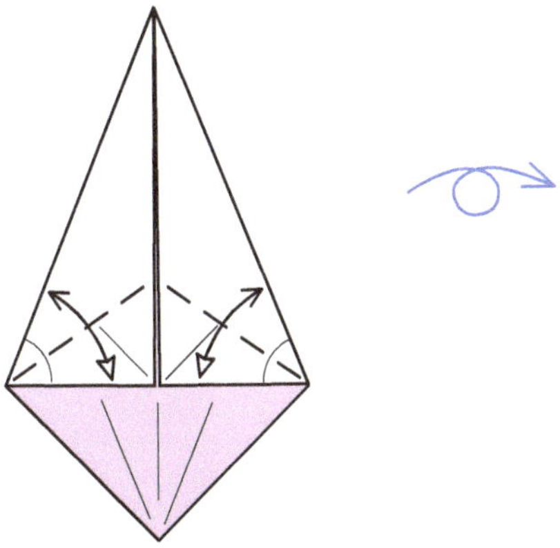

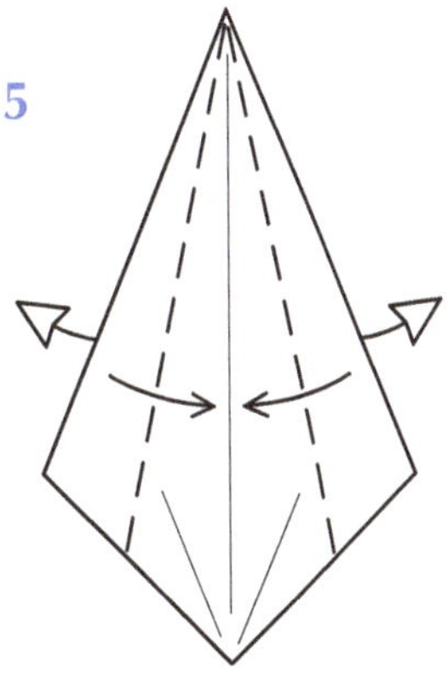

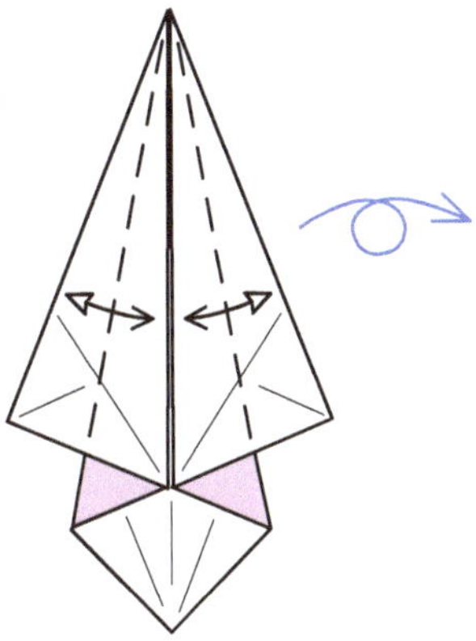

Bibble Thistlebrush 79

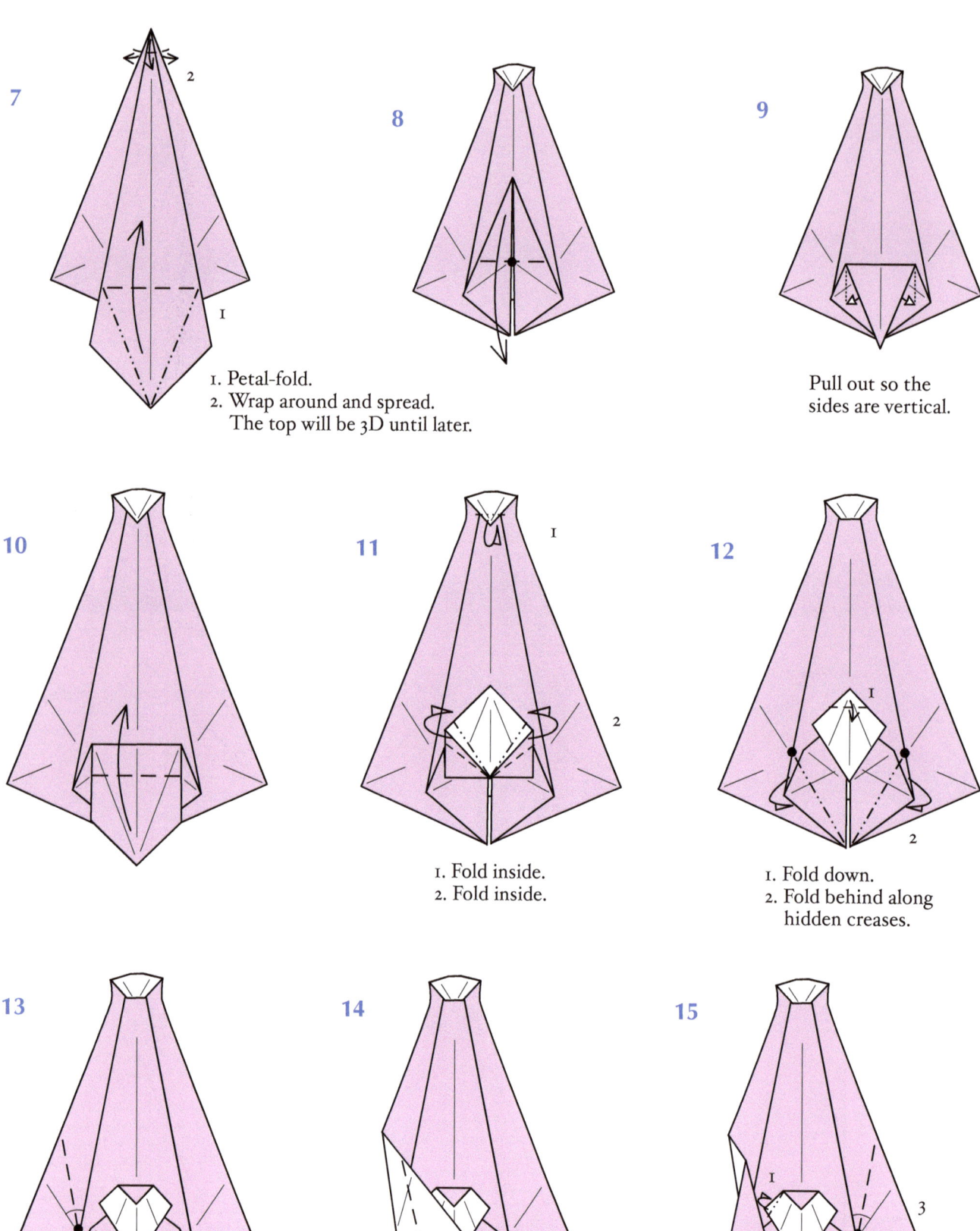

16

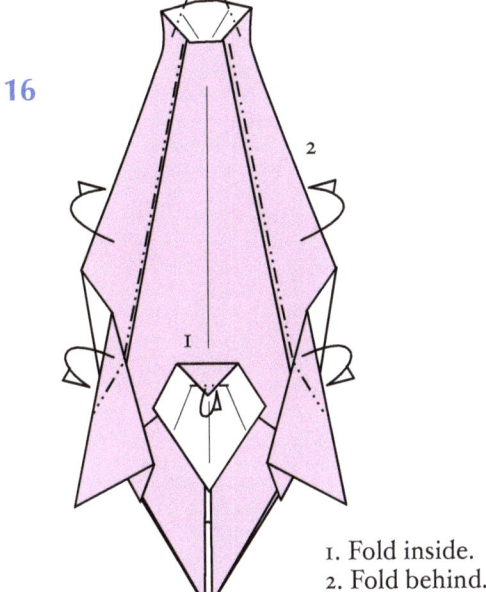

1. Fold inside.
2. Fold behind.

17

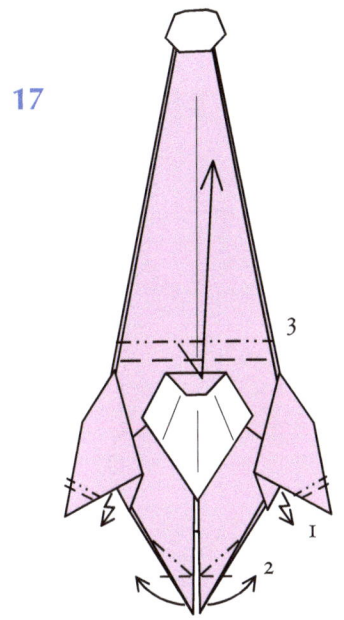

1. Make crimp folds.
2. Make crimp folds.
3. Cover the top of the nose with a pleat fold.

18

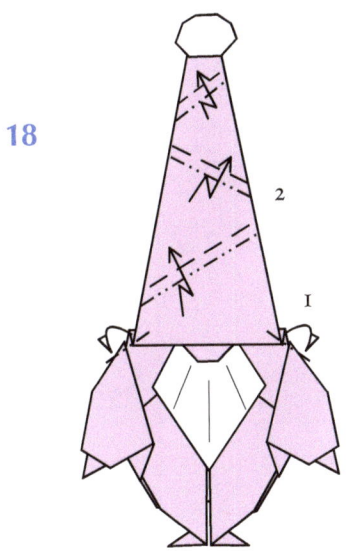

1. Fold behind.
2. Make pleat folds and spread.

19

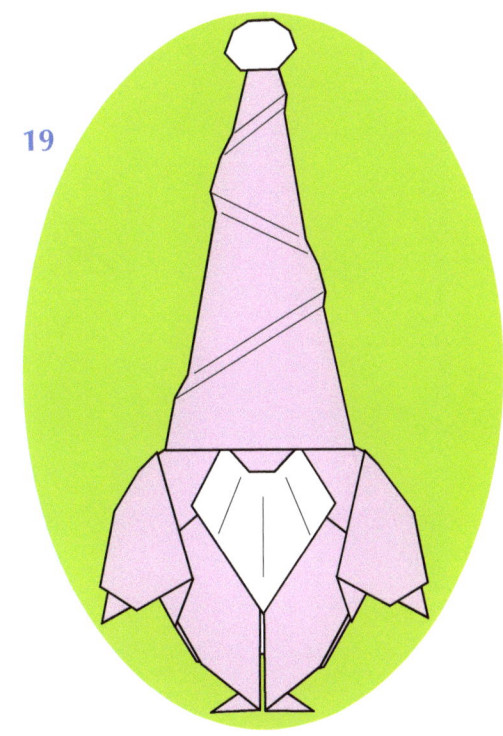

Bibble Thistlebrush

Bibble Thistlebrush 81

Jimble Underbark

Jimble Underbark stores all kinds of berries. He can mimic birdcalls, so the birds fly to him. As they feast on berries, they gift Jimble with twigs, so he can continue adding to his house. He sings to the flowers because they won't judge his voice.

1

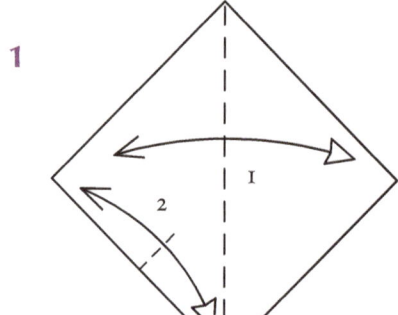

1. Fold and unfold.
2. Fold and unfold on the edge.

2

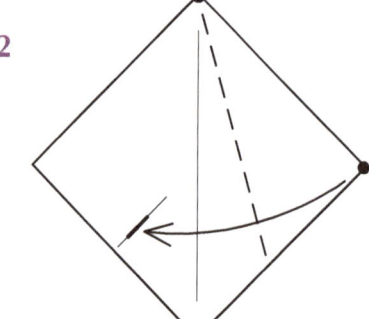

Bring the corner to the line.

3

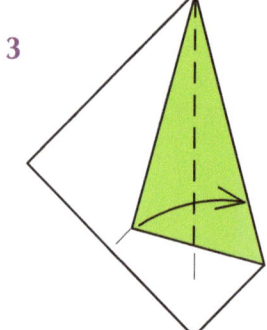

4

Repeat steps 2–3 on the left.

5

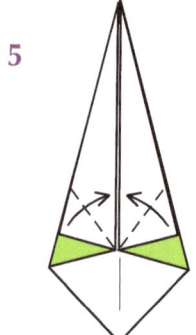

6

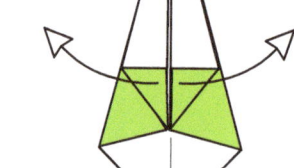

Unfold almost everything.

82   *Magical Origami Gnomes*

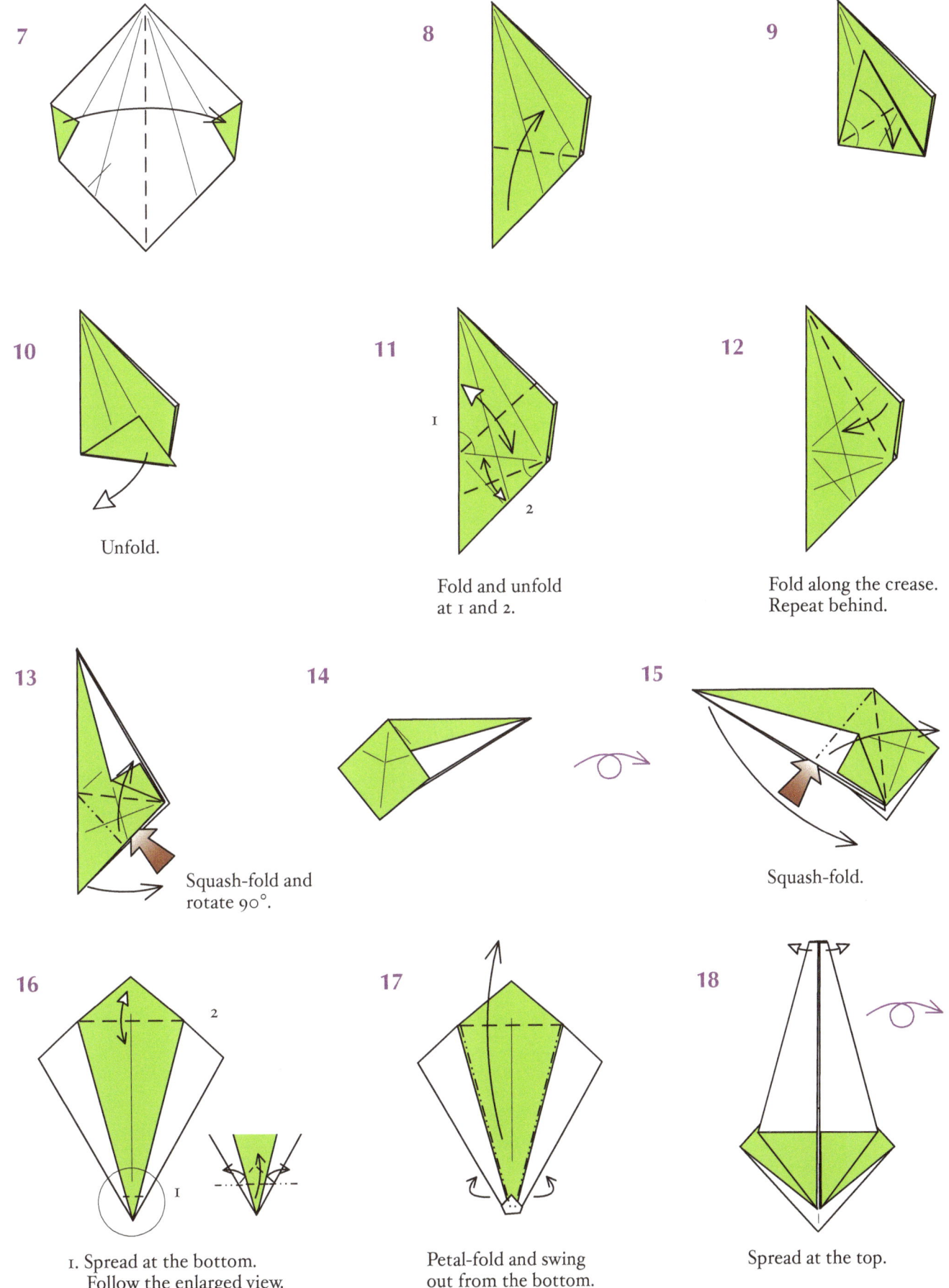

Jimble Underbark 83

19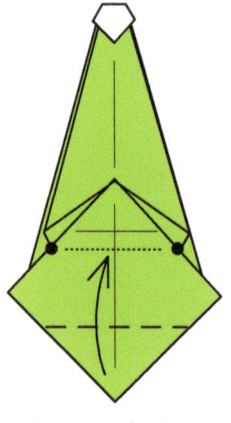
Fold up to the height shown by the dots.

20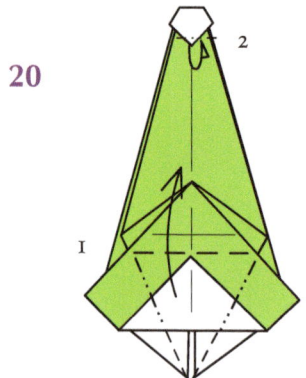
1. Petal-fold.
2. Fold inside.

21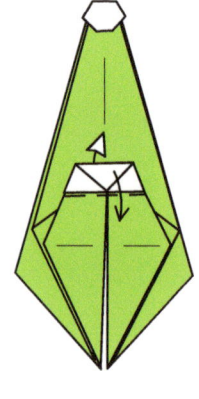
Fold down and swing out from behind.

22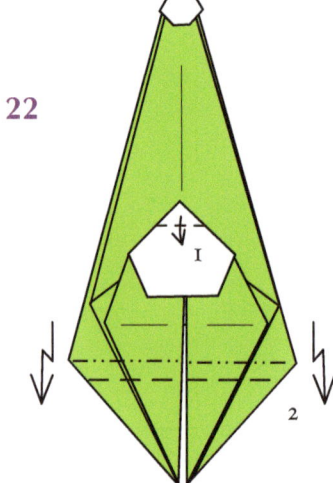
1. Fold down.
2. Make pleat folds.

23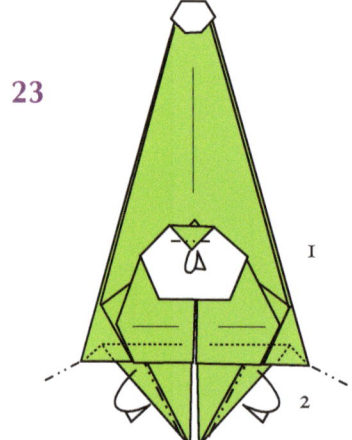
1. Fold inside.
2. Fold behind and make squash folds on the back.

24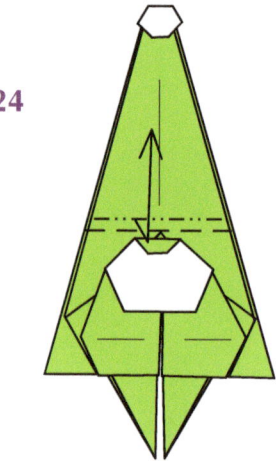
Pleat-fold to cover the top of the nose.

25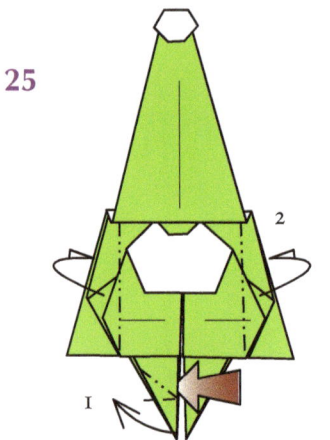
1. Crimp-fold.
2. Fold inside.

26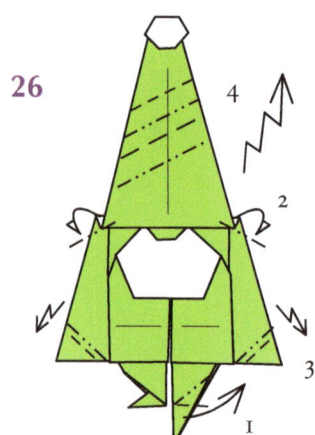
1. Crimp-fold.
2. Fold behind.
3. Make crimp folds.
4. Pleat-fold.

27

Jimble Underbark

84 *Magical Origami Gnomes*

Grindle Mossroot

Grindle Mossroot makes the best hot daffodil drinks, attracting squirrels and rabbits. When they visit, he plays his lute made from spider silk strings, to keep them entertained. Grindle will welcome you with a slice of magnolia cake sprinkled with crunchy bronze chips.

1

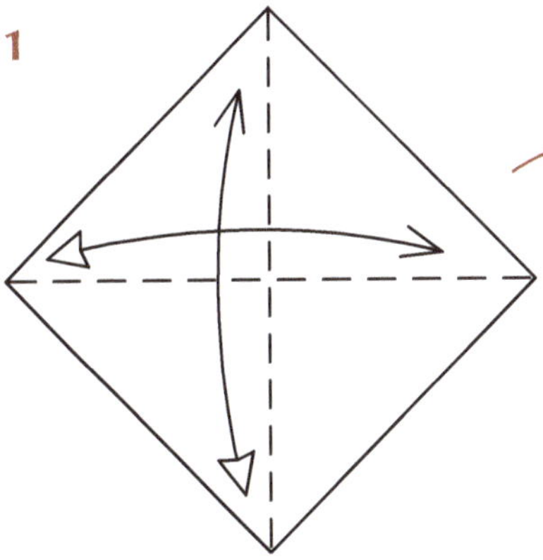

Fold and unfold.

2

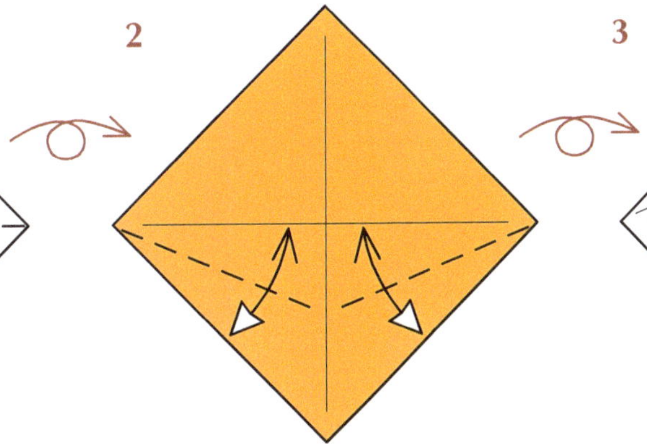

Fold and unfold. Rotate 180°.

3

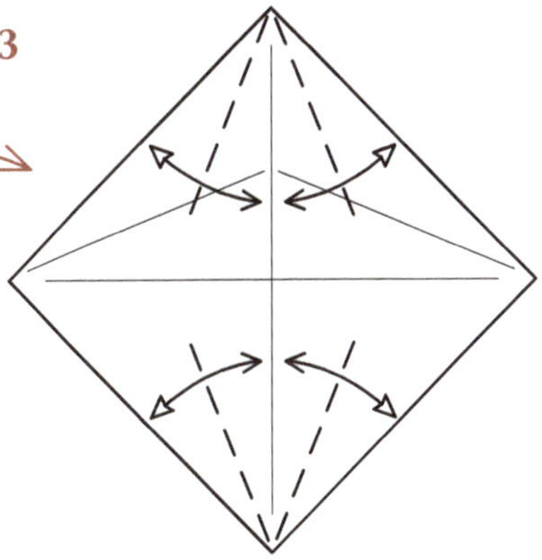

Fold and unfold.

4

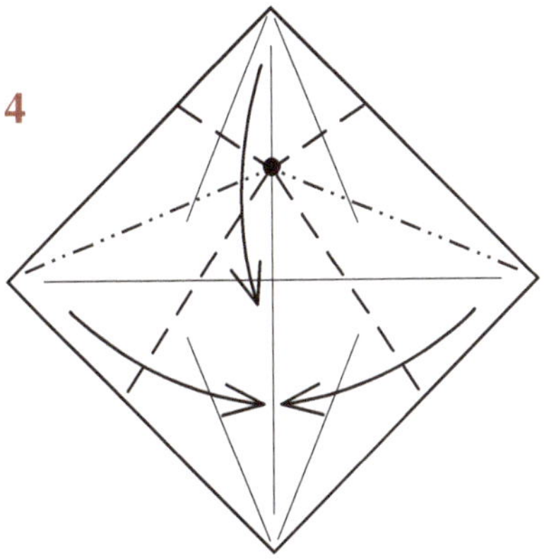

Push in at the dot and fold to the center.

5

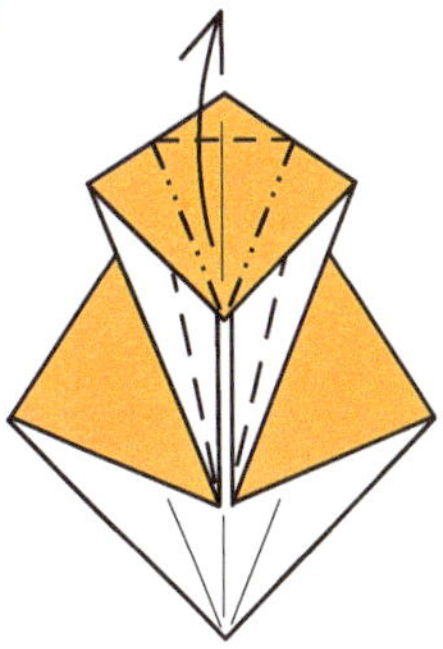

Petal-fold.

6

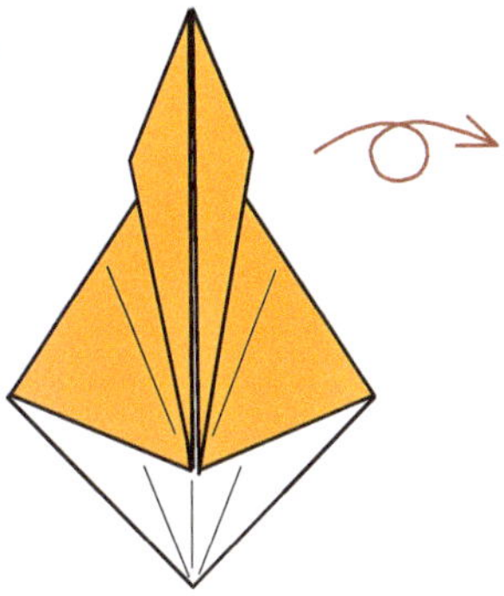

Grindle Mossroot 85

7

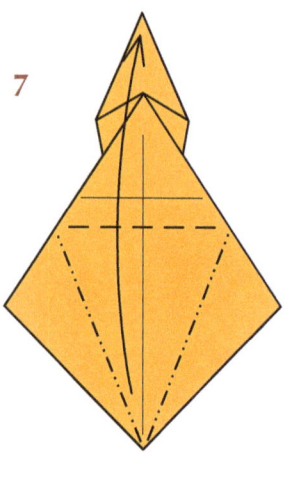

Petal-fold.

8

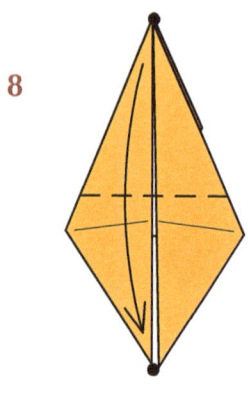

9

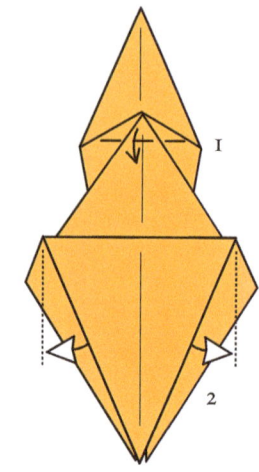

1. Fold down.
2. Pull out to the dotted vertical lines.

10

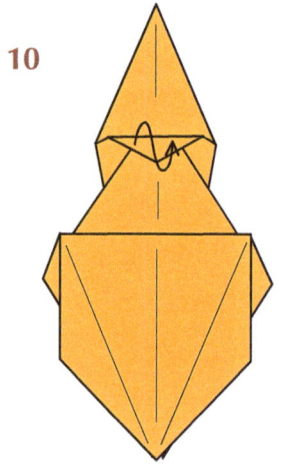

Sink-nose-fold.
(See page 12.)

11

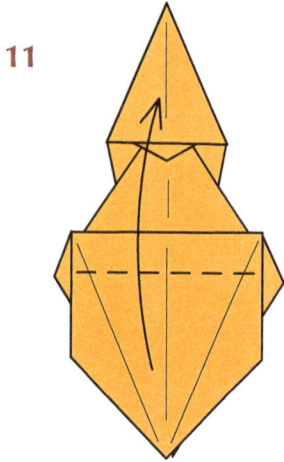

12

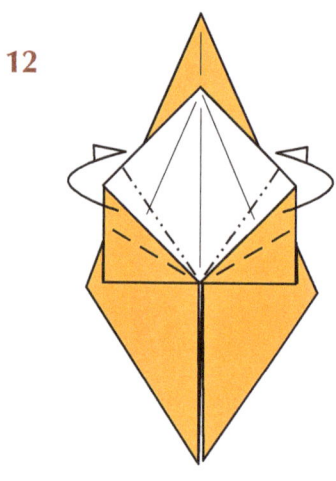

Fold inside.

13

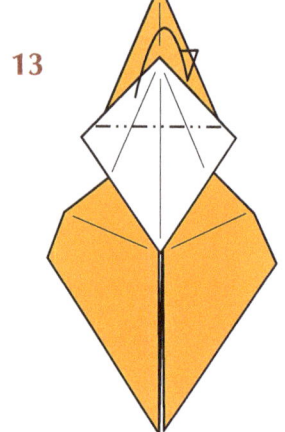

Fold behind.

14

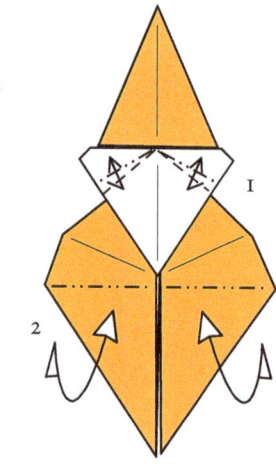

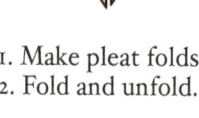

1. Make pleat folds.
2. Fold and unfold.

15

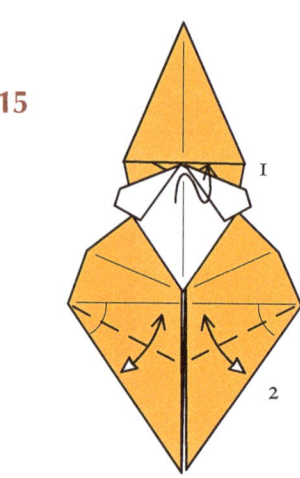

1. Tuck under the nose.
2. Fold and unfold.

86 *Magical Origami Gnomes*

16

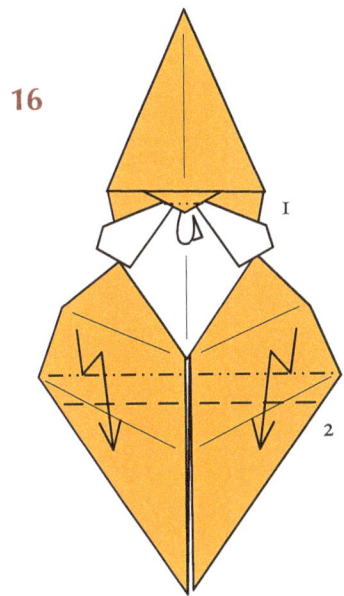

1. Fold inside.
2. Make pleat folds.

17

1. Fold behind at an angle of about 1/3.
2. Make pleat folds.

18

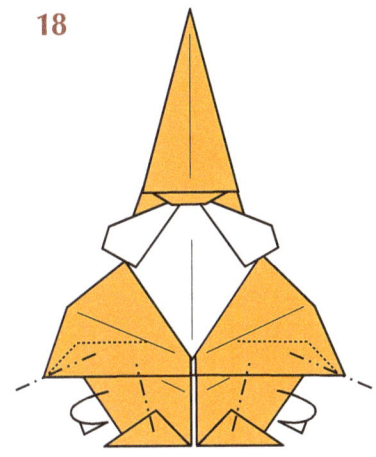

Make squash folds on the layers behind.

19

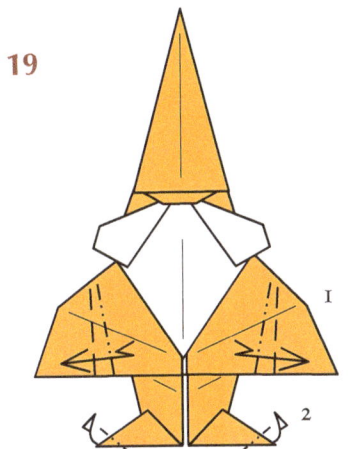

1. Make pleat folds.
2. Fold behind.

20

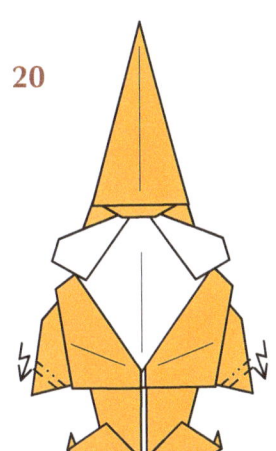

Make pleat folds.

21

Grindle Mossroot

Crimble Bumbleknack

Crimble Bumbleknack tends to the forest bees that make golden honey. When the bees gift him some honey, he spreads in on his favorite oak leaves, for an afternoon snack. He likes telling mindless stories to the daisies because they listen with open petals. In return, he enjoys animal stories since they all have a tail to spin.

1. Fold and unfold.

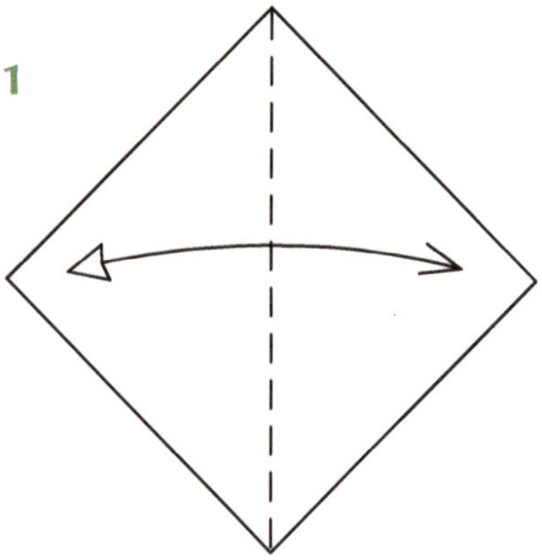

2. Fold to the center and unfold.

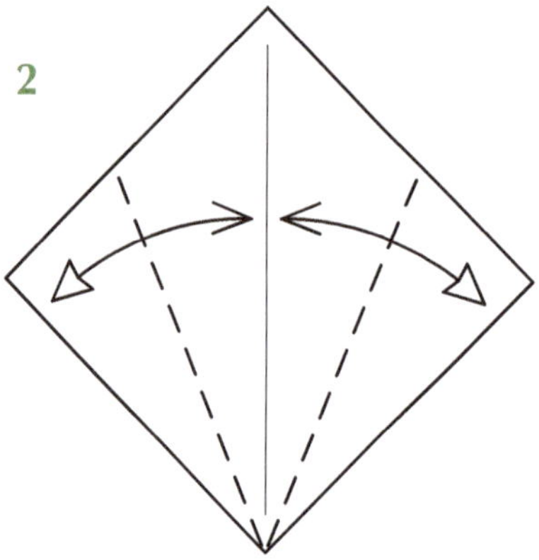

3. Fold and unfold.

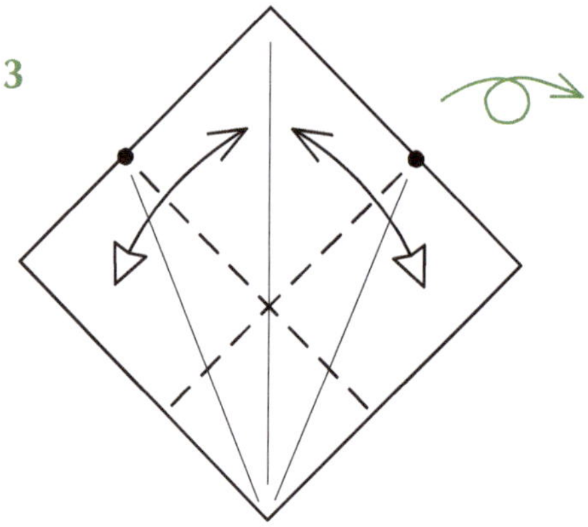

4. Fold and unfold at 1 and 2. Rotate 180°.

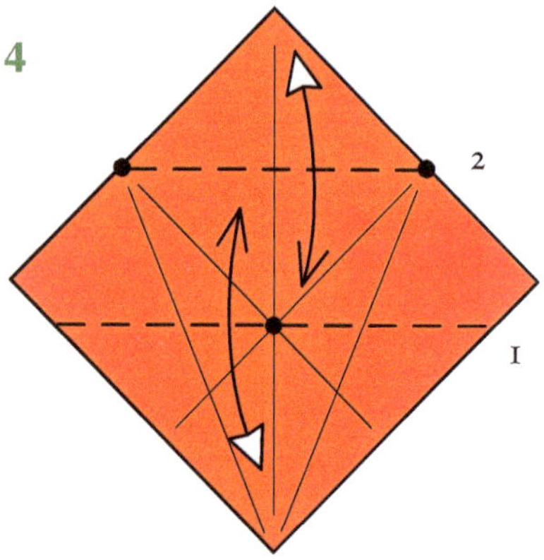

5. Fold along the creases.

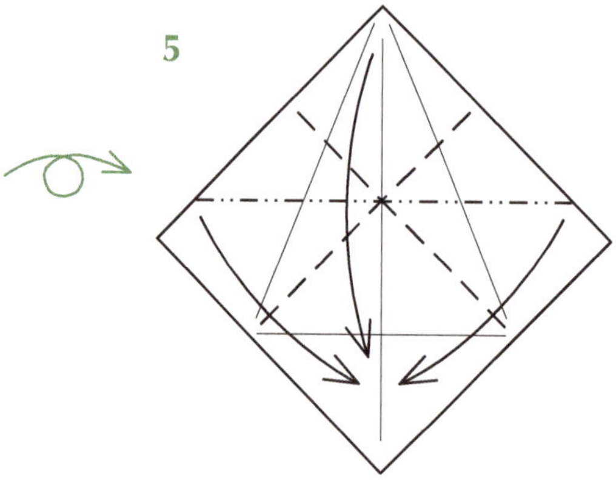

6. Petal-fold.

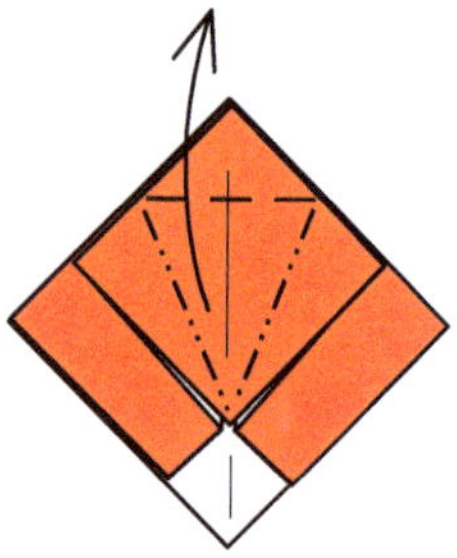

88   *Magical Origami Gnomes*

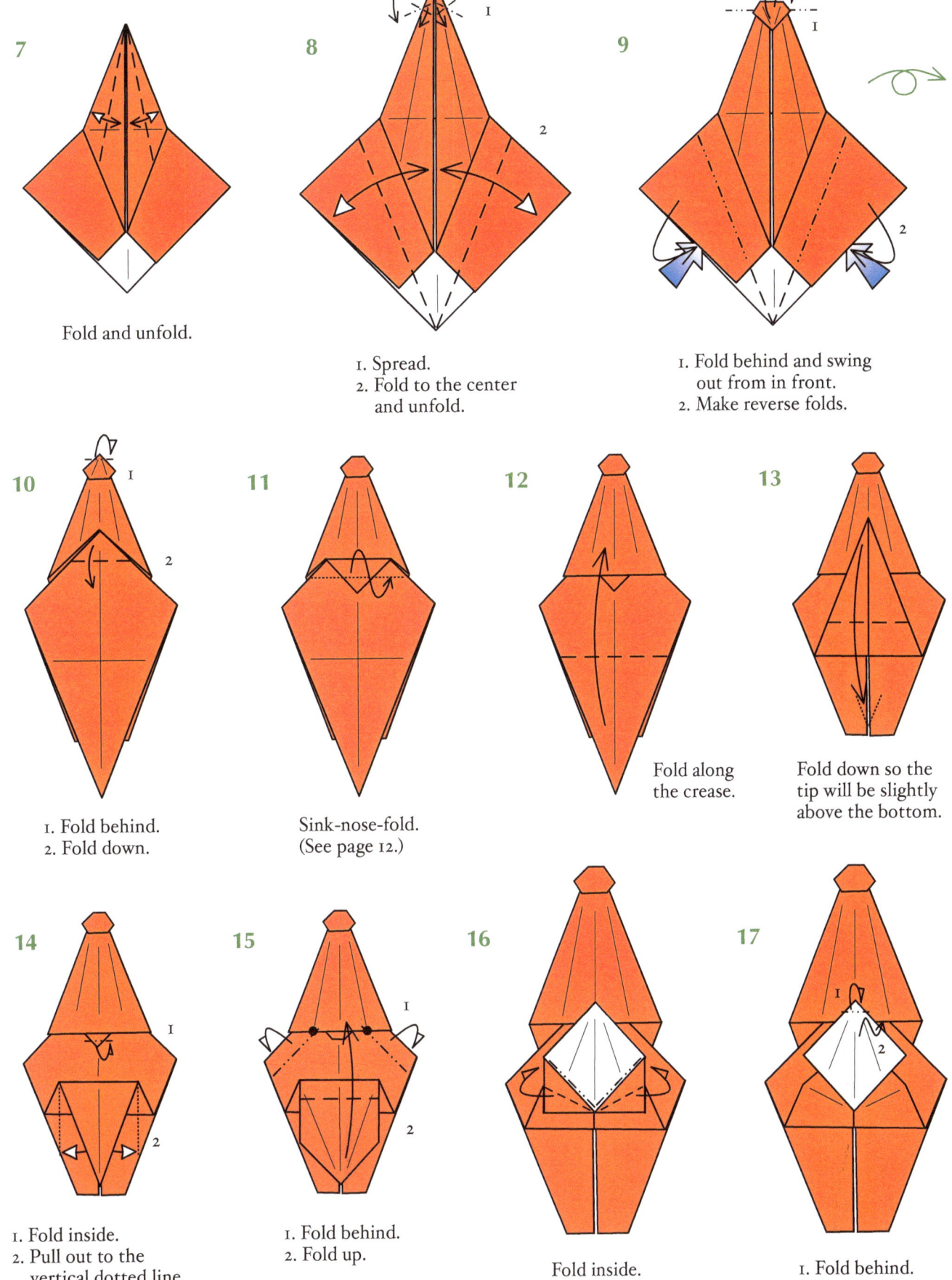

Crimble Bumbleknack 89

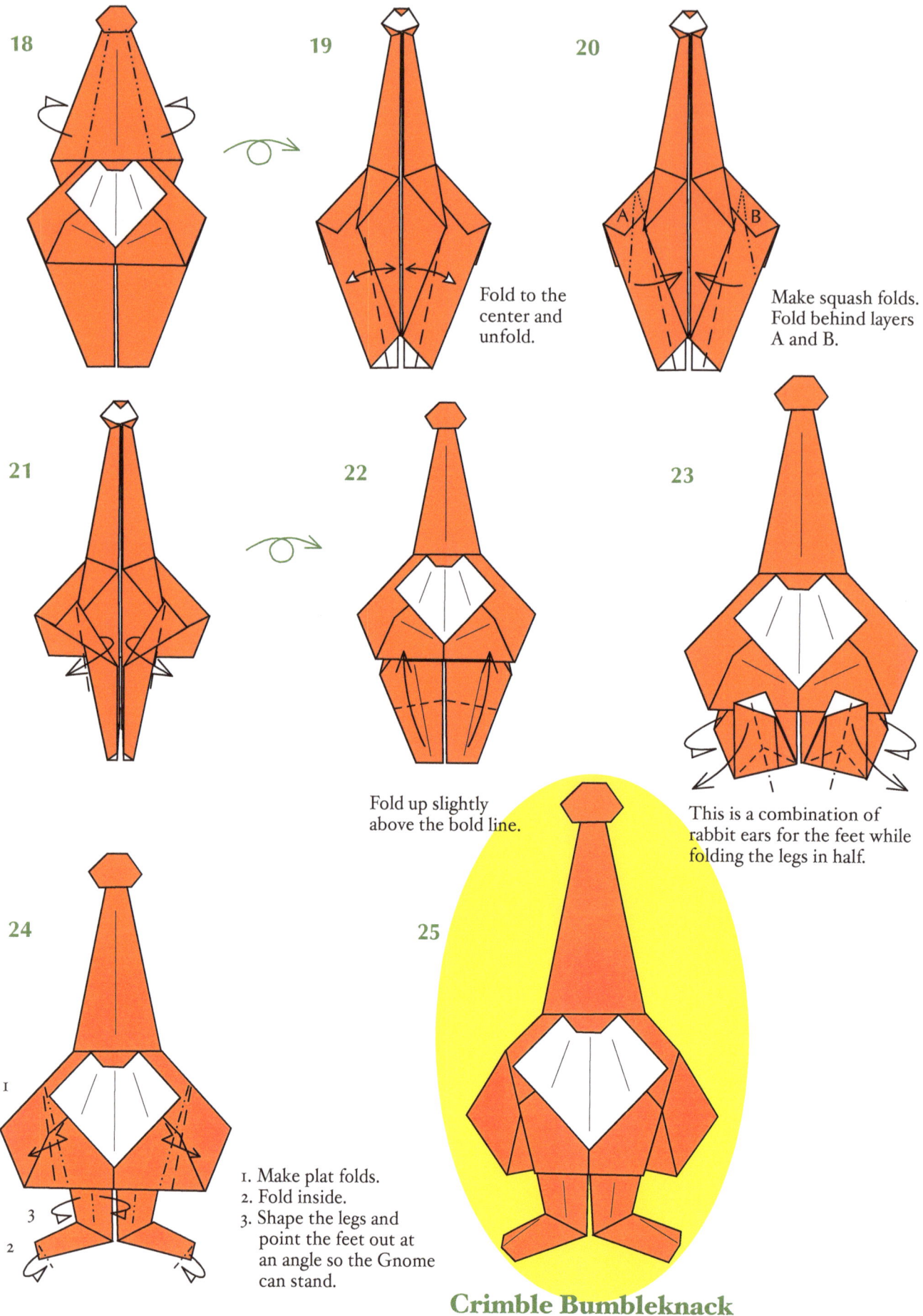

Crimble Bumbleknack

90 *Magical Origami Gnomes*

Wibbin Nutterclap

Wibbin Nutterclap keeps honey and acorns in underground nests. Hedgehogs visit for these treats. Wibbin can strum on the hedgehog's backs to create soothing music for the forest to enjoy. Wibbin is gentle with skunks. He can lead a skunk to water but he can't make him stink.

1

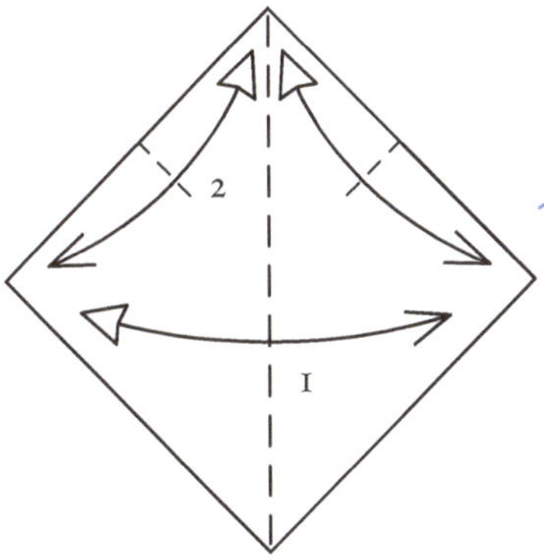

1. Fold and unfold.
2. Fold and unfold on the edges.

2

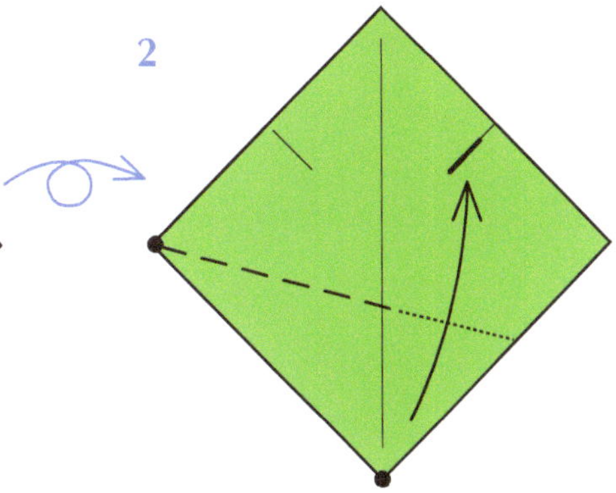

Bring the lower dot to the bold line.

3

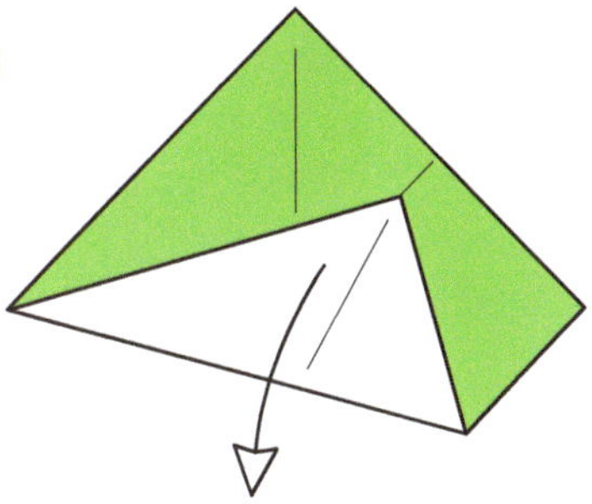

Unfold.

4

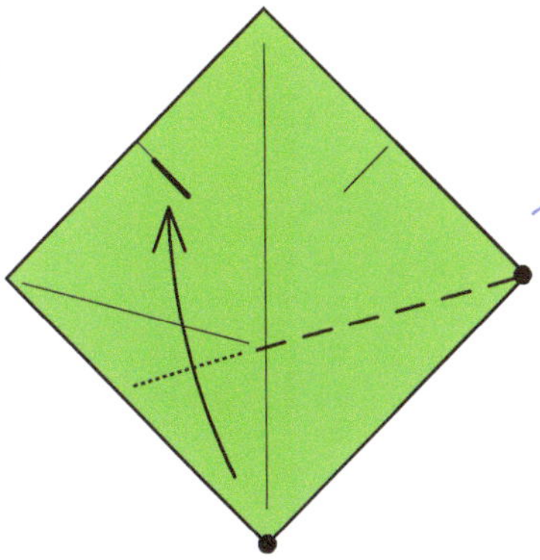

Repeat steps 2–3 in the opposite direction. Rotate 180°.

5

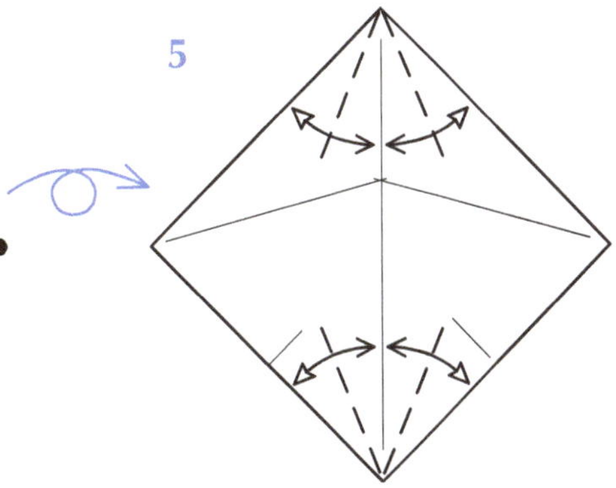

Fold to the center and unfold.

6

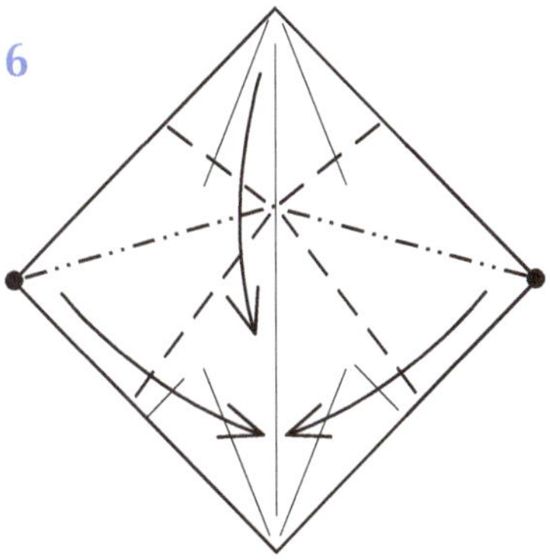

Mountain-fold along the creases and bring the dots to the center line.

Wibbin Nutterclap 91

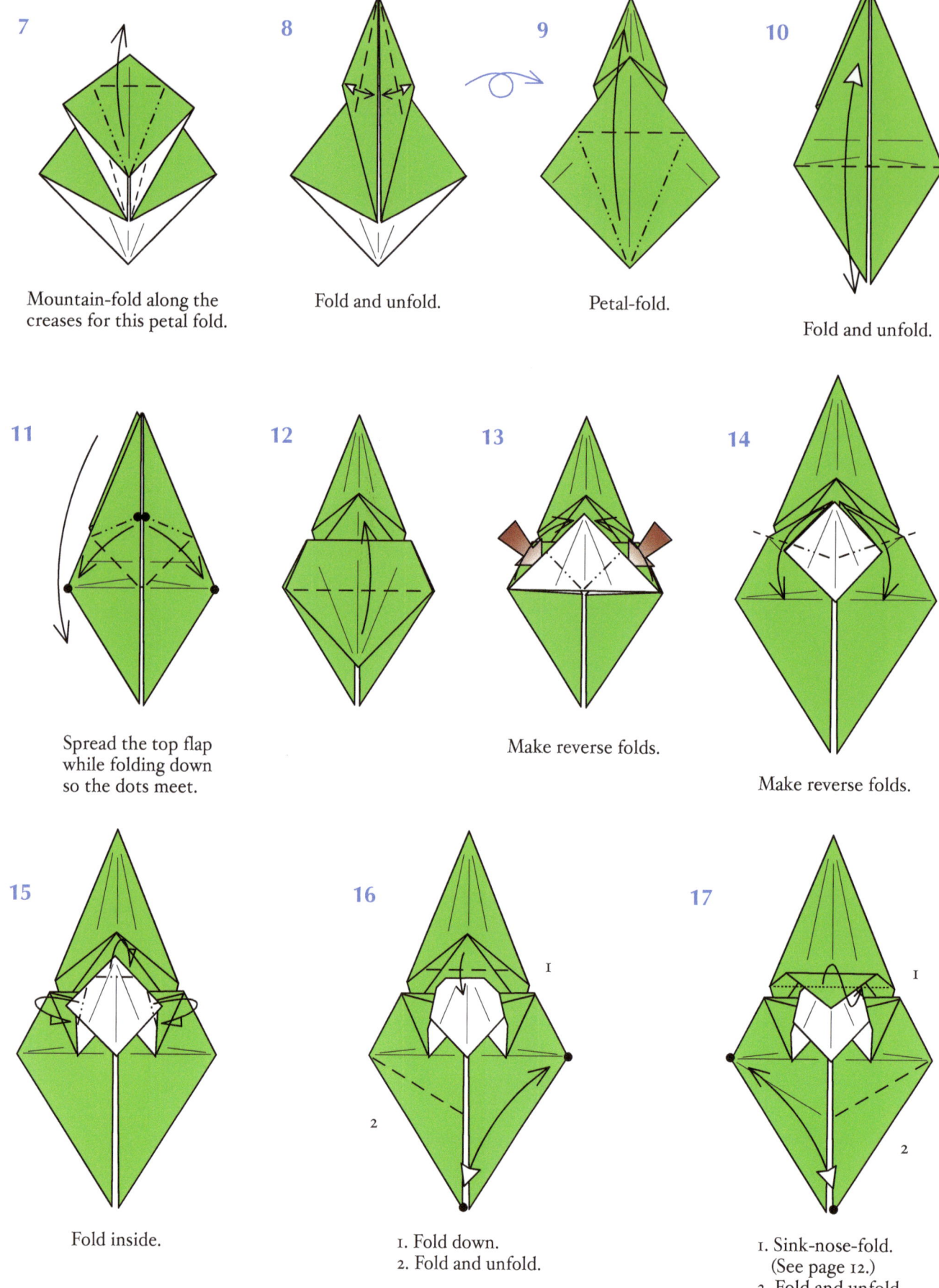

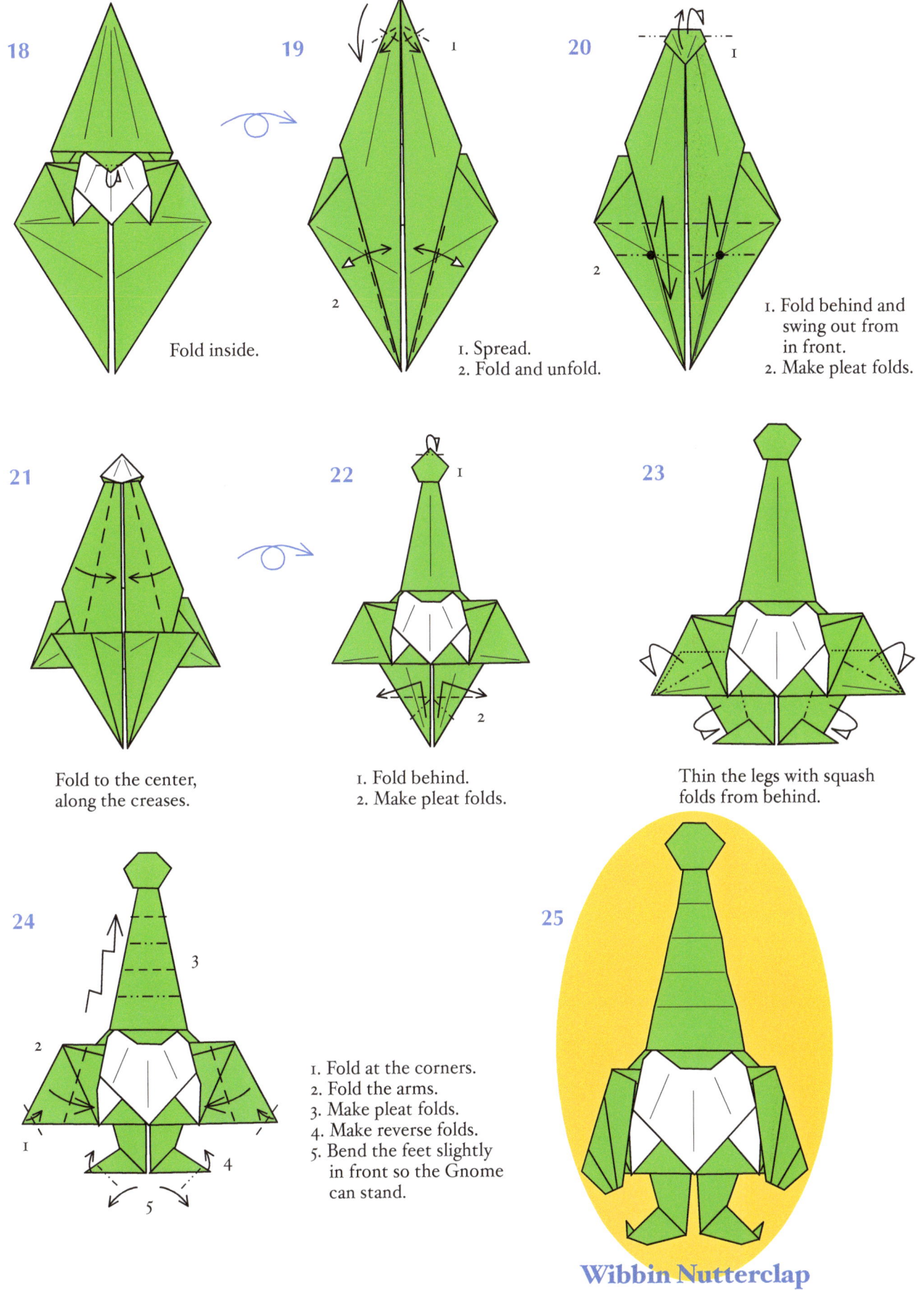

Nockle Fernpocket

Nockle Fernpocket lives near the marshlands of the forest. He rides on frogs and treats them as if they are royalty. He is always counting violets, as long as there are no more than two nearby.

1. 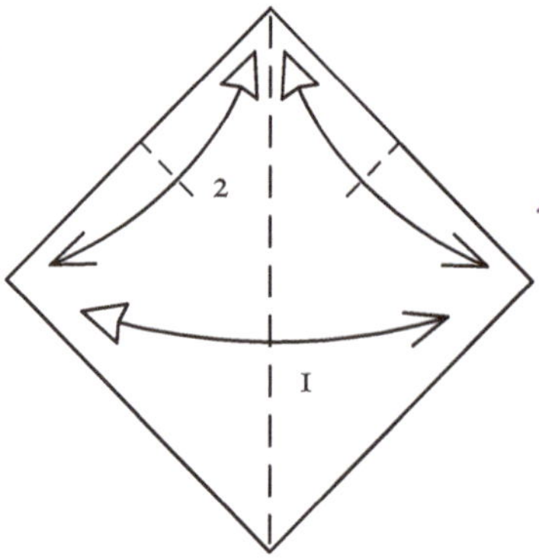
1. Fold and unfold.
2. Fold and unfold on the edges.

2. 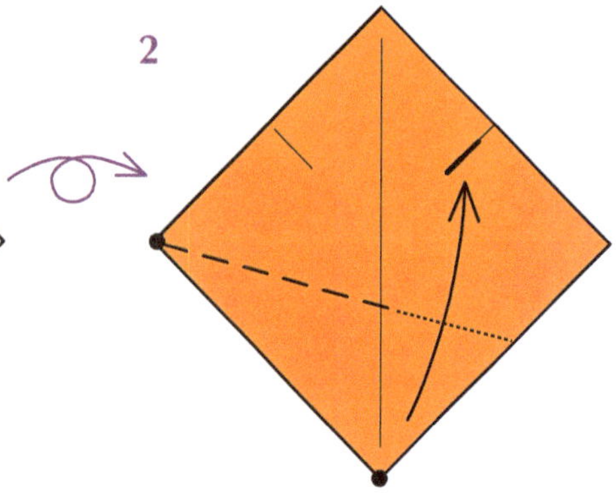
Bring the lower dot to the bold line.

3. 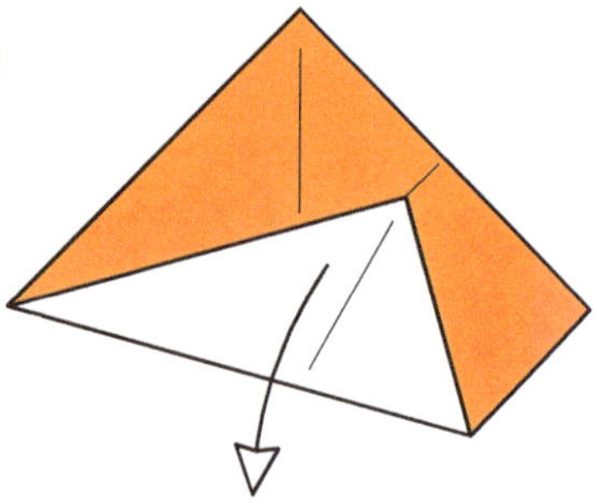
Unfold.

4. 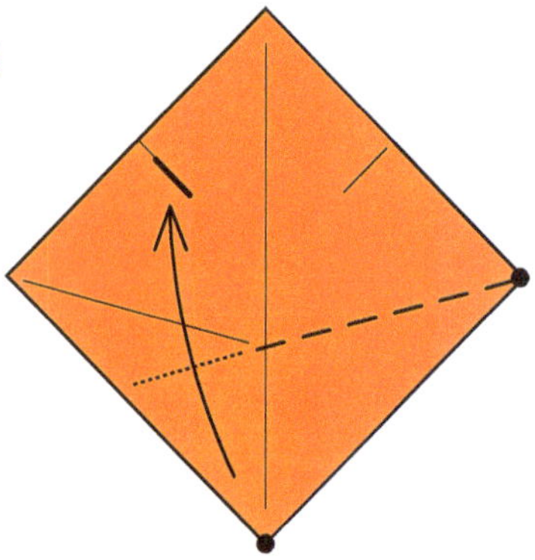
Repeat steps 2–3 in the opposite direction.

5. 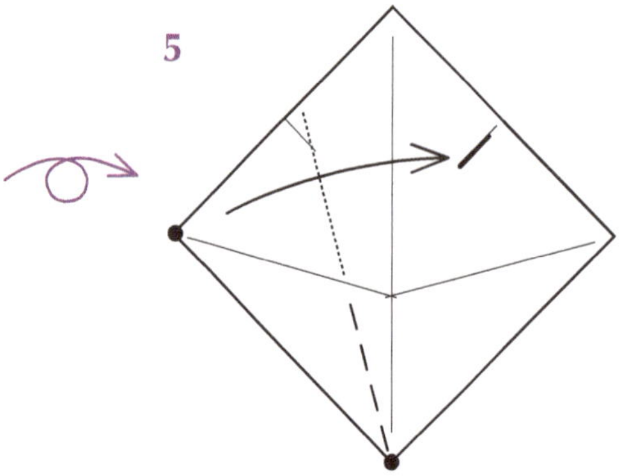
Bring the dot on the left to the bold line.

6. 
Unfold.

94   *Magical Origami Gnomes*

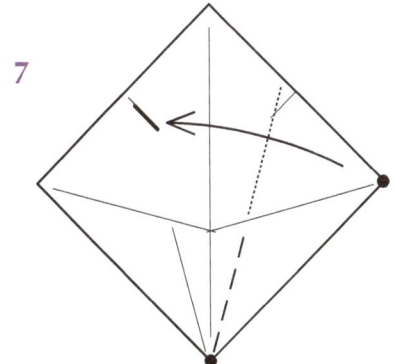

Repeat steps 5–6 on the right. Rotate 180°.

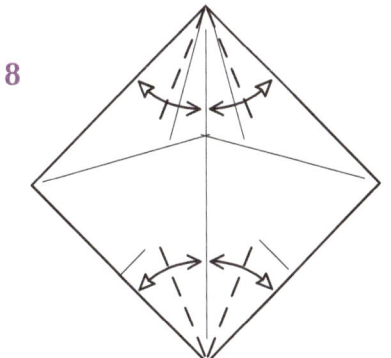

Fold to the center and unfold.

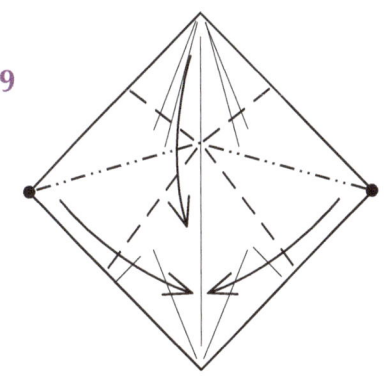

Mountain-fold along the creases and bring the dots to the center line.

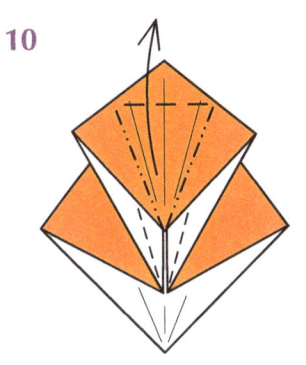

Mountain-fold along the creases for this petal fold.

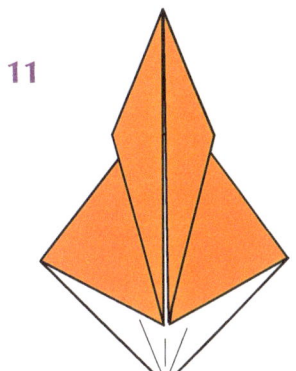

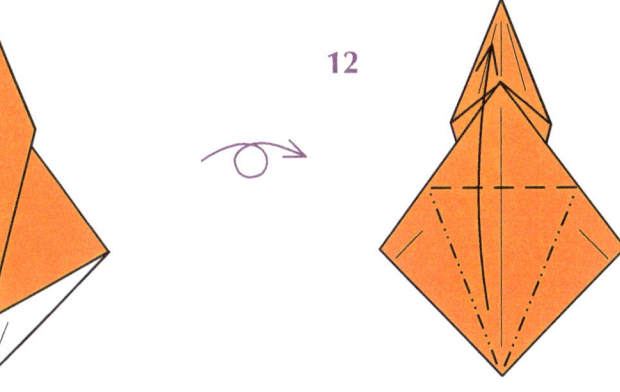

Petal-fold.

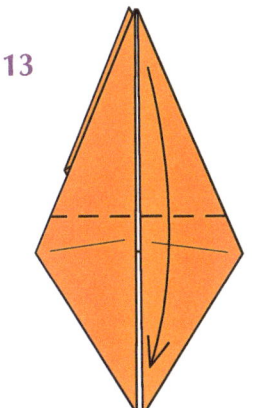

Fold down along the creases.

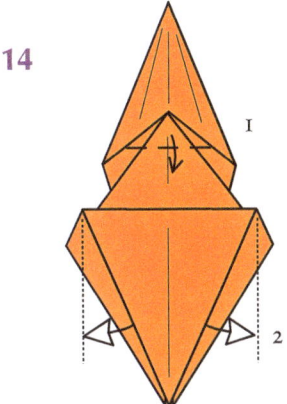

1. Fold down.
2. Pull out to the vertical dotted lines.

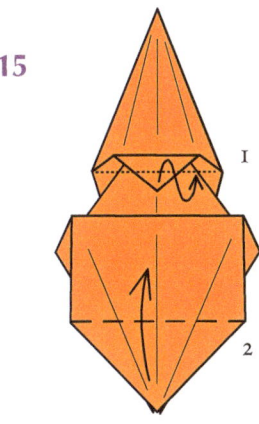

1. Sink-nose-fold. (See page 12.)
2. Fold up.

Nockle Fernpocket 95

16
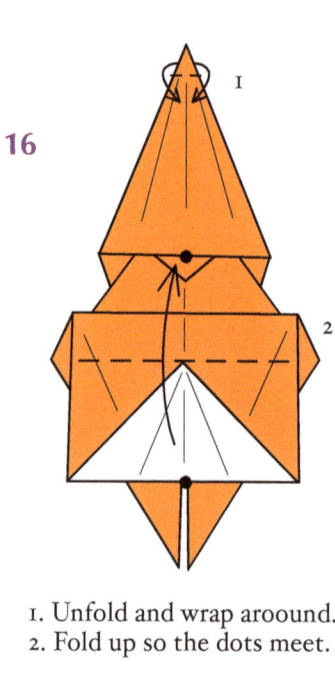
1. Unfold and wrap around.
2. Fold up so the dots meet.

17
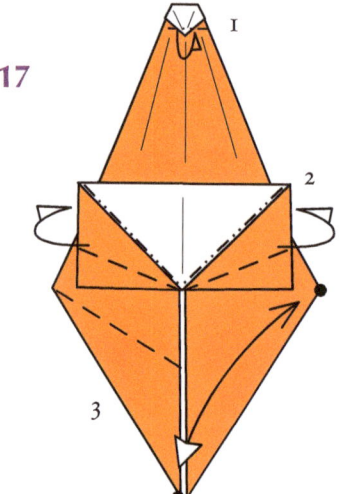
1. Fold inside.
2. Fold inside.
3. Fold and unfold.

18
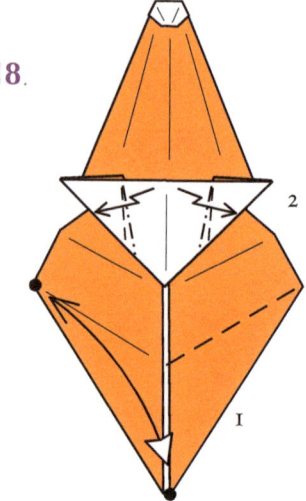
1. Fold and unfold.
2. Make crimp folds.

19
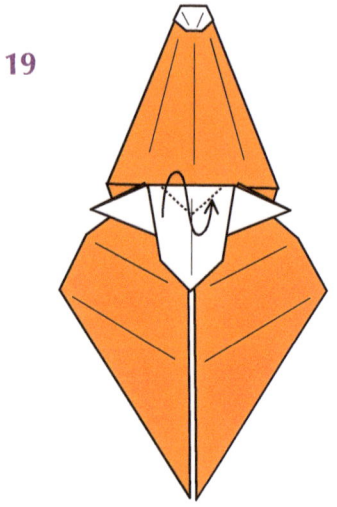
Note the angle of the mustache. Tuck under the nose.

20
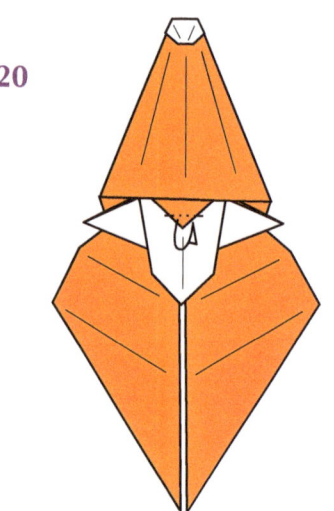

21
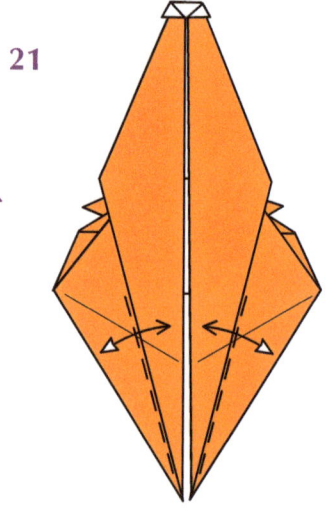
Fold and unfold.

22
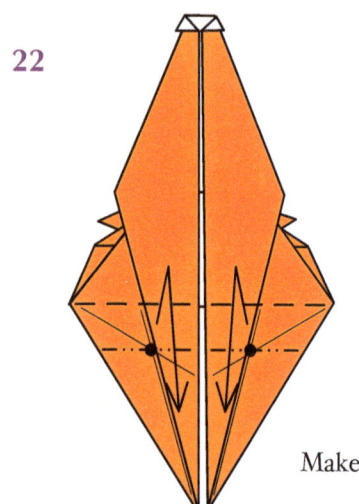
Make pleat folds.

23
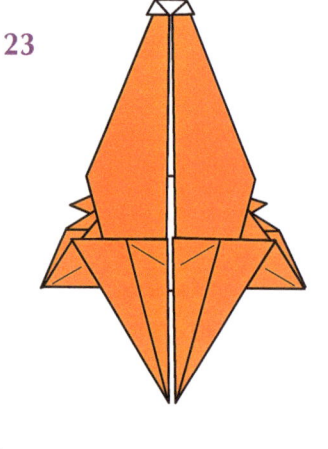

24
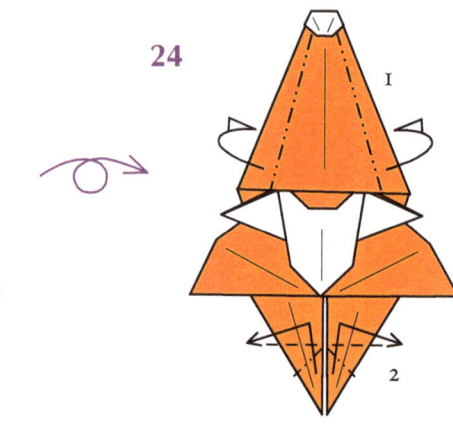
1. Fold behind along the creases.
2. Make pleat folds.

25

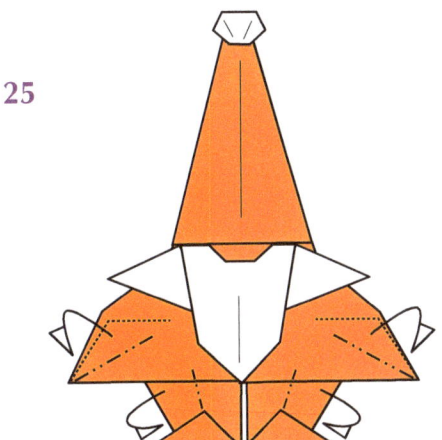

Thin the legs with squash folds from behind.

26

1. Make pleat folds.
2. Make pleat folds.

27

1. Make pleat folds.
2. Make reverse folds.
3. Bend the feet slightly in front so the Gnome can stand.

28

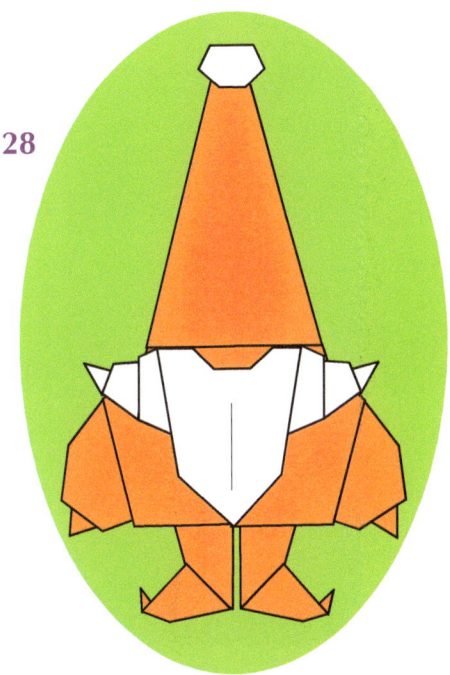

Nockle Fernpocket

Mischievous Gnomes of the North

At every corner of GnomeLand in the North, mischievous gnomes are up to no good. They are wild-hearted and endlessly curious. Their usually harmless pranks, gleeful chaos, and clever illusions always surprise someone. Some speak in rhymes and make others around them speak in riddles. Others disappear in mid-conversation for dramatic effect. Fold these carefully or they will turn into crumpled rocks.

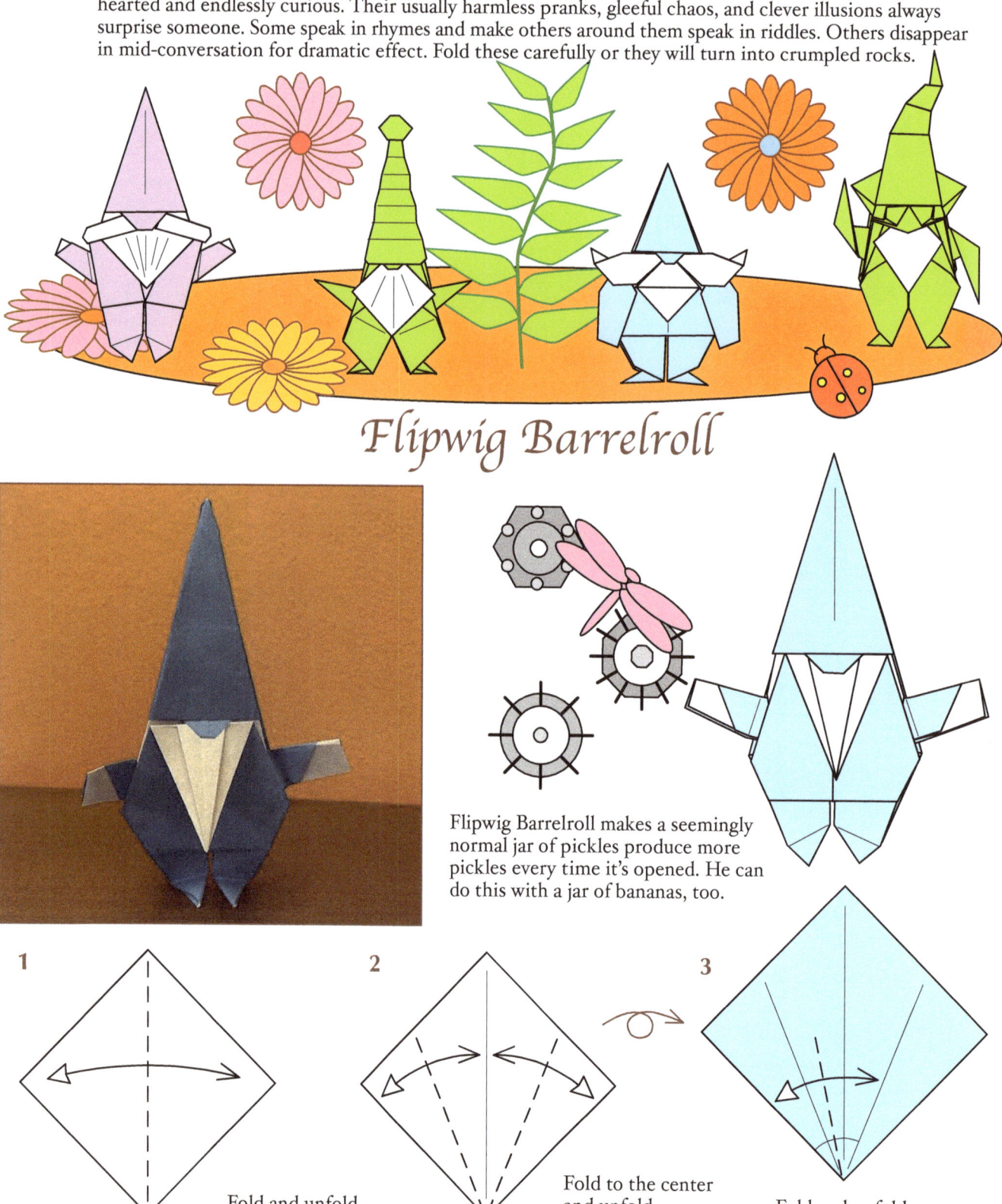

Flipwig Barrelroll

Flipwig Barrelroll makes a seemingly normal jar of pickles produce more pickles every time it's opened. He can do this with a jar of bananas, too.

1. Fold and unfold.
2. Fold to the center and unfold.
3. Fold and unfold.

98 *Magical Origami Gnomes*

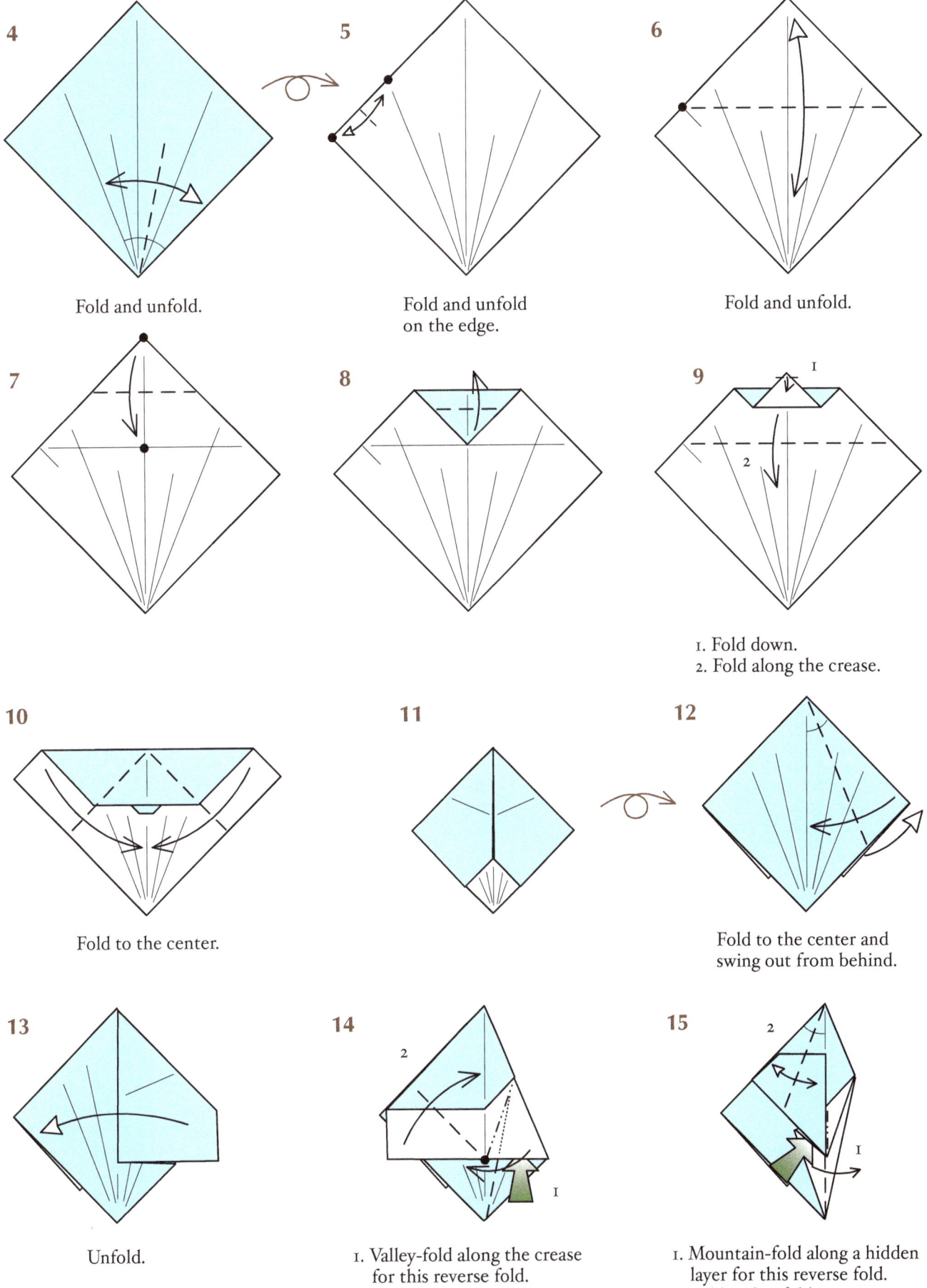

Flipwig Barrelroll 99

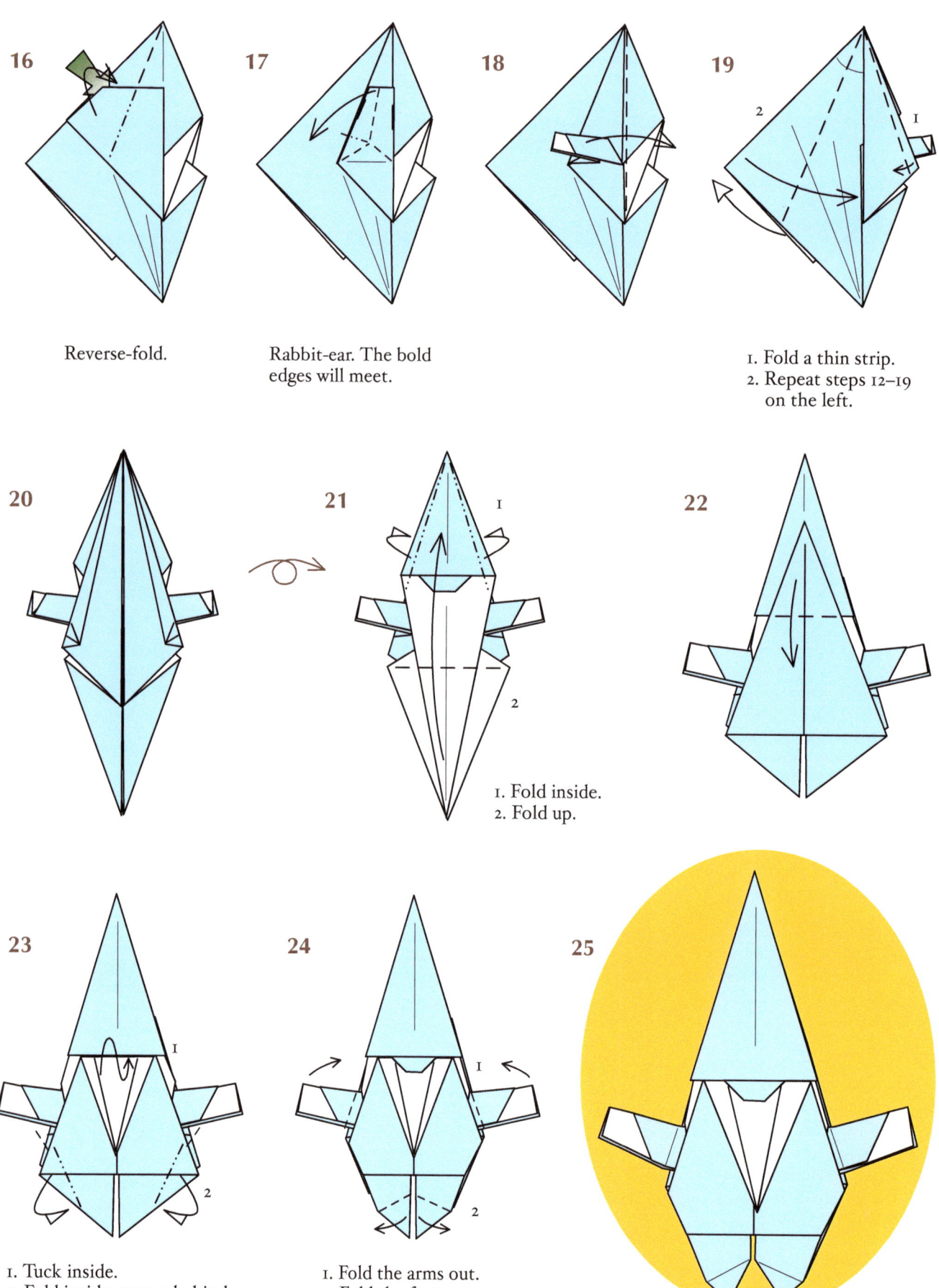

16. Reverse-fold.

17. Rabbit-ear. The bold edges will meet.

19.
1. Fold a thin strip.
2. Repeat steps 12–19 on the left.

21.
1. Fold inside.
2. Fold up.

23.
1. Tuck inside.
2. Fold inside, repeat behind.

24.
1. Fold the arms out.
2. Fold the feet out so the Gnome can stand.

Flipwig Barrelroll

100 *Magical Origami Gnomes*

Tottik Grumbleflick

Tottik Grumbleflick wears 7 rings on each finger. He makes teacups appear in someone's hands when they are trying to be serious. If you can't be helpful, be hilarious.

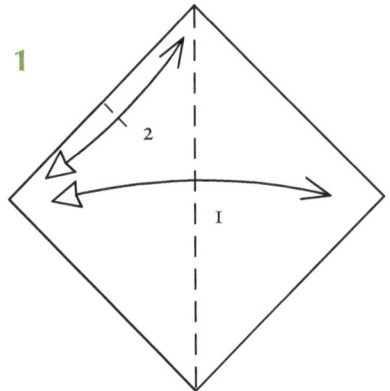

1. Fold and unfold.
2. Fold and unfold on the edge.

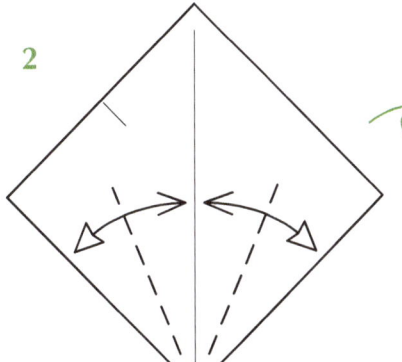

Fold to the center and unfold.

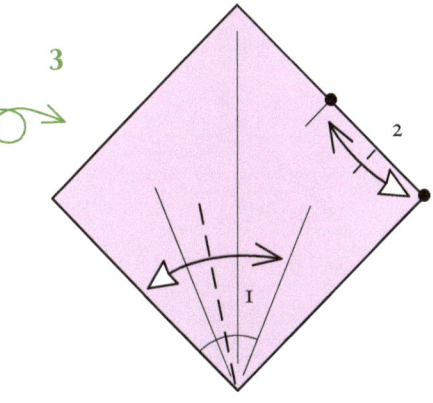

1. Fold and unfold.
2. Fold and unfold on the edge.

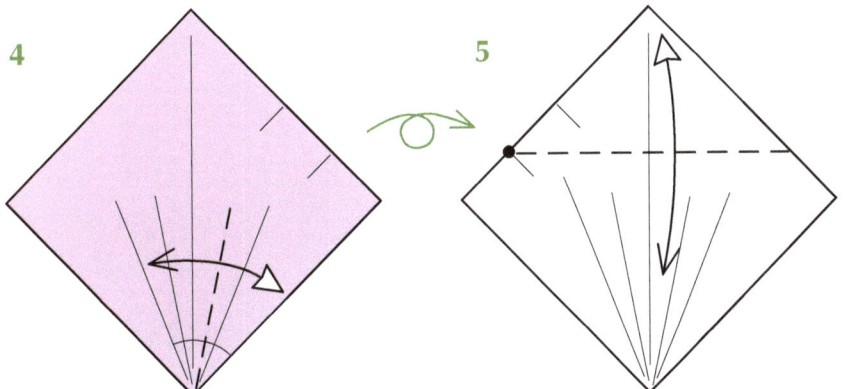

Fold and unfold.

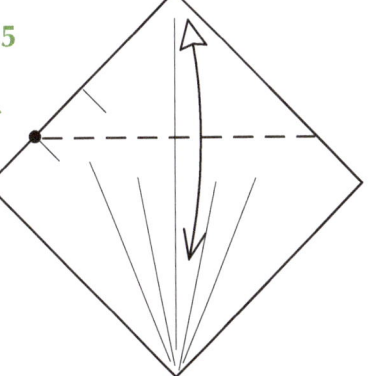

Fold and unfold.

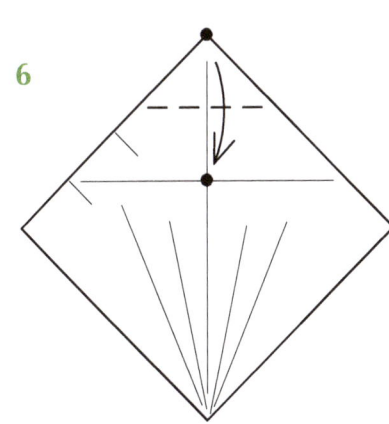

Tottik Grumbleflick 101

7
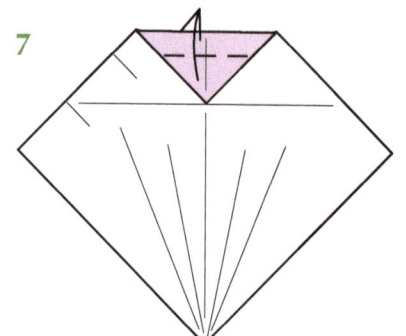

8
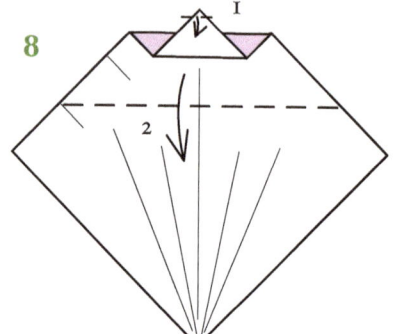

1. Fold down.
2. Fold along the crease.

9

Fold to the center.

10

11
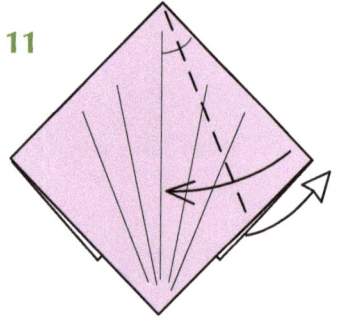

Fold to the center and swing out from behind.

12
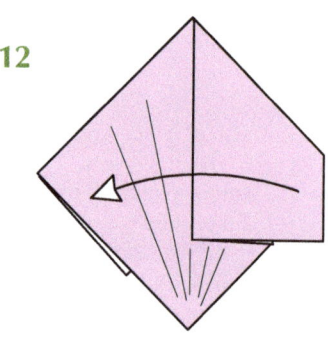

Unfold.

13
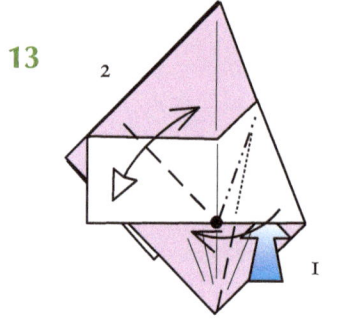

1. Valley-fold along the crease for this reverse fold.
2. Fold and unfold the top flap.

14
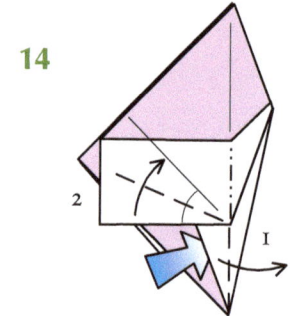

1. Mountain-fold along a hidden layer for this reverse fold.
2. Fold up.

15
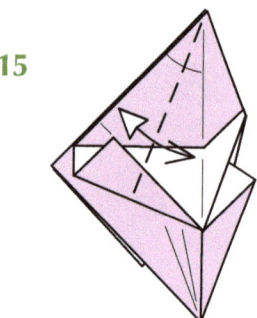

Fold and unfold the top flap.

16
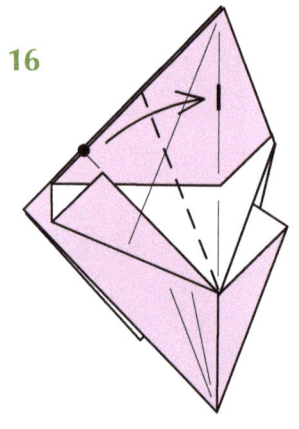

17
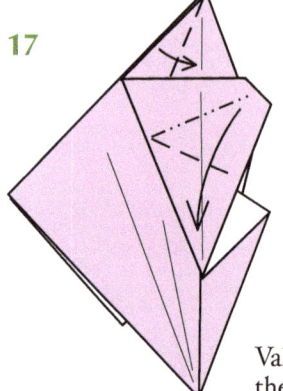

Valley-fold along the creases for this squash fold.

18
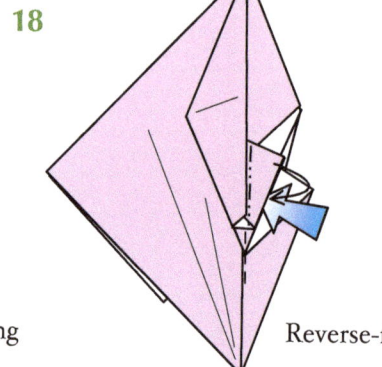

Reverse-fold.

102 *Magical Origami Gnomes*

19

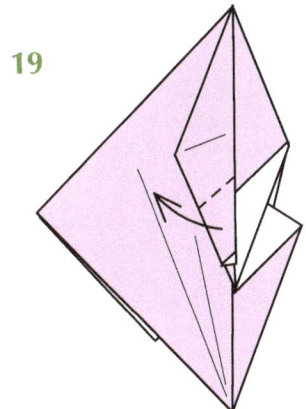

Spread-squash-fold.

20

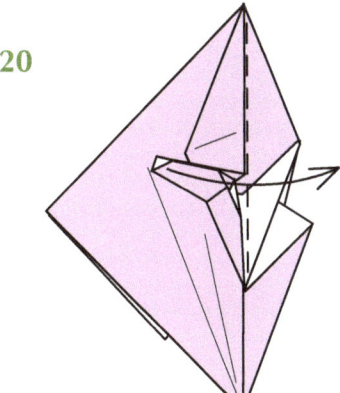

21

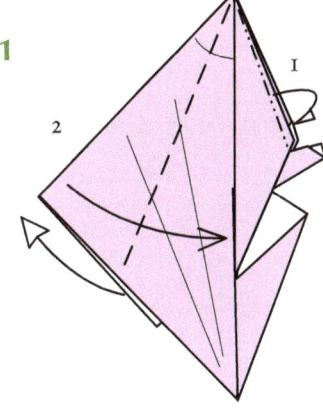

1. Fold a thin strip inside.
2. Repeat steps 11–21 on the left.

22

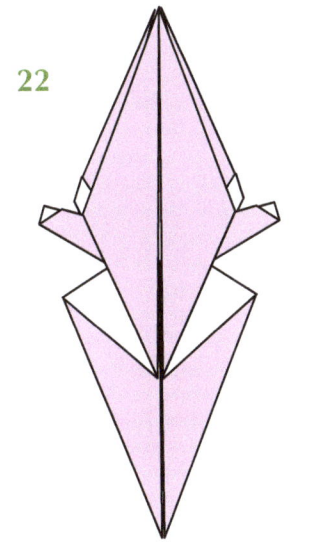

23

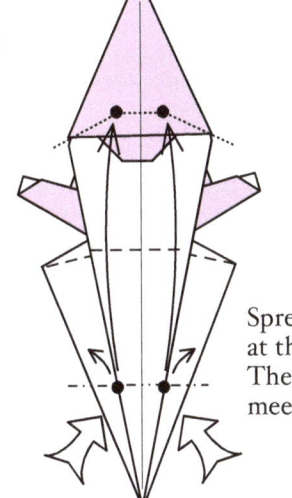

Spread and puff out at the lower dots. The lower dots will meet the upper ones.

24

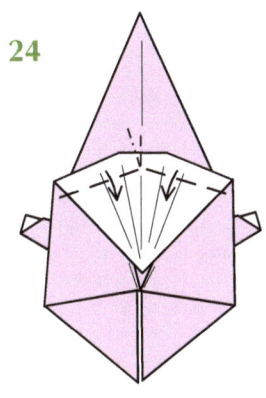

Fold two strips down.

25

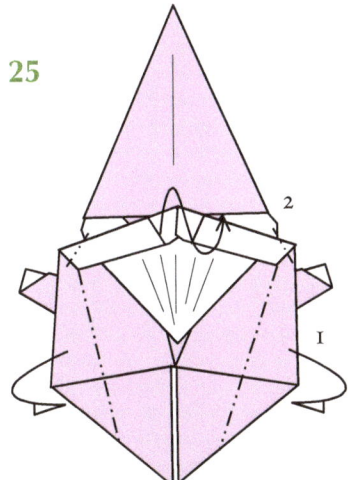

1. Fold inside.
2. Tuck inside.

26

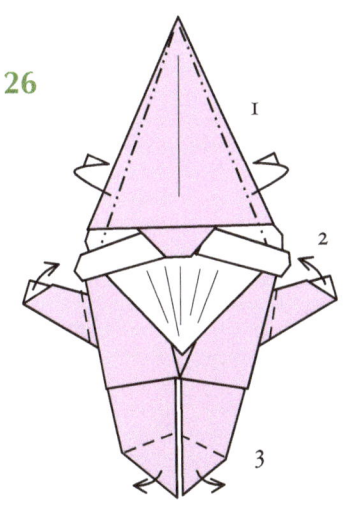

1. Fold inside.
2. Fold the arms out.
3. Fold the feet out so the Gnome can stand.

27

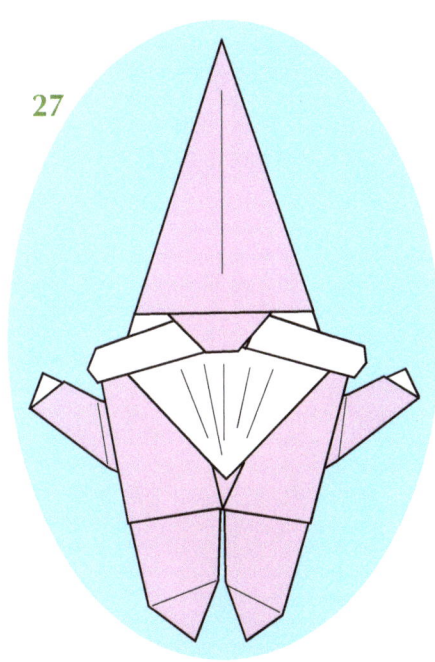

Tottik Grumbleflick

Tottik Grumbleflick 103

Driggol Driftnettle

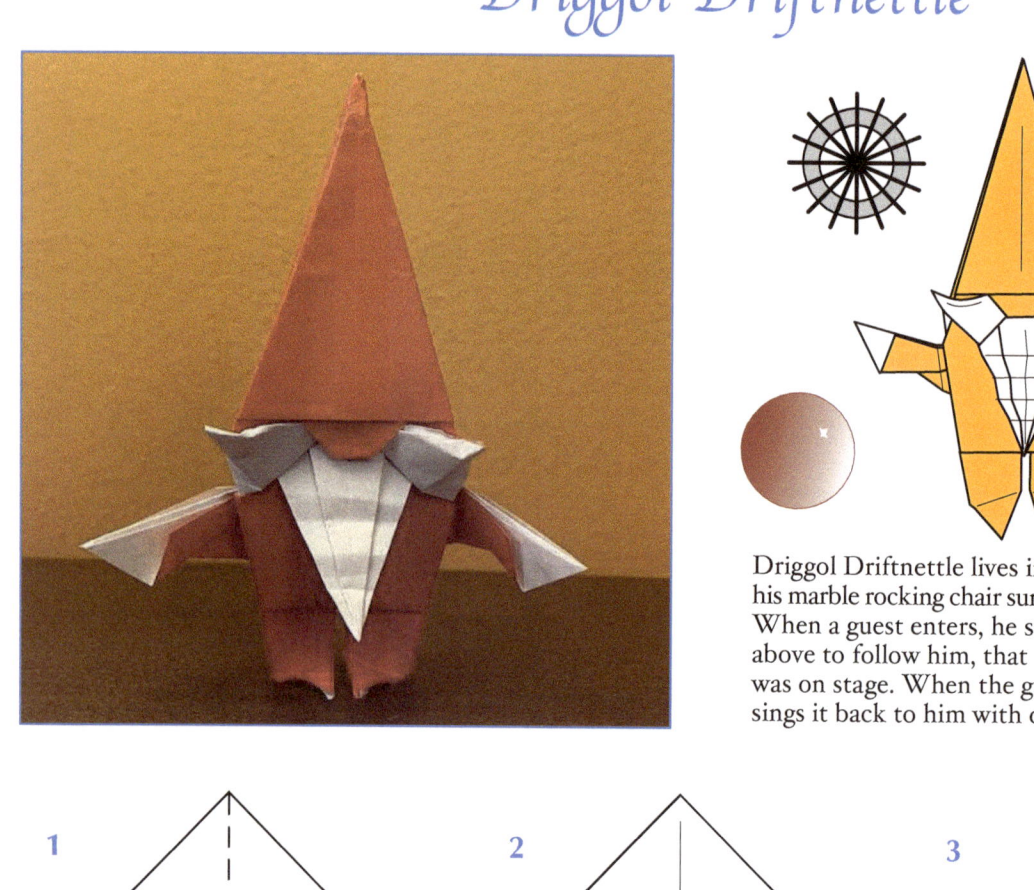

Driggol Driftnettle lives in a cave and relaxes on his marble rocking chair surrounded by blue crystals. When a guest enters, he summons glowworms above to follow him, that illuminates him as if he was on stage. When the guest speaks, the echo sings it back to him with operatic excitement.

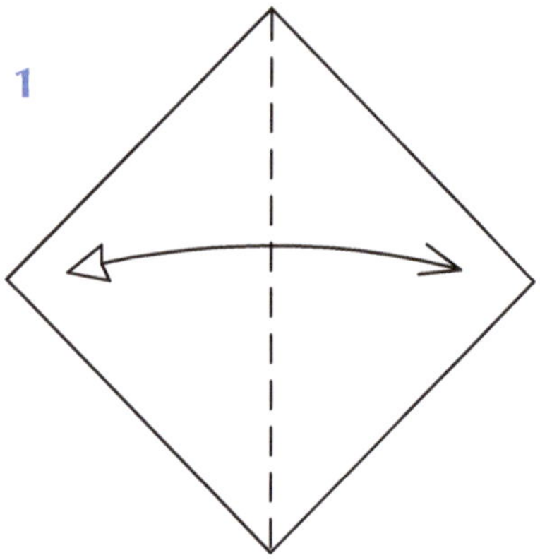

1. Fold and unfold.

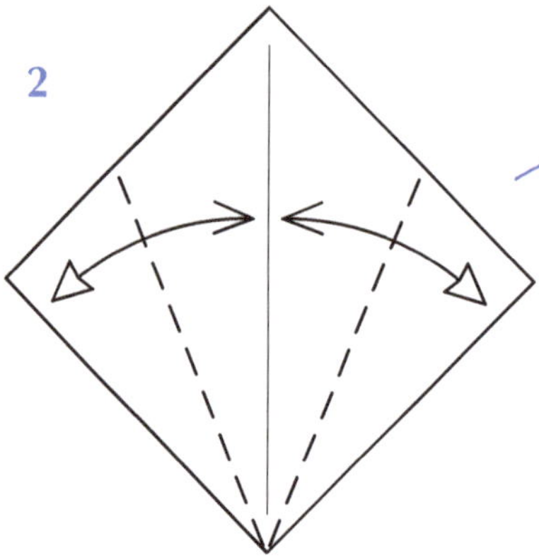

2. Fold to the center and unfold.

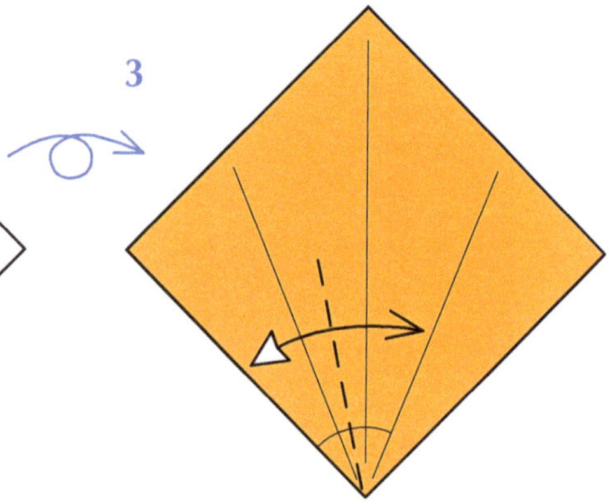

3. Fold and unfold.

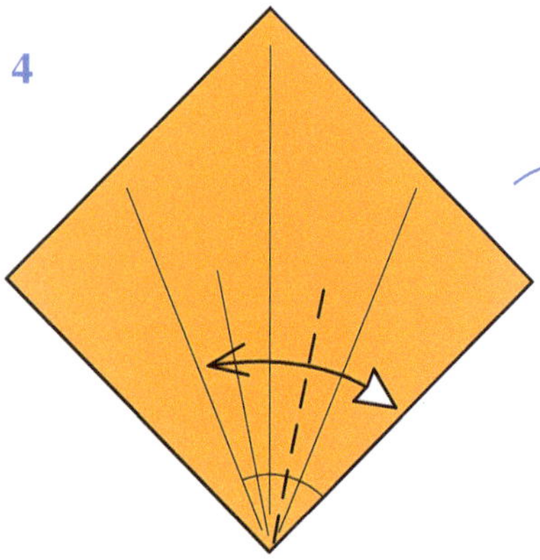

4. Fold and unfold.

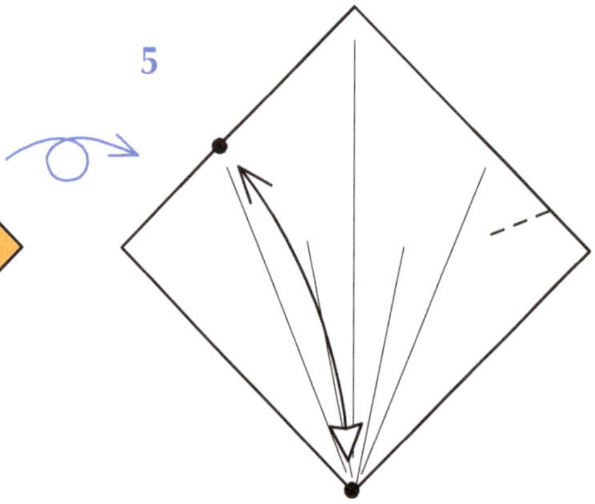

5. Fold and unfold on the edge.

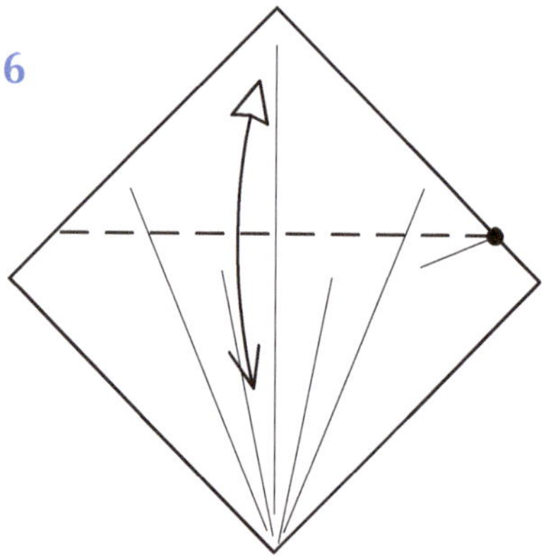

6. Fold and unfold.

104   *Magical Origami Gnomes*

7

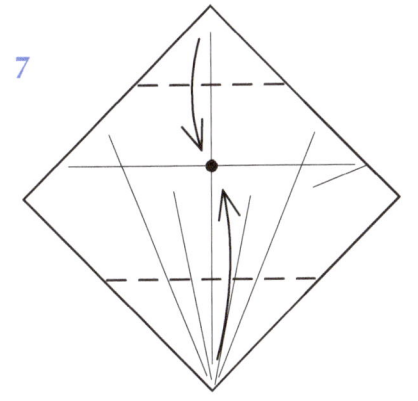

8

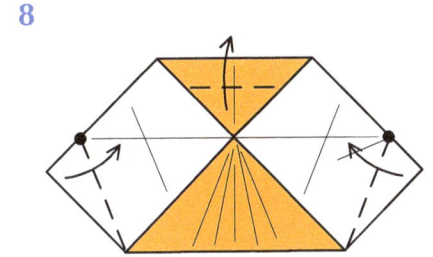

9

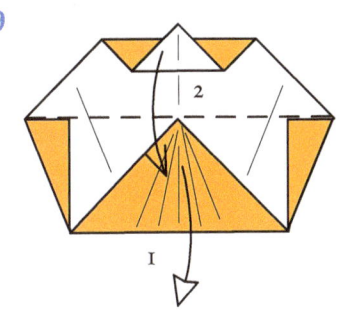

1. Unfold.
2. Fold along the crease.

10

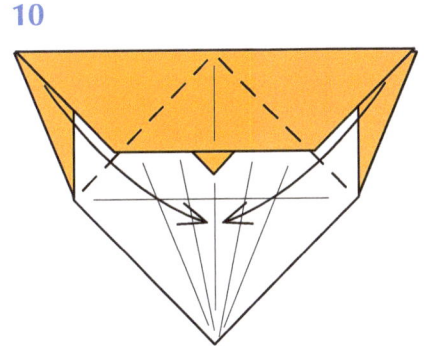

Fold to the center.

11 12

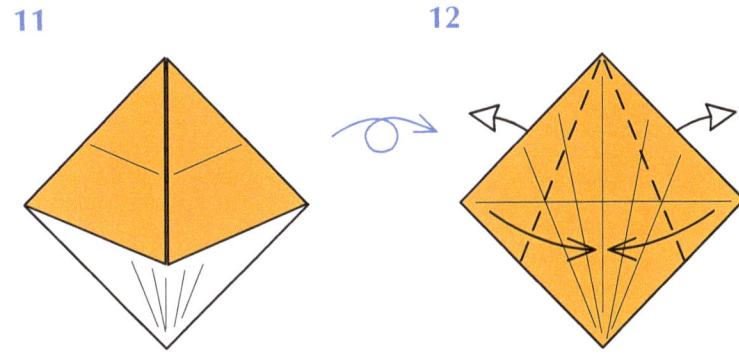

Fold to the center and swing out from behind.

13

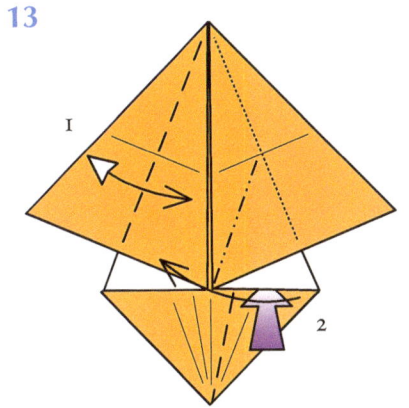

1. Fold and unfold.
2. Valley-fold along the crease for this reverse fold.

14

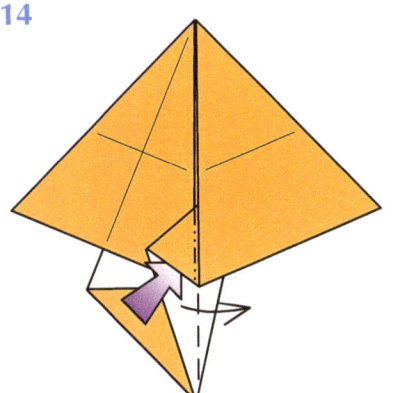

Reverse-fold.

15

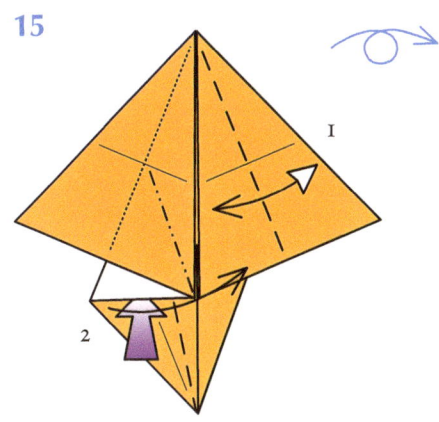

Repeat steps 13–14 in the opposite direction.

Driggol Driftnettle 105

16

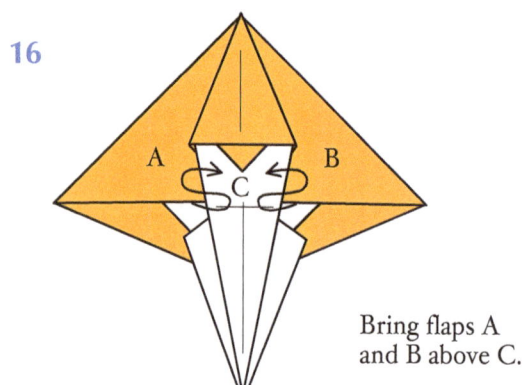

Bring flaps A and B above C.

17

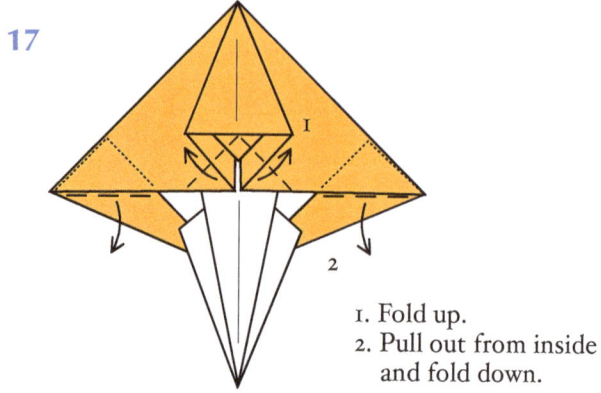

1. Fold up.
2. Pull out from inside and fold down.

18

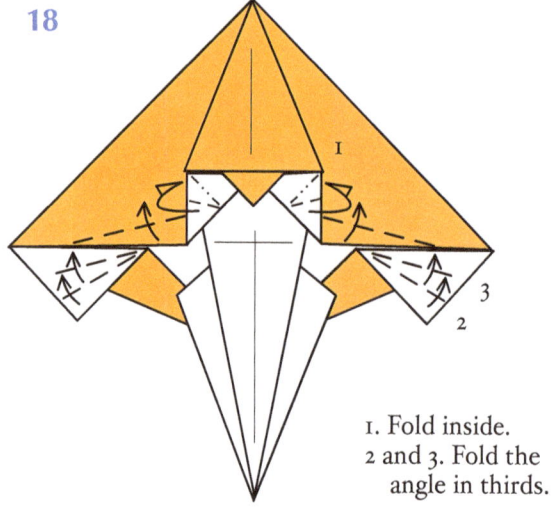

1. Fold inside.
2 and 3. Fold the angle in thirds.

19

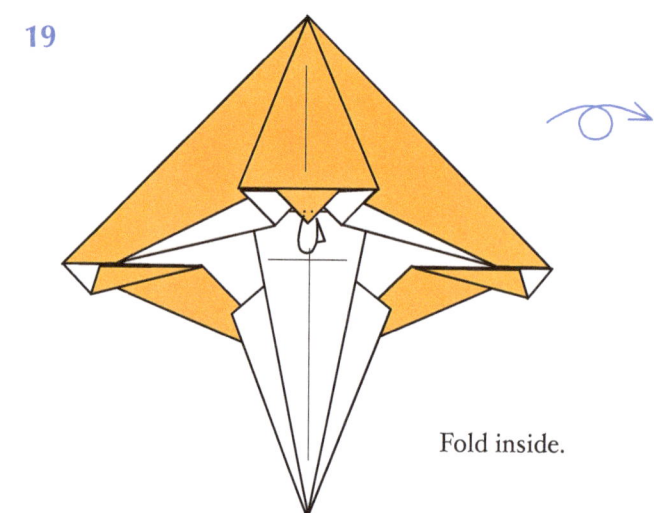

Fold inside.

20

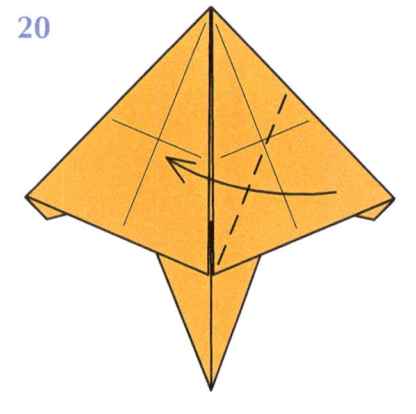

21

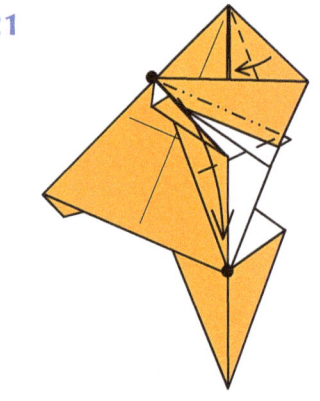

Squash-fold.

22

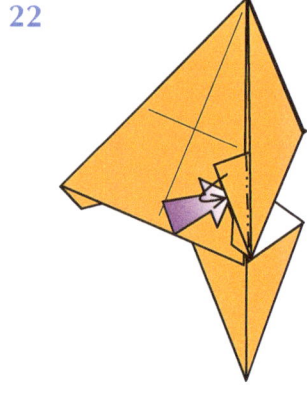

Reverse-fold.

106 *Magical Origami Gnomes*

23

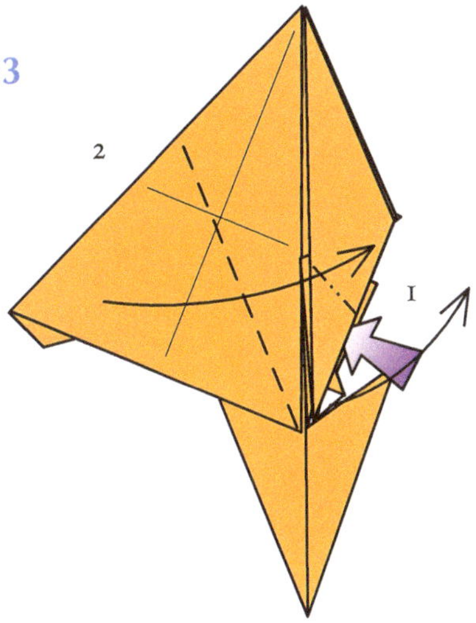

1. Reverse-fold.
2. Repeat steps 20–23 on the left.

24

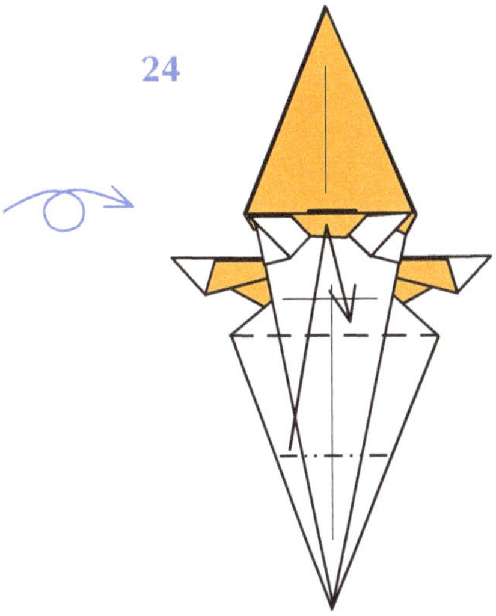

Pleat-fold so the mountain line meets the bold line.

25

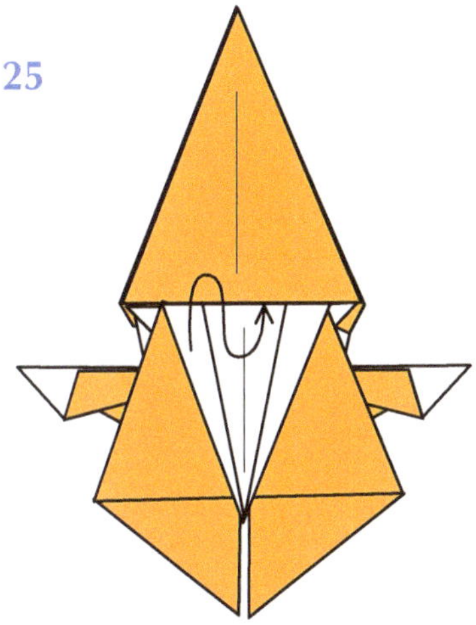

Tuck inside.

26

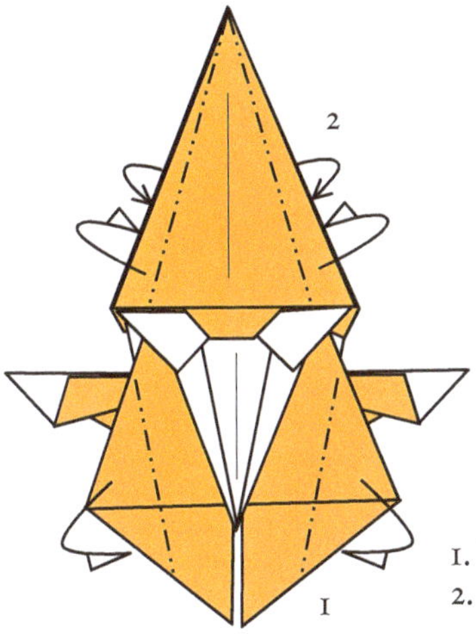

1. Fold inside.
2. Fold inside, repeat behind.

27

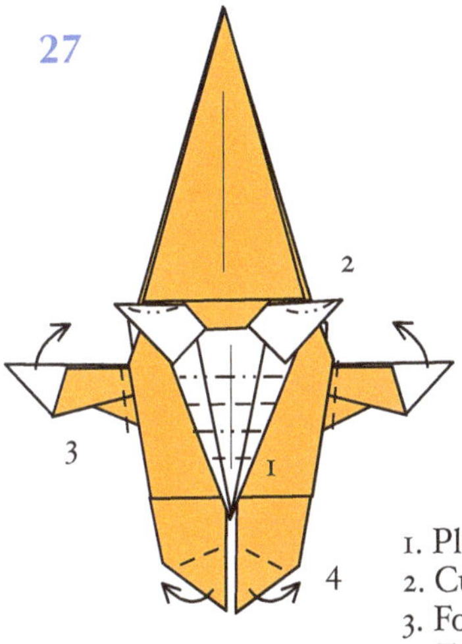

1. Pleat-fold the beard.
2. Curl the mustache.
3. Fold the arms out.
4. Fold the feet out so the Gnome can stand.

28

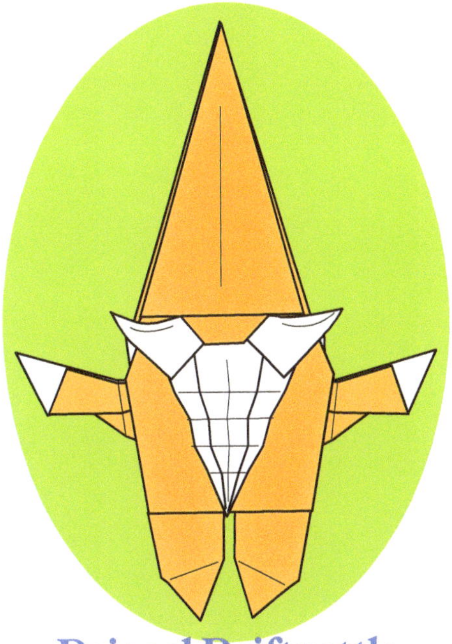

Driggol Driftnettle

Driggol Driftnettle 107

Margold Eggwobble

Margold Eggwobble is always holding buttercups. He makes butterflies and dragonflies fly out of shoes. When he's in a pickle, he summons his bones and owls.

1. Fold and unfold.

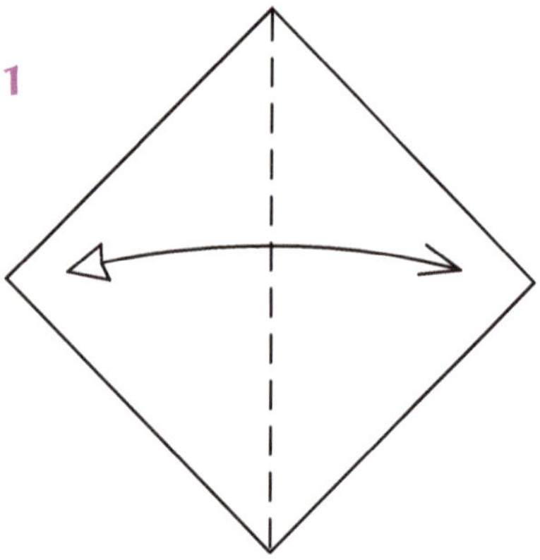

2. Fold to the center and unfold.

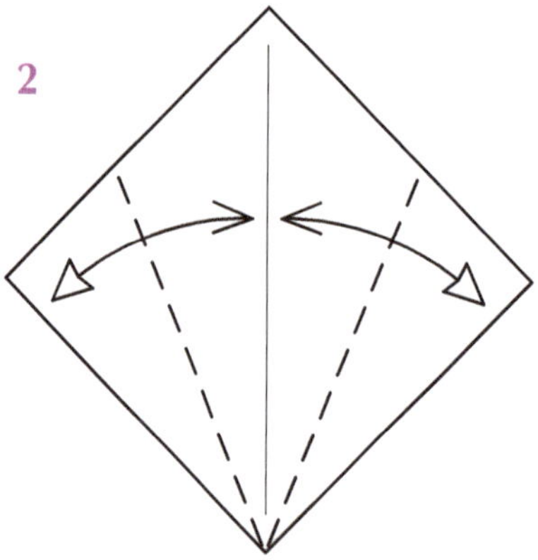

3. Fold and unfold.

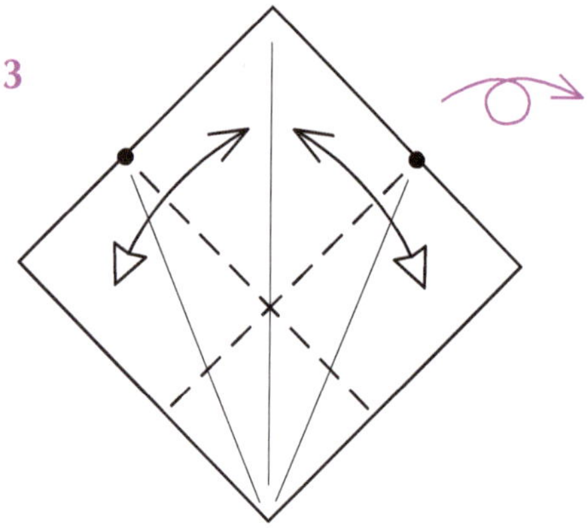

4. Fold and unfold at 1 and 2. Rotate 180°.

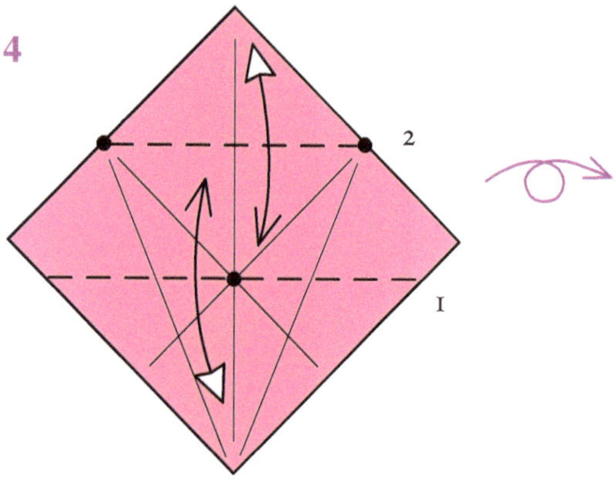

5. Fold along the creases.

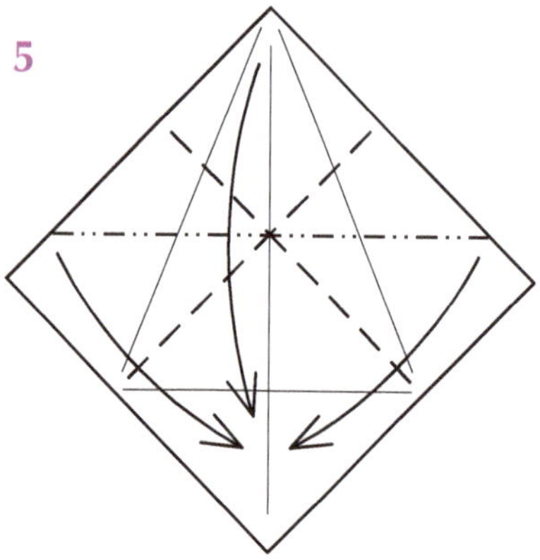

6. Petal-fold.

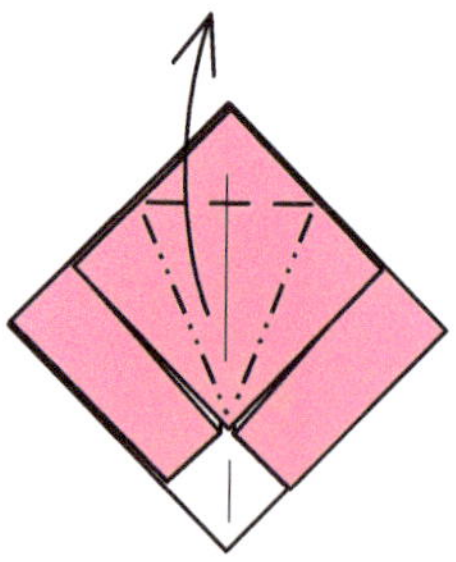

108   *Magical Origami Gnomes*

7

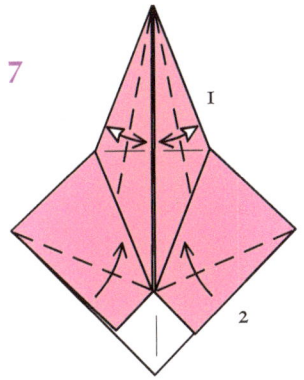

1. Fold and unfold.
2. Fold up.

8

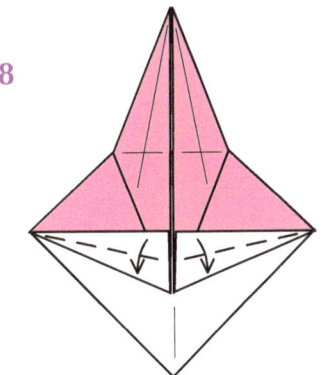

9

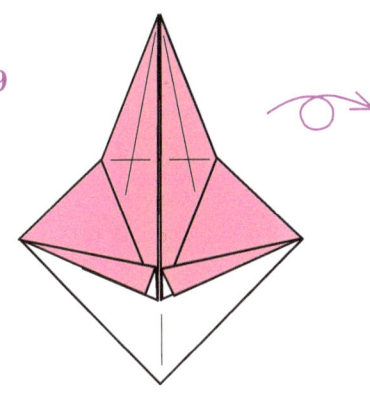

10

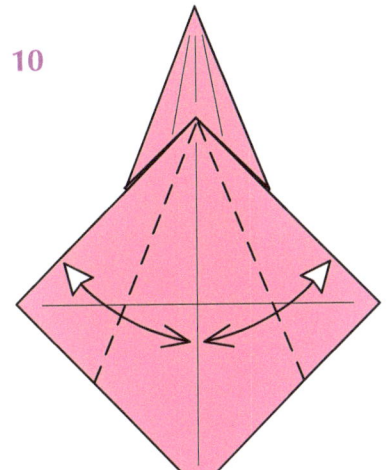

Fold to the center and unfold.

11

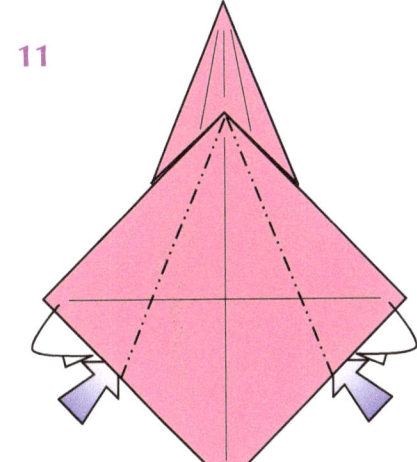

Make reverse folds.

12

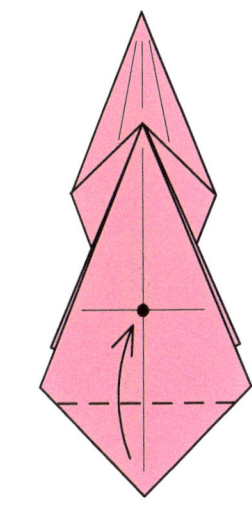

13

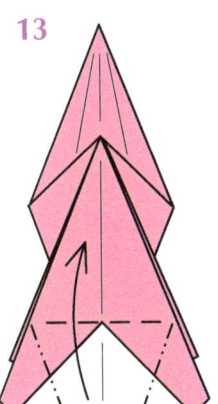

Petal-fold.

14

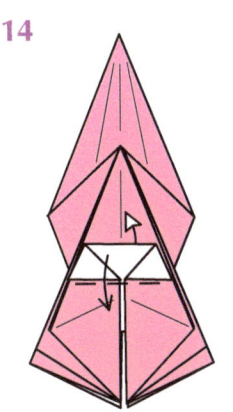

Fold down and swing out from inside.

15

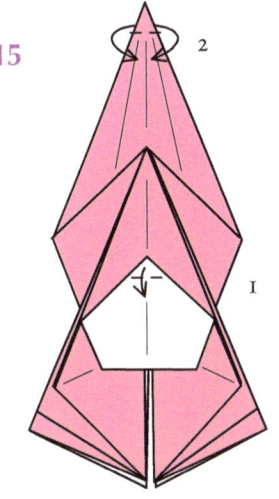

1. Fold down.
2. Unfold and wrap around.

16

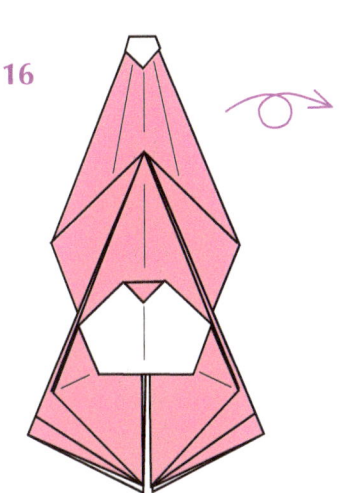

Margold Eggwobble 109

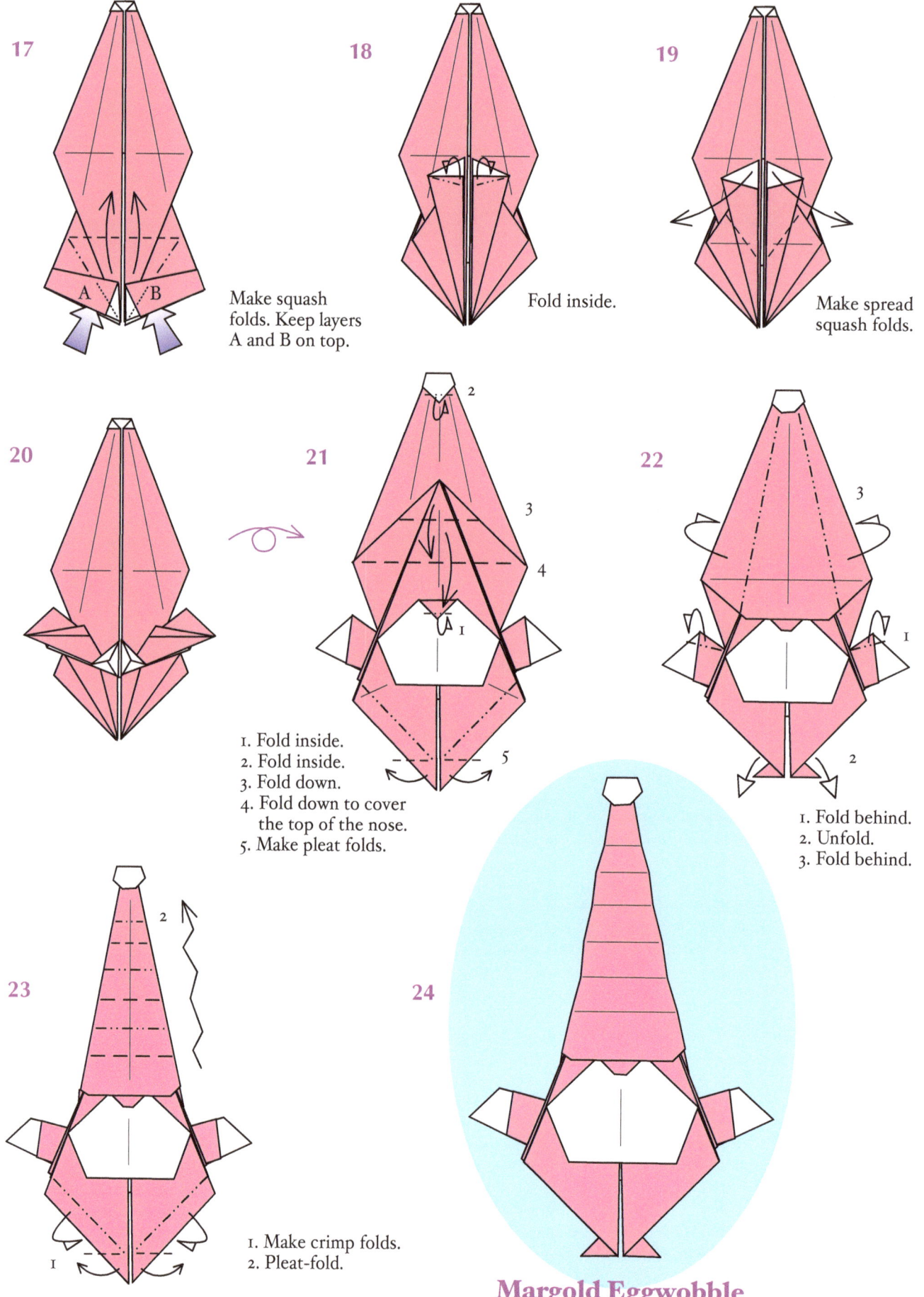

Fizzle Nimblecheek

Fizzle Nimblecheek summons a magic pickle spell. When a character picks up a pickle, it politely introduces itself and asks for a name. Upon a response it will add: What a beautiful name.

1

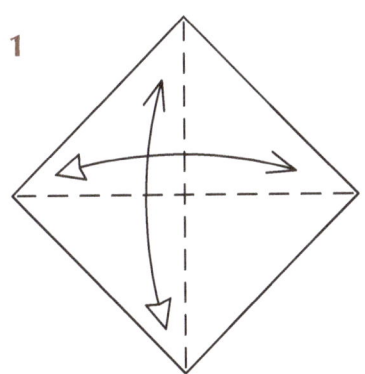

Fold and unfold.

2

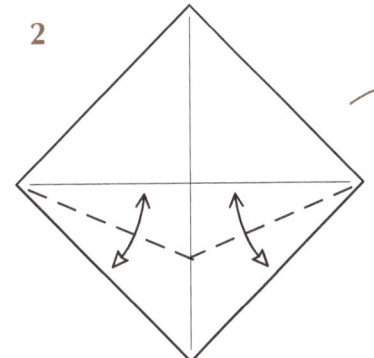

Fold to the center and unfold.

3

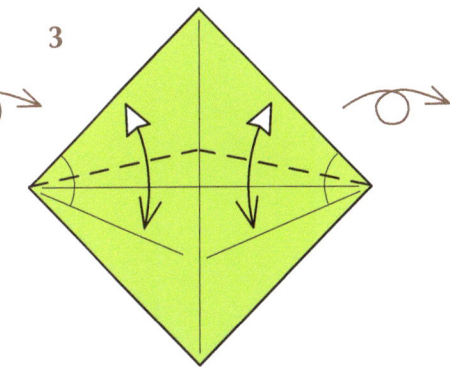

Fold and unfold.

4

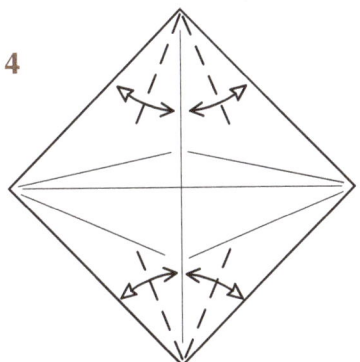

Fold to the center and unfold.

5

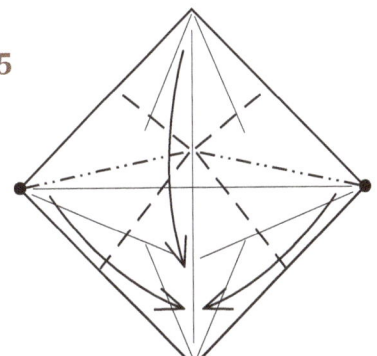

Mountain-fold along the creases and bring the dots to the vertical line in the center.

6

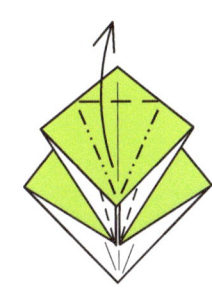

Petal-fold.

Fizzle Nimblecheek 111

7

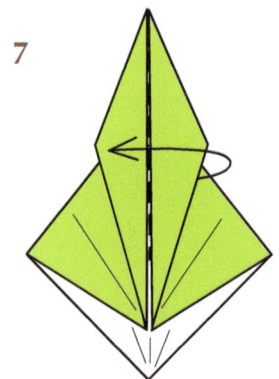

8

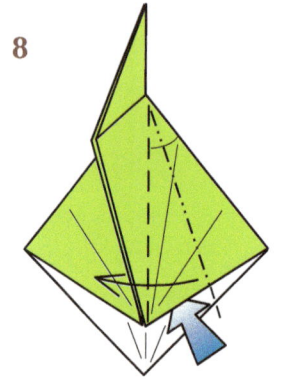

Squash-fold.

9

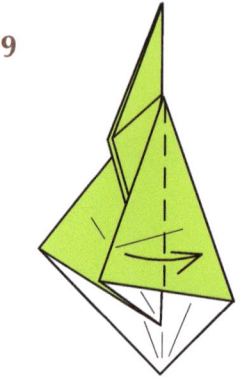

10

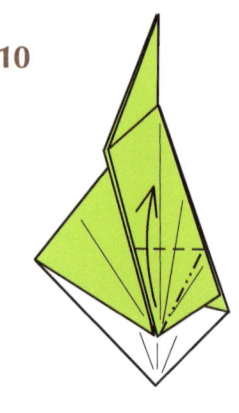

Squash-fold.

11

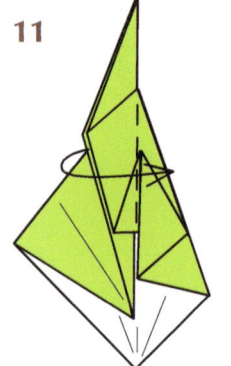

12

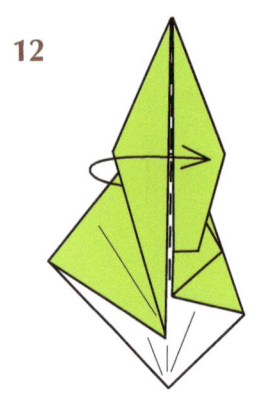

Repeat steps 7–11 in the opposite direction.

13

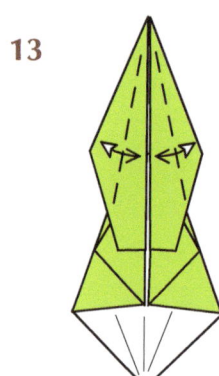

Fold to the center and unfold.

14

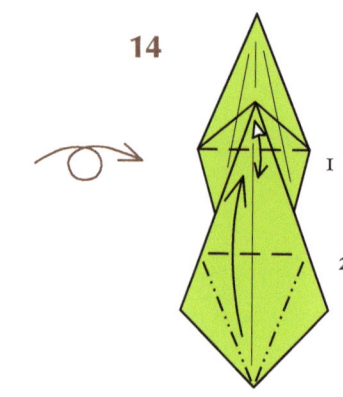

1. Fold and unfold.
2. Petal-fold.

15

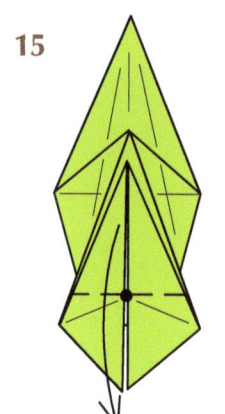

16

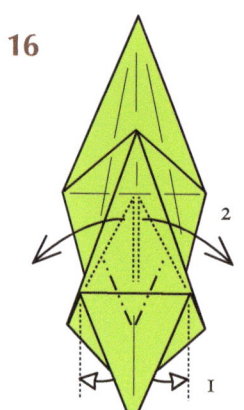

1. Pull out to the vertical dotted lines.
2. Make reverse folds on the hidden flaps to form the arms.

17

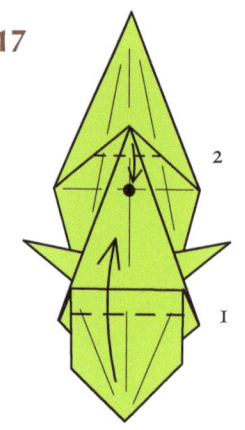

1. Fold up.
2. Fold down.

18

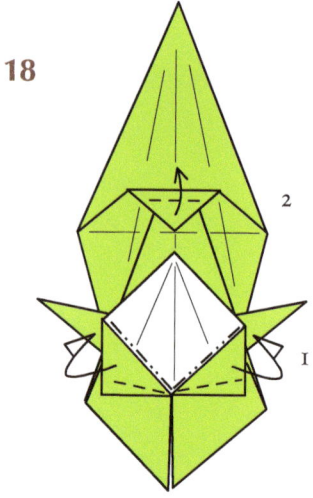

1. Fold inside.
2. Fold up.

112 *Magical Origami Gnomes*

19

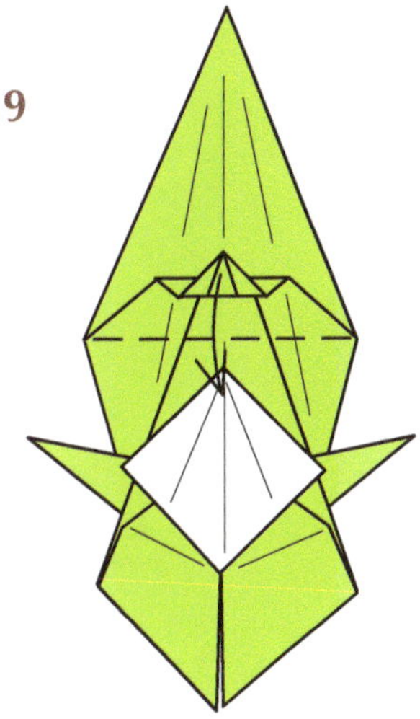

20

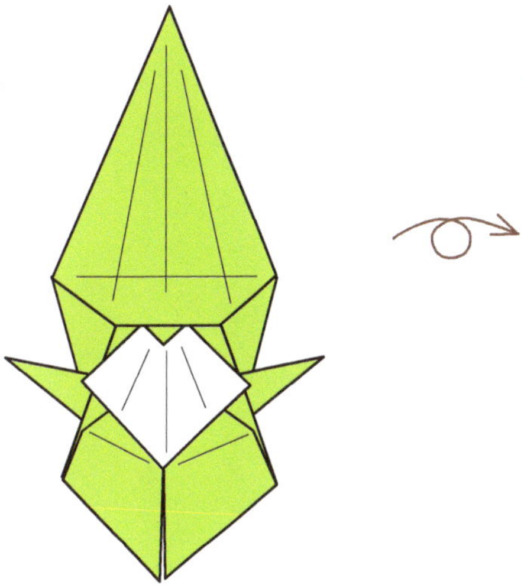

21
1. Spread. 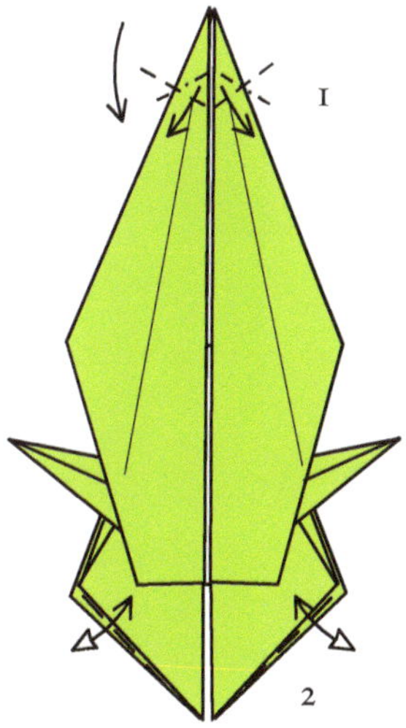
2. Fold and unfold.

22 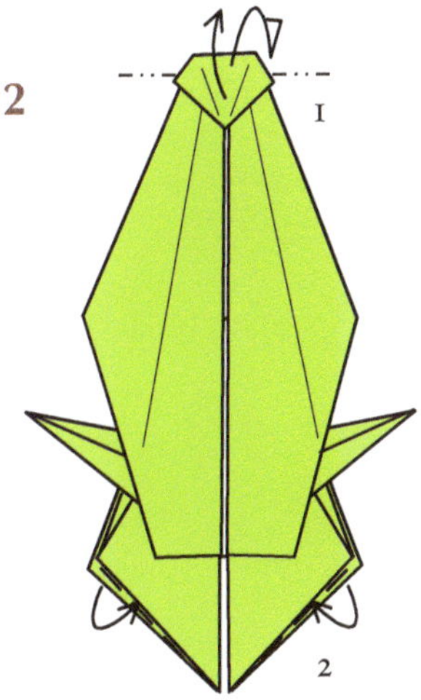
1. Fold behind and swing out from in front.
2. Tuck inside.

23 
Fold along the creases.

24 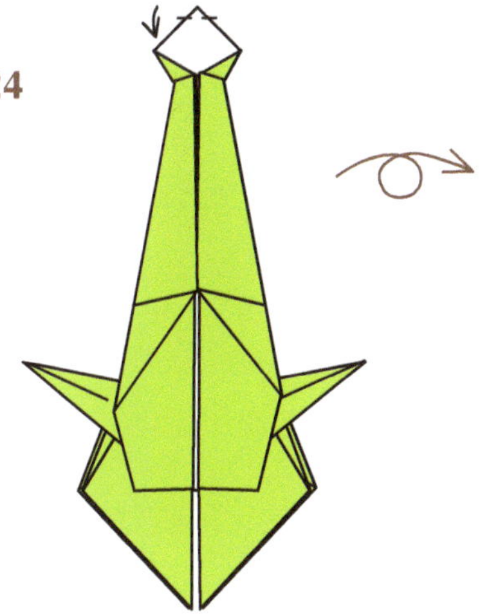
Fold down.

25 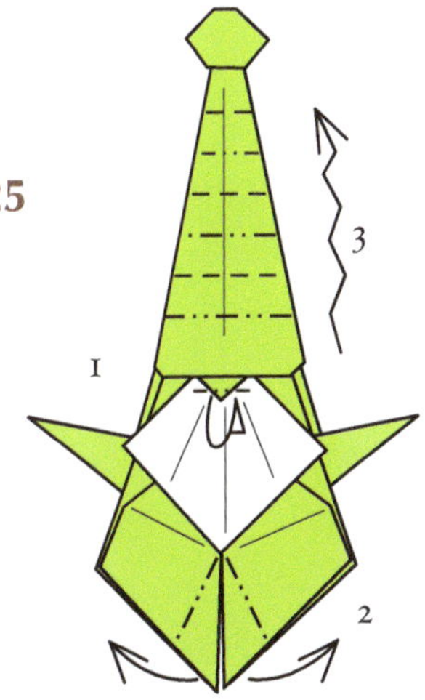
1. Fold inside.
2. Make reverse folds.
3. Pleat-fold.

26

Fizzle Nimblecheek

Fizzle Nimblecheek 113

Vibble Noodlebop

Vibble Noodlebop makes spoons stick to hands and won't let go. It is Vibble's favorite spell on outings with relatives while dining under weeping willow trees. One of the months in GnomeLand is Cucumbvember. What's the name of the other month?

1. Fold and unfold.

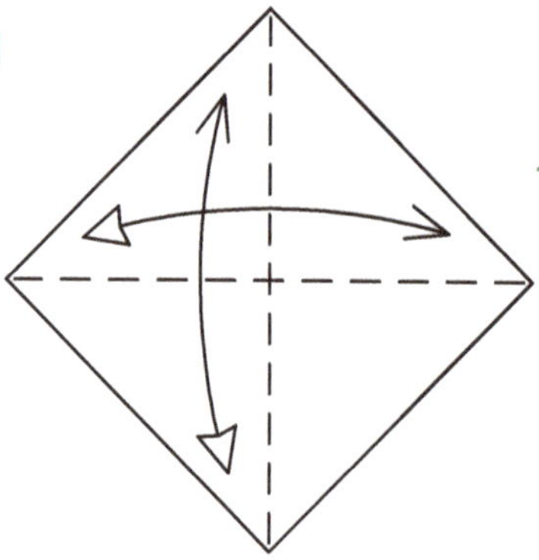

2. Fold and unfold on the edge.

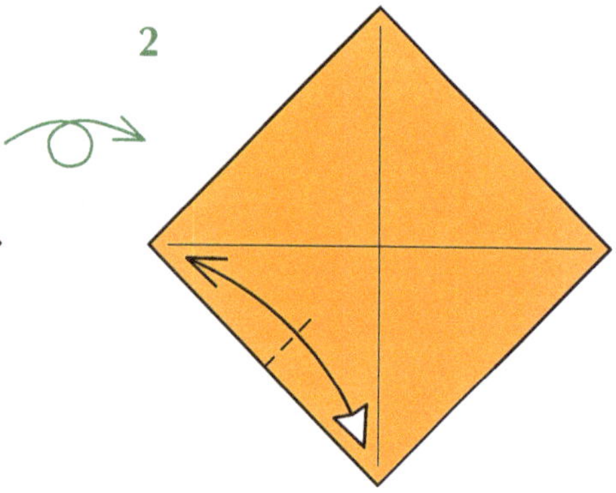

3. Fold and unfold on the diagonal.

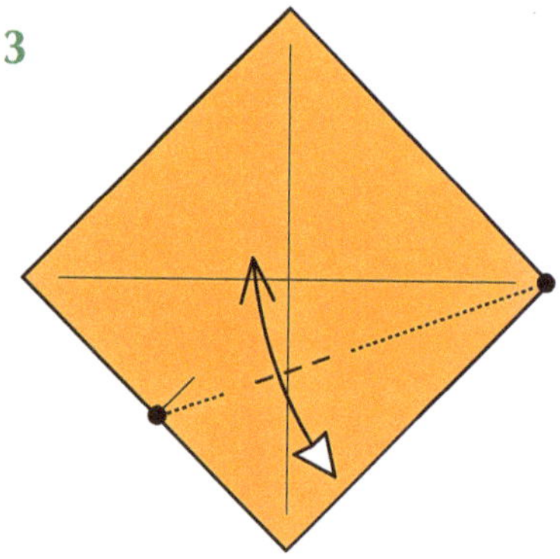

4. Fold and unfold.

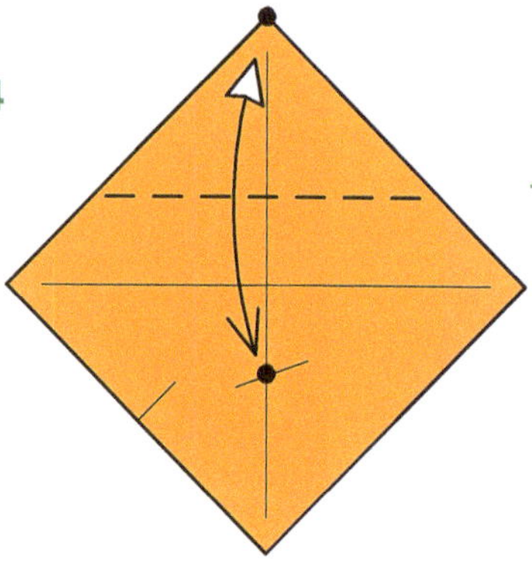

5. Fold and unfold.

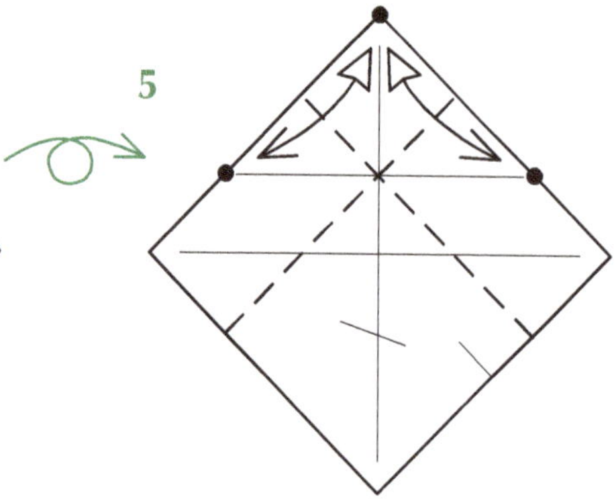

6.

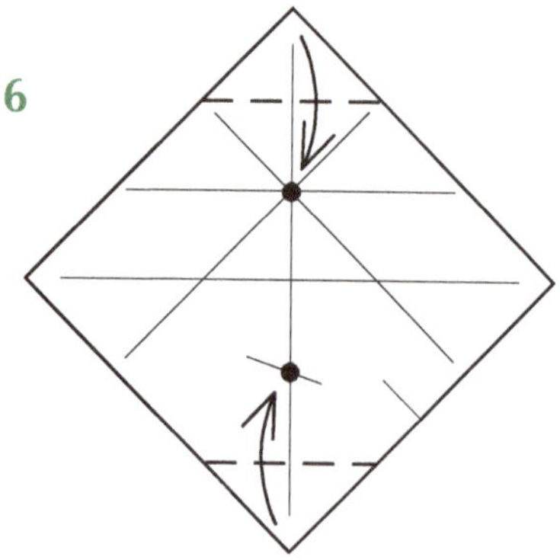

114 *Magical Origami Gnomes*

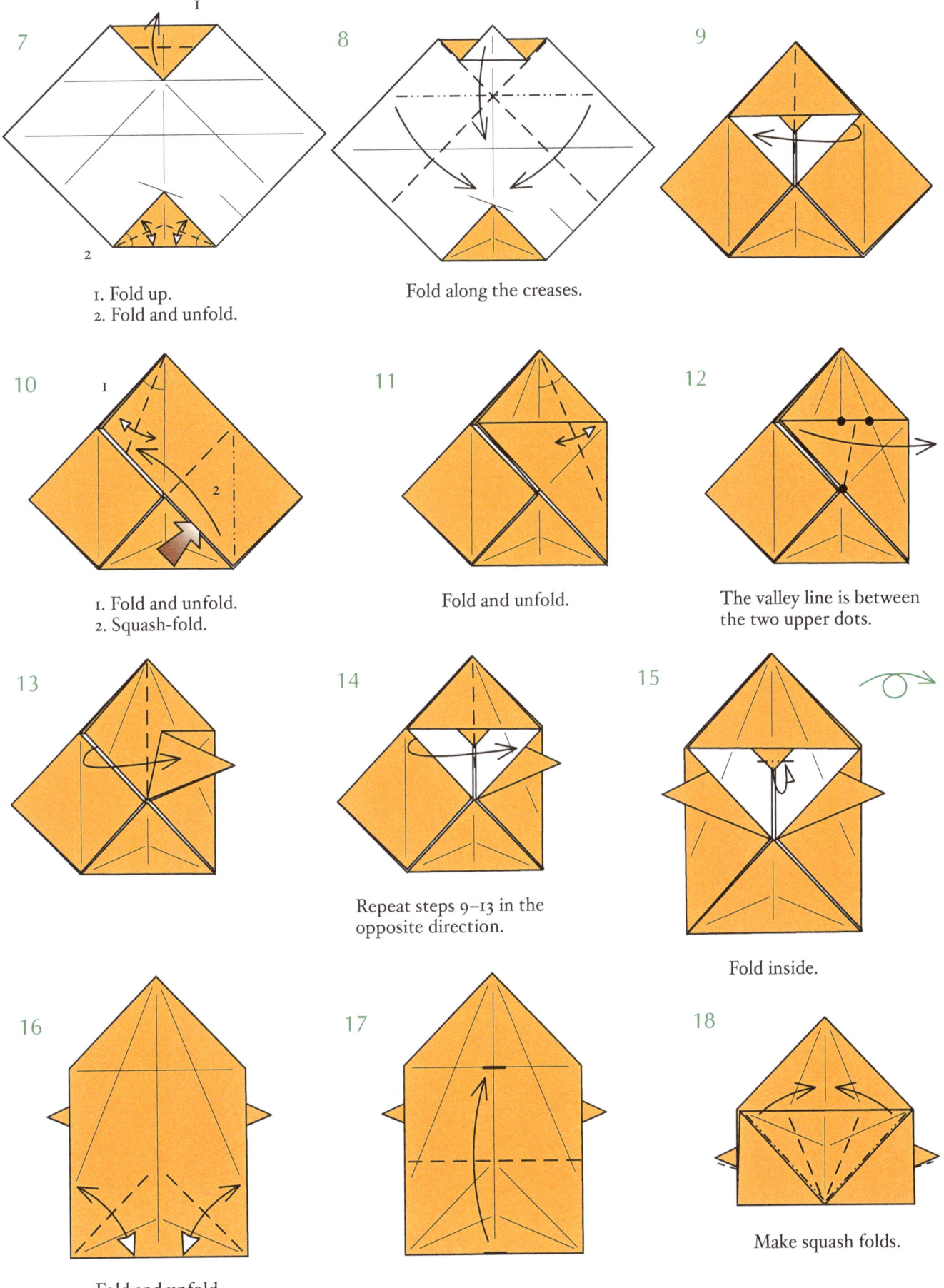

Vibble Noodlebop

19
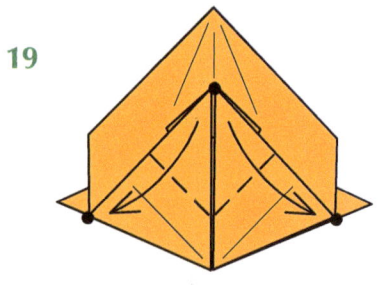
Make squash folds.

20

21
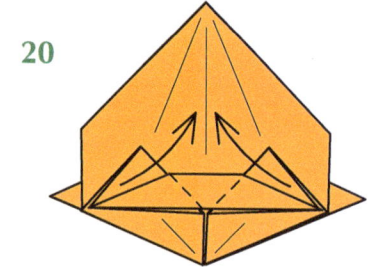
Petal-fold.

22

23
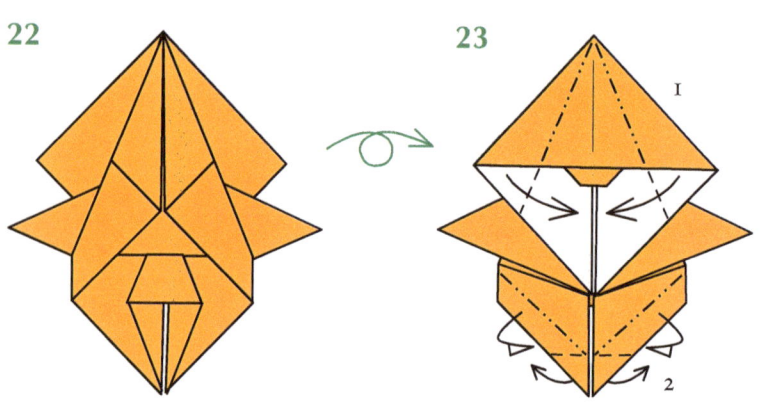
1. Make reverse folds.
2. Make crimp folds.

24
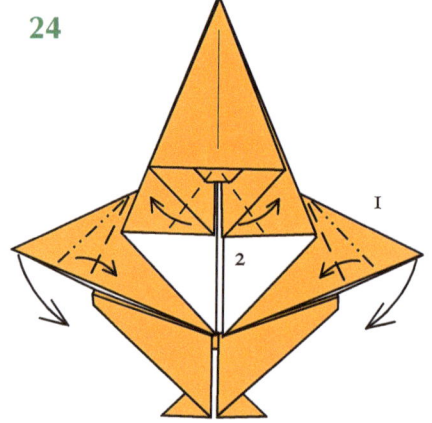
1. Make squash folds.
2. Fold up.

25
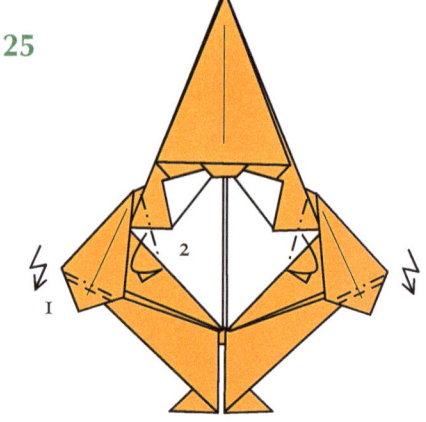
1. Make pleat folds.
2. Fold inside.

26
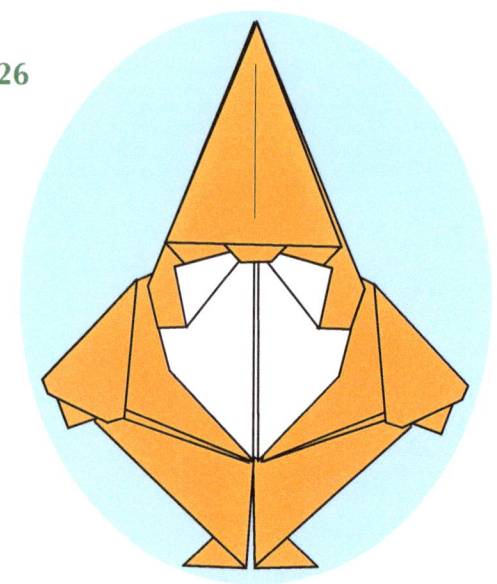

Vibble Noodlebop

116 *Magical Origami Gnomes*

Zindle Snickerdash

Zindle Snickerdash makes their victims see everyone with giant, twirling mustaches until they take off their hats and break the spell.

1

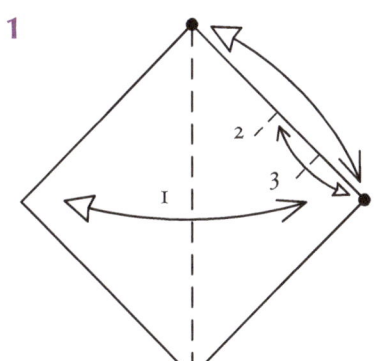

Fold and unfold at 1, 2, and 3.

2

Fold and unfold along the diagonal.

3

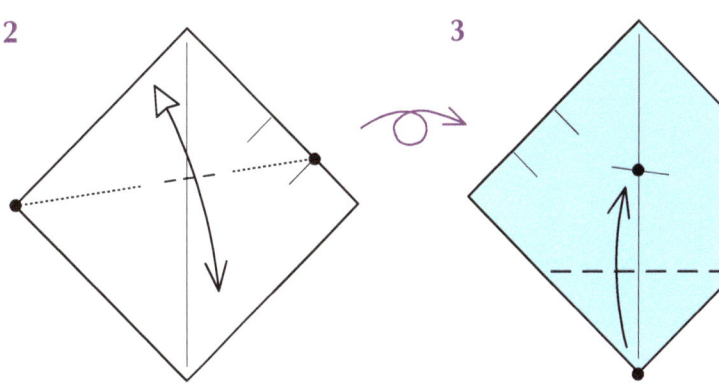

4

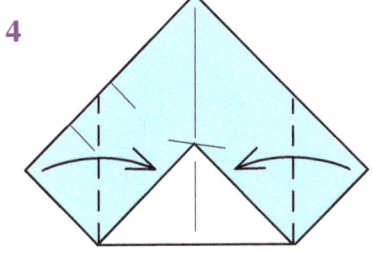

5

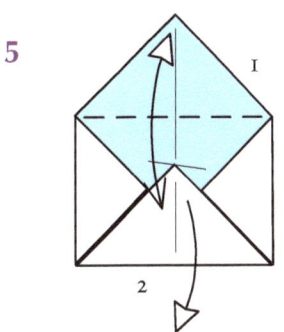

1. Fold and unfold.
2. Unfold.

6

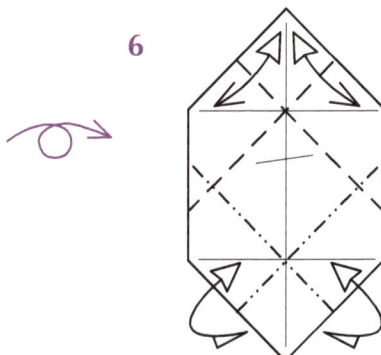

Fold and unfold.

Zindle Snickerdash 117

7

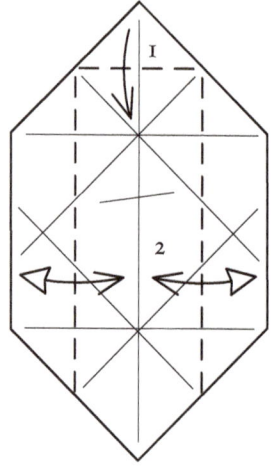

1. Fold down.
2. Fold and unfold the top layer.

8

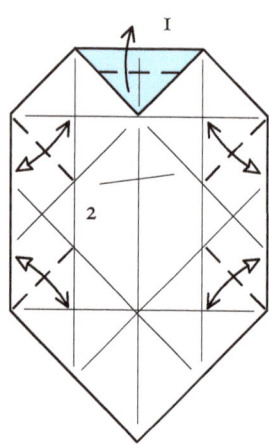

1. Fold up.
2. Fold and unfold.

9

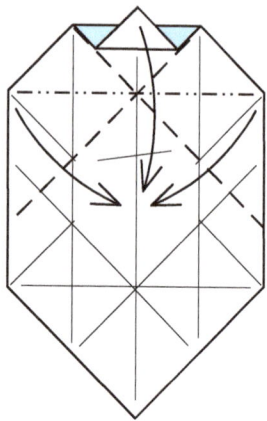

Fold along the creases.

10

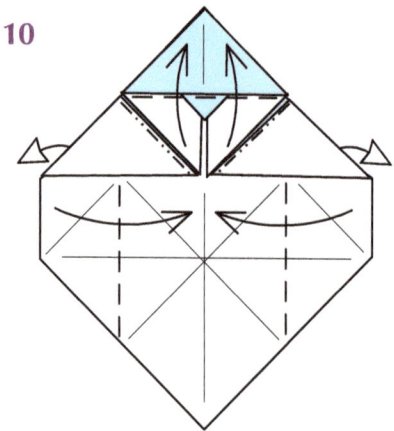

Make squash folds and swing out from behind.

11

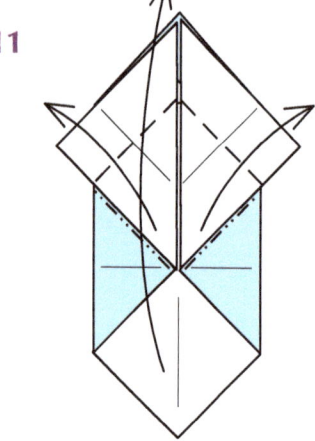

Petal-fold.

12

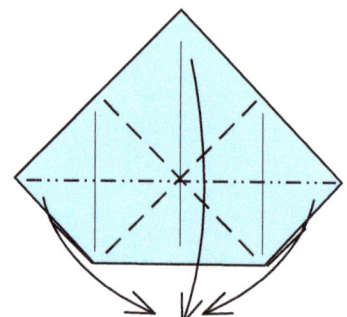

Fold along the creases.

13

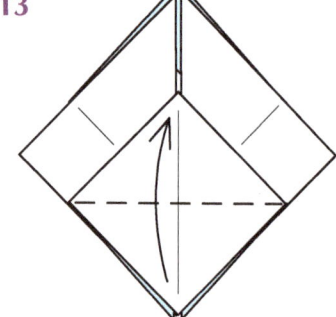

14

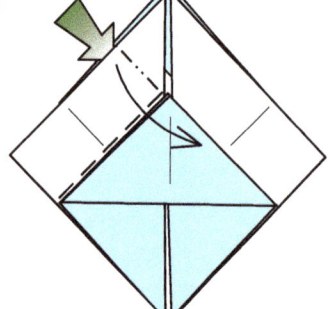

Squash-fold.

15

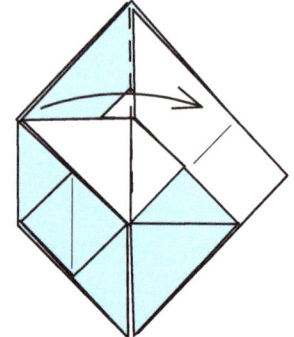

118 *Magical Origami Gnomes*

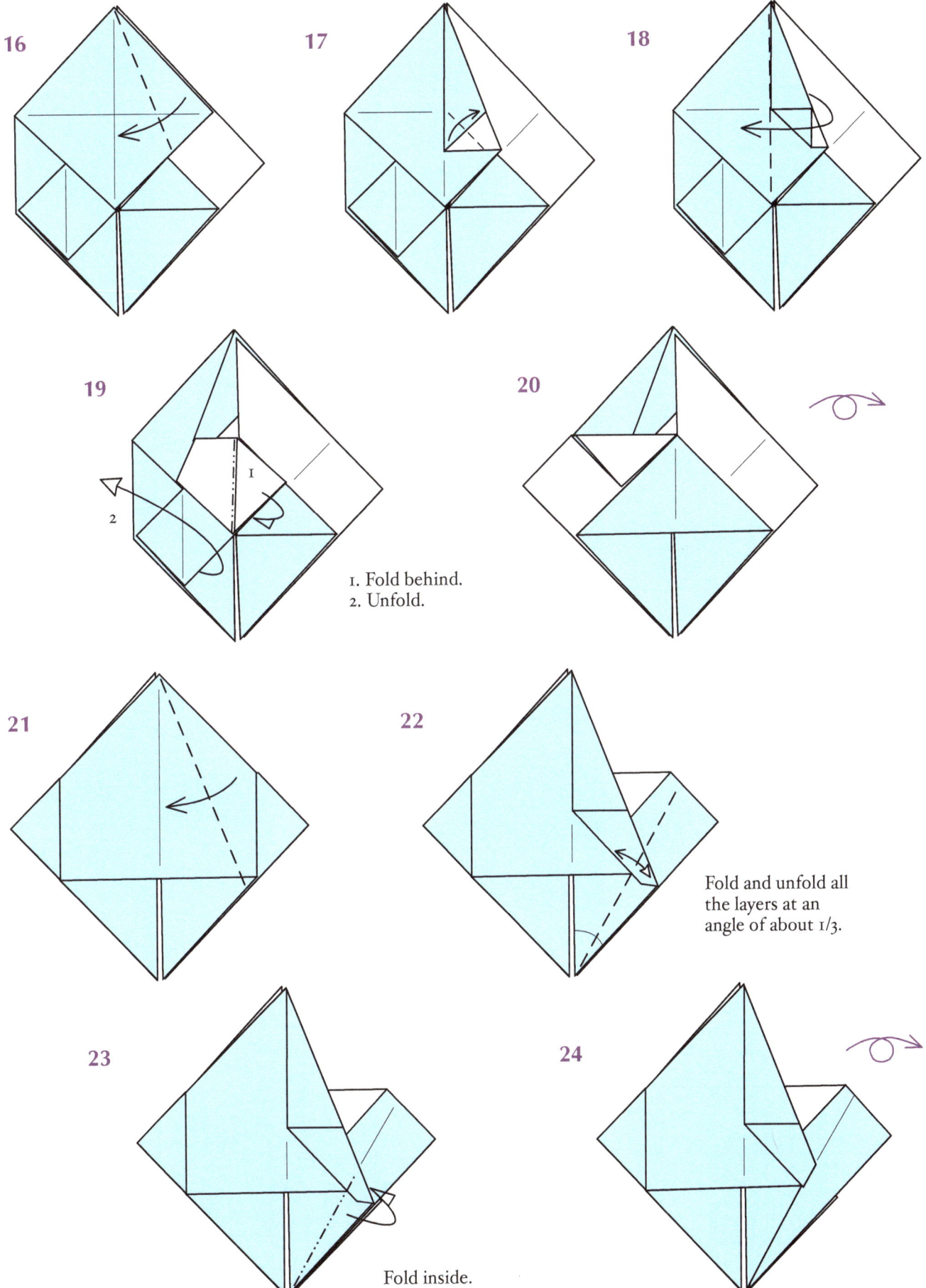

Zindle Snickerdash 119

25

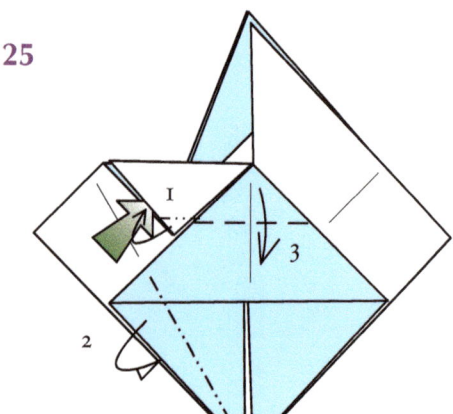

1. Reverse-fold.
2. Fold inside along the crease.
3. Fold down.

26

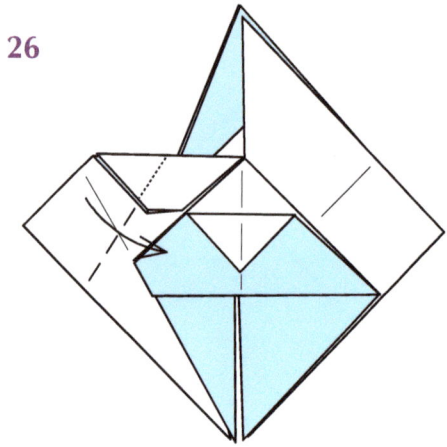

27

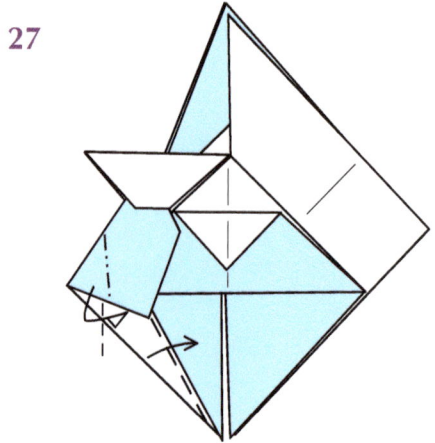

Reverse-fold.

28

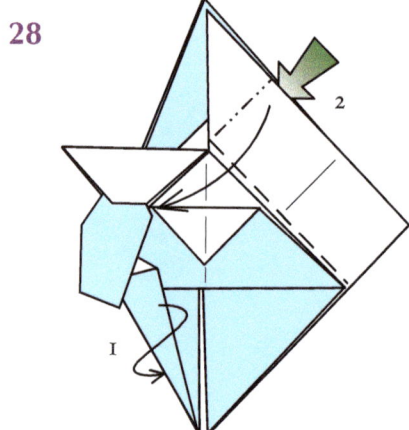

1. Tuck inside.
2. Repeat steps 14–28 on the right.

29

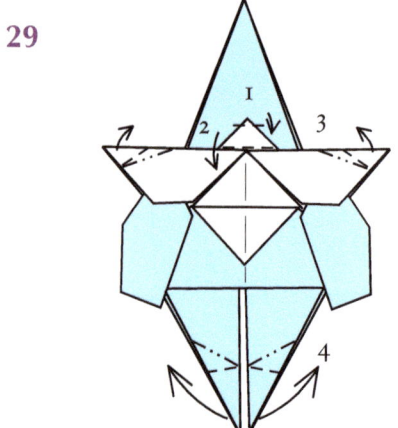

1. Fold down.
2. Fold down.
3. Make pleat folds.
4. Make crimp folds.

30

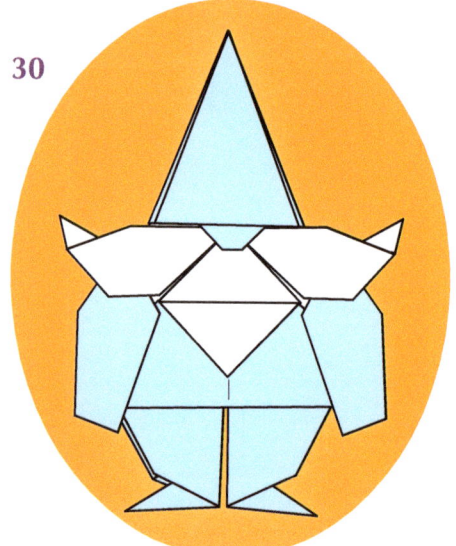

Zindle Snickerdash

Sprolla Mucklestomp

Sprolla Mucklestomp bakes all kinds of delicious-looking pastries. When bitten, it emits a loud party horn noise, all the paintings on the wall fall and are replaced with pickles taped to the wall.

1

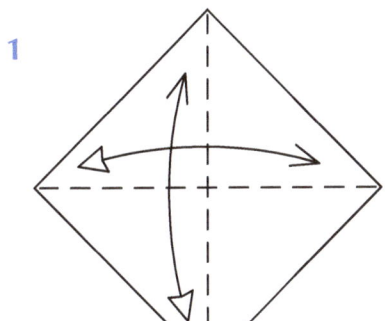

Fold and unfold.

2

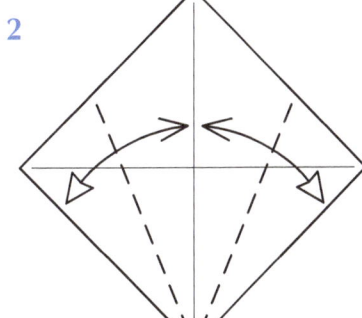

Fold to the center and unfold.

3

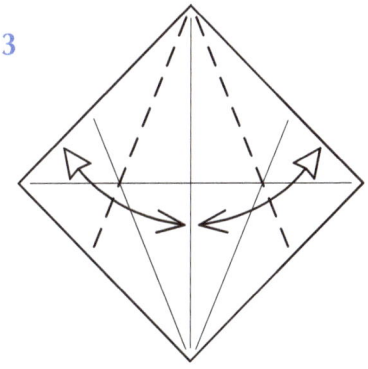

Fold to the center and unfold.

4

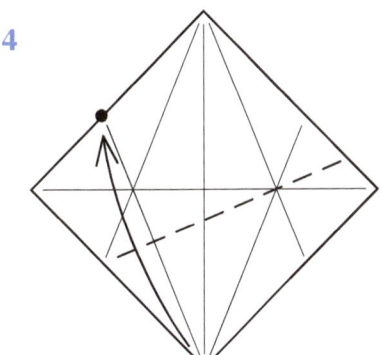

5

Squash-fold.

6

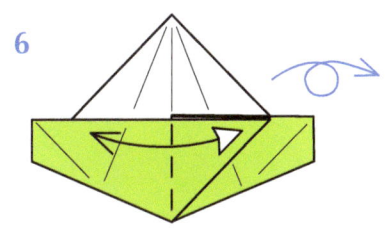

Fold and unfold. Rotate 180°.

Sprolla Mucklestomp 121

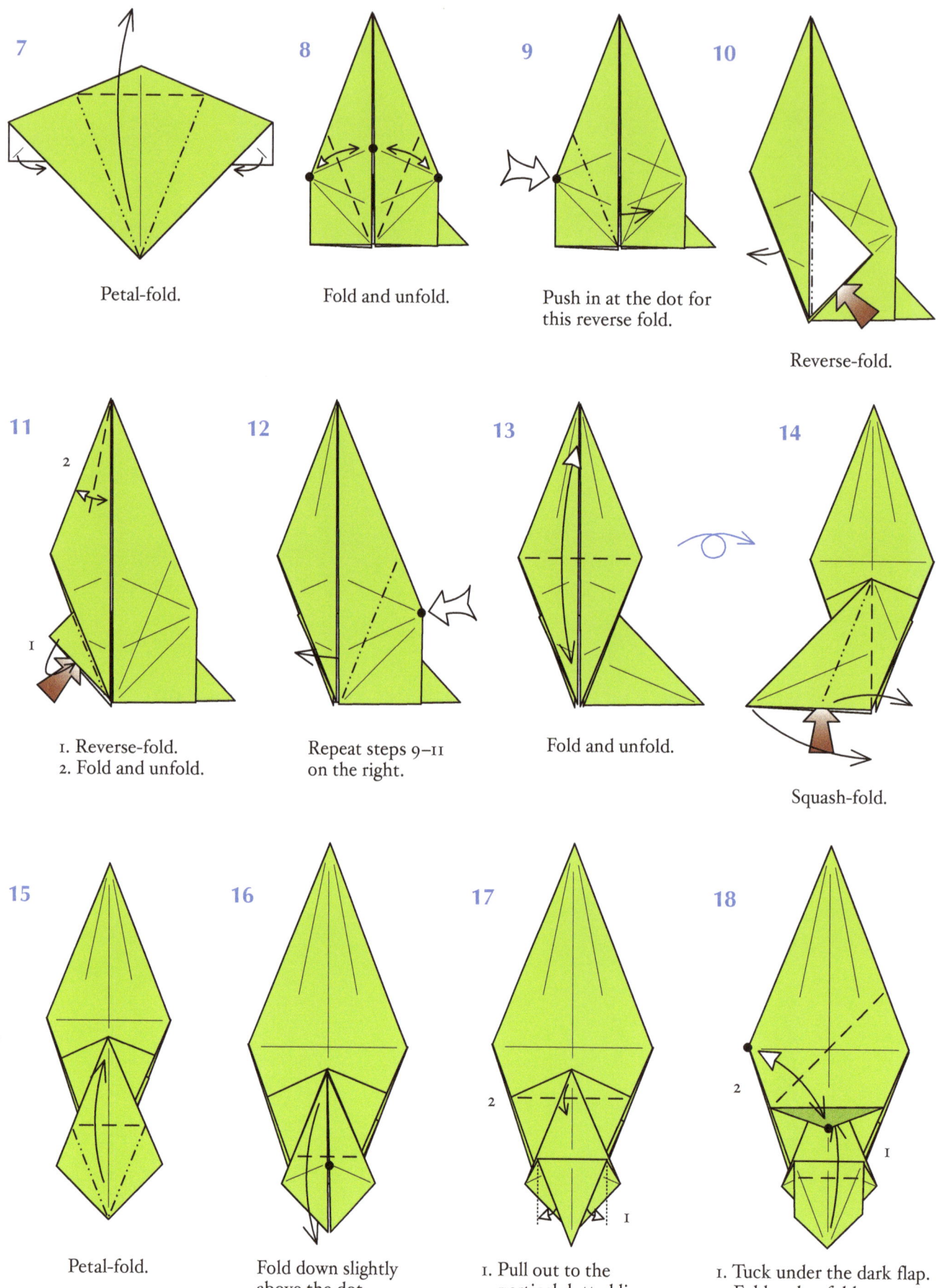

122 *Magical Origami Gnomes*

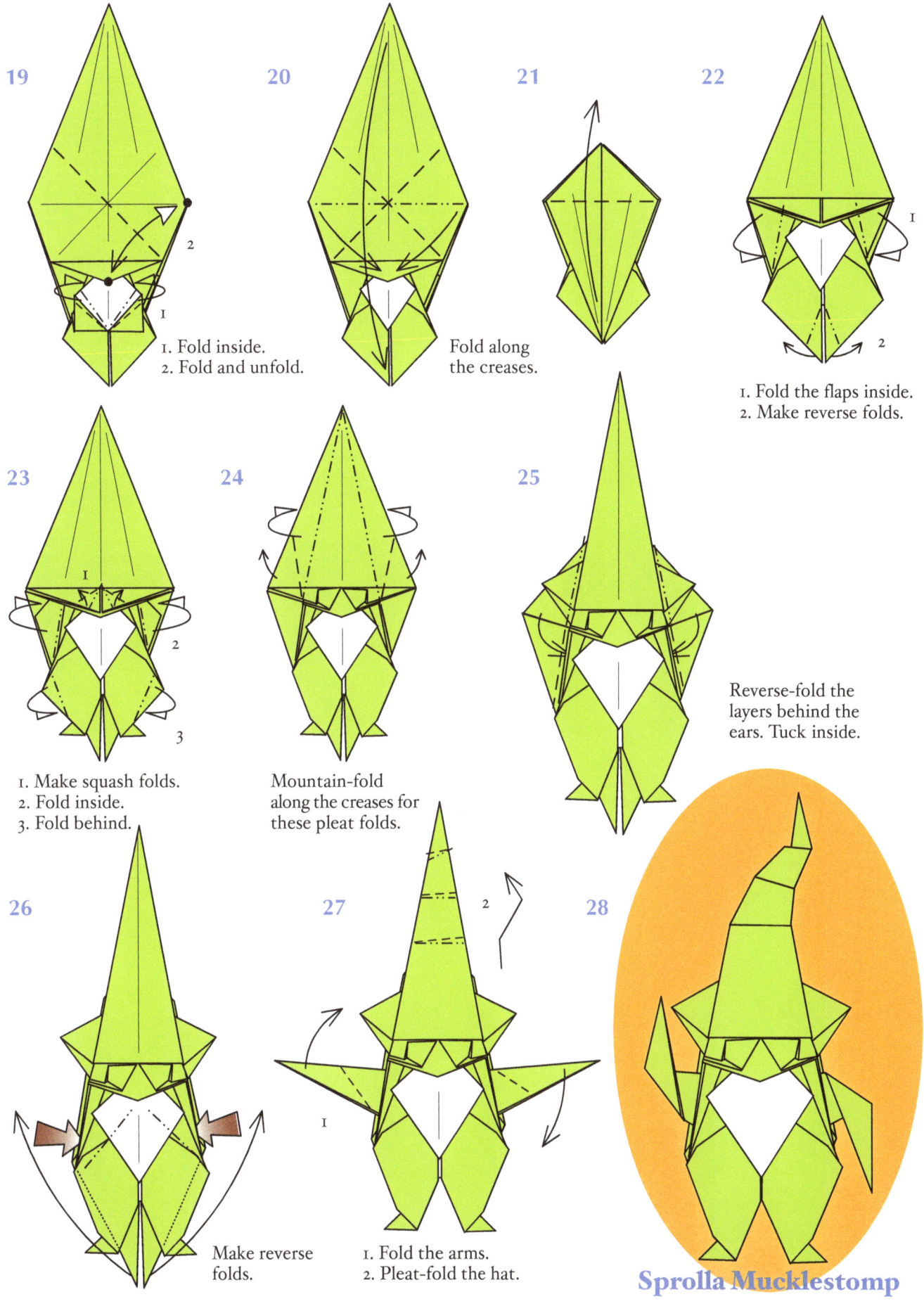

Sprolla Mucklestomp

Jibber Kelpwhistle

Jibber Kelpwhistle always sports fancy shoes and wears a super-tall hat. He makes everything taste better, makes hats seem so comfortable that you will want to sleep in them, and makes piles of gifts appear at the front door every day. Every time you open the pantry door, there will be dozens of bluebell-mushroom tarts, with just the right amount of moss toppings. A porcupine will guard your cottage at night. New colorful shoes with curly tips greet you every morning. Raccoons hidden in corners of each room are ready to offer refreshing pickles while whirling machinery on the ceiling creates rainbows. Butterflies and bluejays glisten in the distance. There's no place like Gnome.

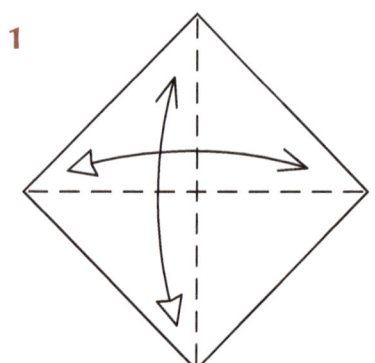

1

Fold and unfold.

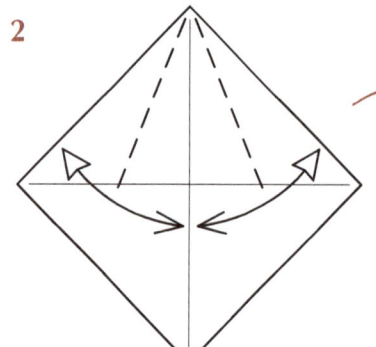

2

Fold to the center and unfold.

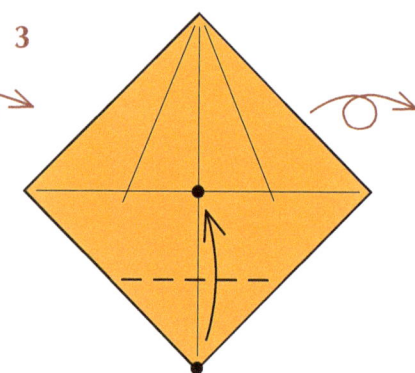

3

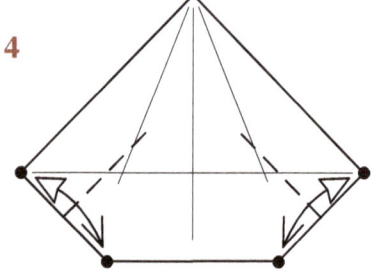

4

Fold and unfold.

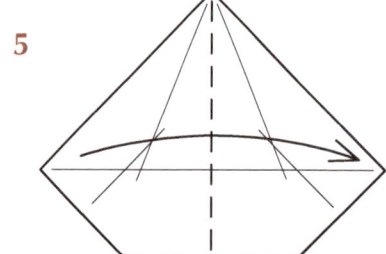

5

6

Squash-fold and rotate.

124 *Magical Origami Gnomes*

7

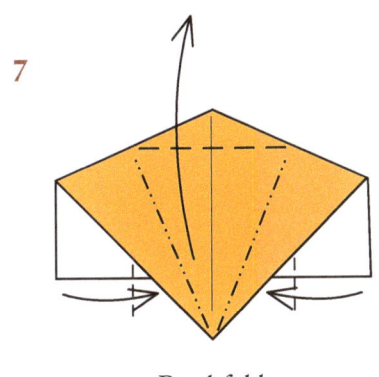

Petal-fold.

8

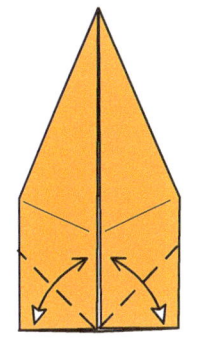

Fold and unfold along the creases.

9

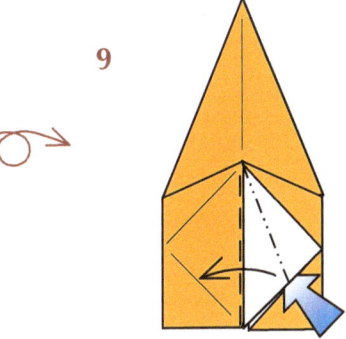

Squash-fold.

10

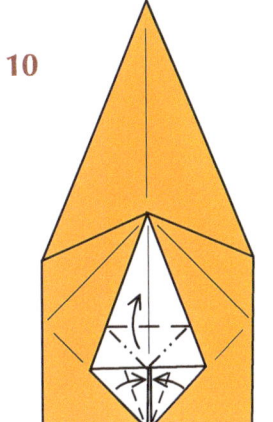

Petal-fold.

11

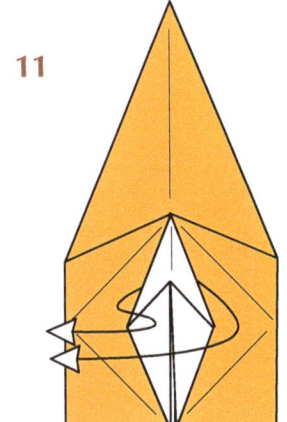

Double-unwrap-fold. (See page 13.)

12

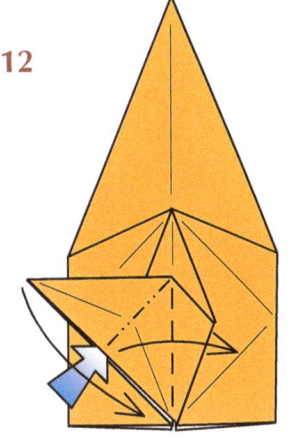

Squash-fold.

13

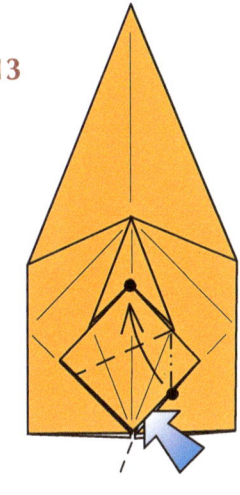

Squash-fold.

14

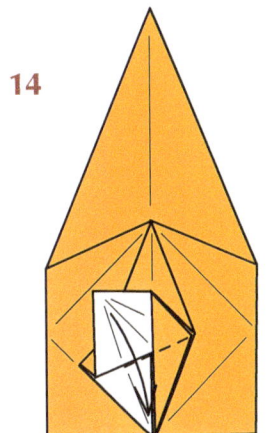

15

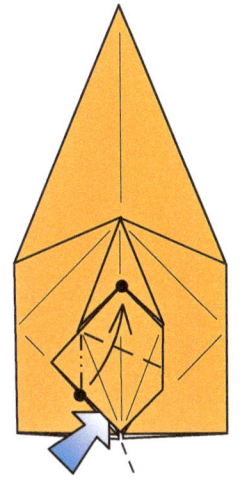

Repeat steps 13–14 in the opposite direction.

16

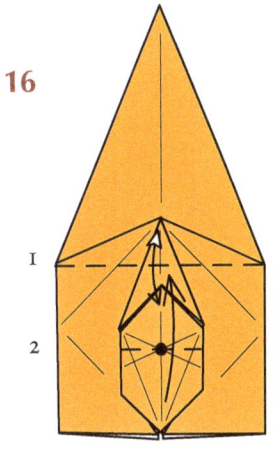

1. Fold and unfold.
2. Fold up.

17

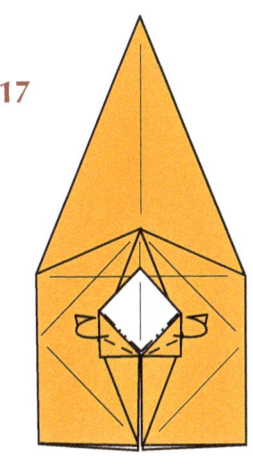

Fold inside.

Jibber Kelpwhistle 125

18

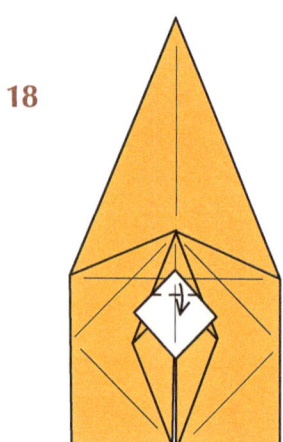

19

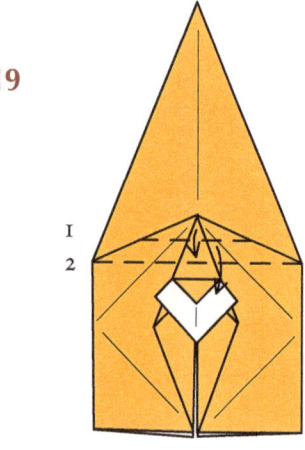

1. Fold to the crease.
2. Fold along the crease.

20

Fold inside.

21

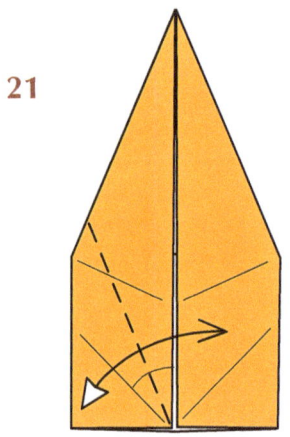

Fold and unfold.

22

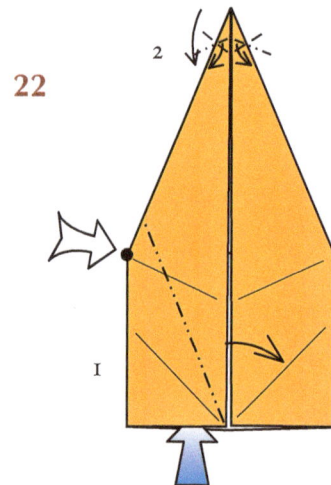

1. Push in at the dot for this reverse fold.
2. Spread.

23

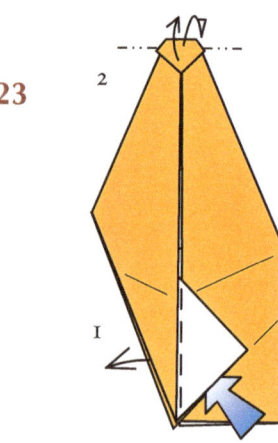

1. Reverse-fold.
2. Fold up and swing out from behind.

24

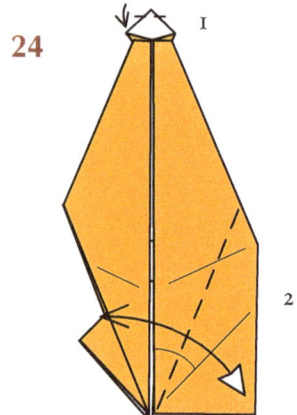

1. Fold down.
2. Repeat steps 21–23 at the bottom on the right.

25

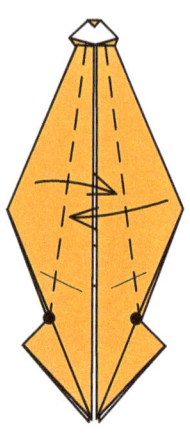

Divide the angle in thirds.

26

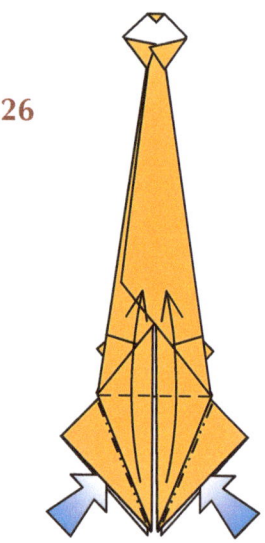

Make squash folds.

126 *Magical Origami Gnomes*

27

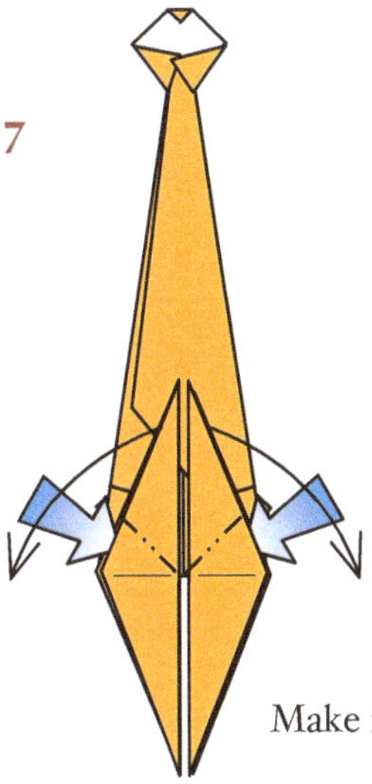

Make reverse folds.

28

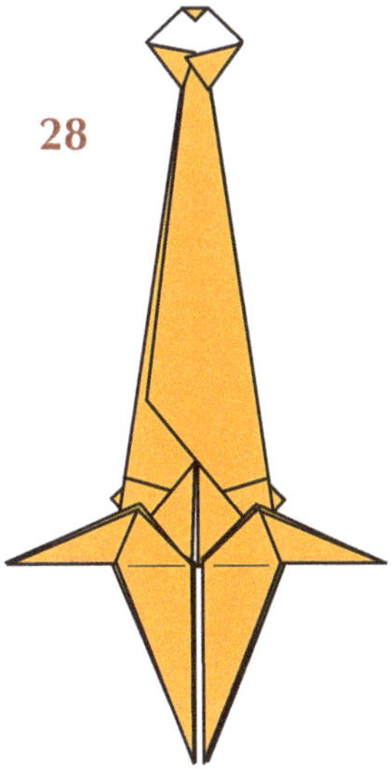

29

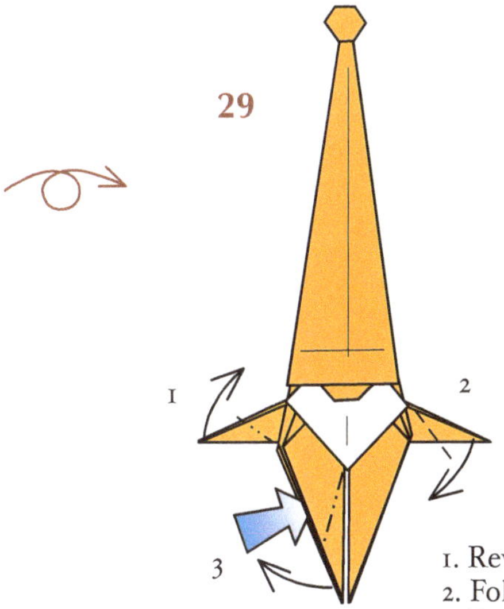

1. Reverse-fold.
2. Fold down.
3. Reverse-fold.

30

Magnified view.

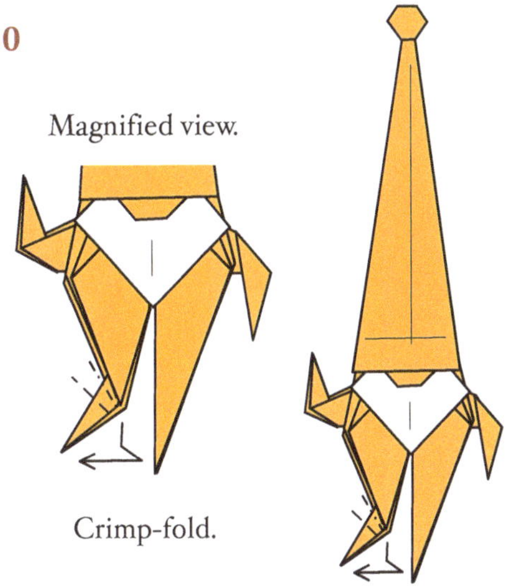

Crimp-fold.

31

Magnified view.

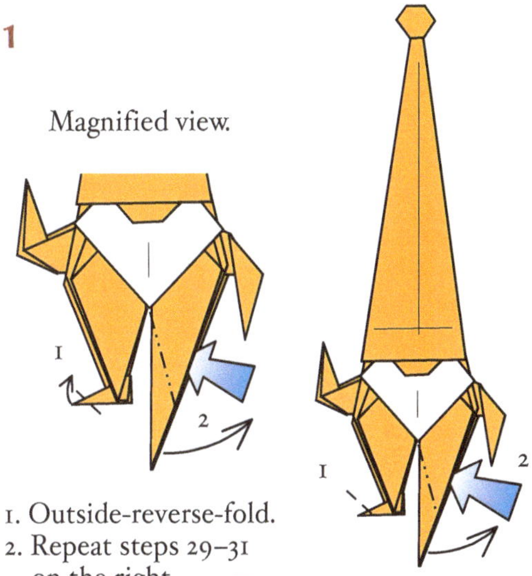

1. Outside-reverse-fold.
2. Repeat steps 29–31 on the right.

32

1. Pleat-fold.
2. Spread the feet at the bottom so the Gnome can stand.

33

Jibber Kelpwhistle

Jibber Kelpwhistle 127

www.ingramcontent.com/pod-product-compliance
Ingram Content Group UK Ltd.
Pitfield, Milton Keynes, MK11 3LW, UK
UKHW052121230426
12049UKWH00009BA/141